A Greek and Arabic Lexicon (GALex)

Fascicle 10
بعد to بشر

Handbook of Oriental Studies
Handbuch der Orientalistik

Section 1, The Near and Middle East

Edited by

Maribel Fierro (Madrid)
M. Şükrü-Hanioğlu (Princeton)
Kees Versteegh (Nijmegen)

VOLUME 11

A Greek and Arabic Lexicon

Edited by

Gerhard Endress
Dimitri Gutas

FASCICLE 10

The titles published in this series are listed at brill.com/ho1

A Greek and Arabic Lexicon
(GALex)

Materials for a Dictionary of the Mediæval Translations from Greek into Arabic

Edited by

Gerhard Endress and Dimitri Gutas

Fascicle 10

بعد to بشر

Compiled by

Rüdiger Arnzen, Gerhard Endress and Dimitri Gutas

BRILL

LEIDEN · BOSTON
2013

The editors wish to acknowledge with gratitude the financial assistance provided by the European Research Council (ERC Project Ideas, Advanced Grant 249431 «Greek into Arabic»), for the project "Glossarium Graeco-Arabicum" of the Ruhr-Universität Bochum, toward the completion of this project, as well as the financial support of the Provost's Fund, Yale University, and the Viscusi Fund, Department of Near Eastern Languages and Civilizations at Yale, for the research toward the preparation of this fascicle.

Scholars interested in contributing to the Lexicon in any form (glossaries, additions, corrections) will receive updated materials on request. Please direct inquiries to one of the editors:

Prof. Dr Gerhard Endress
Seminar für Orientalistik und Islamwissenschaften
Ruhr-Universität Bochum, GB 2
44780 Bochum, Germany
E-mail: gerhard.endress@ruhr-uni-bochum.de
URL: http://www.ruhr-uni-bochum.de/orient/GlossariumGraecoArabicum/

Prof. Dr Dimitri Gutas
Department of Near Eastern Languages and Civilizations
Yale University, 316 Hall of Graduate Studies
P. O. Box 208236
New Haven, CT 06520-8236, USA
E-mail: dimitri.gutas@yale.edu

The Roman and Greek texts were set in the ANDRON typeface
© by Andreas Stötzner <http://www.signographie.de>

Library of Congress Control Number: 2012952306

ISSN 0169-9423
ISBN 978-90-04-21213-8 (paperback)

This book is printed on acid-free paper.

FSC
www.fsc.org
MIX
Paper from responsible sources
FSC® C109576

Printed by Printforce, the Netherlands

ADDITIONS TO THE LIST OF SOURCES

Arist. Eth. Nic.

= Aristoteles: *Ethica Nicomachea.* – *Aristotelis Ethica Nicomachea.* Ed. I. Bywater. Oxonii 1894. Repr. 1962. (Scriptorum Classicorum Bibliotheca Oxoniensis.)

➢ *K. al-Aḫlāq al-musammā bi-Nīqūmāḫiyā.*

¶ *The Arabic version of the* Nicomachean Ethics. Ed. by Anna A. Akasoy and Alexander Fidora, with an introduction and annotated translation by Douglas M. Dunlop. Leiden [etc.] 2005. (Aristoteles Semitico-Latinus, vol. 17.)

In *GALex,* vol. I (letter *alif*), references are to:

¶ Badawī = Badawī, ʿAbd-al-Raḥmān: *al-Aḫlāq,* taʾlīf Arisṭūṭālīs, tarǧamat Isḥāq b. Ḥunayn. al-Kuwayt 1979. – Ref. to | page | . | line | *Badawī.*

¶ Axelroth = Axelroth, Dorothy G.: *An analysis of the Arabic translation of Book Ten of Aristotle's Nicomachean Ethics.* Diss. Philadelphia, Dropsie College, 1968. – Ref. to | page | . | line | *Axelroth.*

¶ Arberry = Arthur John Arberry: 'The Nicomachean Ethics in Arabic'. In: *Bulletin of the School of Oriental and African Studies*; 17 (1955) 1–9 [specimen ed. of book IX, 1].

Schmidt / Ullmann = Ernst A. Schmidt, Manfred Ullmann, *Aristoteles in Fes: zum Wert der arabischen Überlieferung der "Nikomachischen Ethik" für die Kritik des griechischen Textes.* Heidelberg: Winter, 2012.

Ullmann NE I = Manfred Ullmann, *Die Nikomachische Ethik des Aristoteles in arabischer Übersetzung*; Teil 1. Wortschatz. Wiesbaden : Harrassowitz, 2011.

Ullmann NE II = Manfred Ullmann, *Die Nikomachische Ethik des Aristoteles in arabischer Übersetzung*; Teil 2: Überlieferung, Textkritik, Grammatik. Wiesbaden : Harrassowitz, 2012.

Cass. Bass. Geopon.

= *Geoponica sive Cassiani Bassi scholastici De re rustica eclogae,* rec. Henricus Beckh. Leipzig: Teubner, 1895. – Ref. to | book |, | chapter | . | section | .

➢ *K. al-Filāḥa al-yūnāniyyya li-Qusṭūs ibn Lūqā al-Rūmī.*

¶ Ed. Wāʾil ʿAbd-al-Raḥīm Iʿbīd. ʿAmmān 1420/1999. – References from: Ullmann, *WGAÜ, Suppl.*

Ceb. Tab.

= *Cebetis Tabula.* — Ed. Karl Praechter: *Cebetis Tabula,* rec. Carolus Praechter. Lipsiae: Teubner, 1893. — Ref. to | page | . | line | .

➢ Qābis.

¶ Arabic text in ʿAbd-al-Raḥmān Badawī, ed., Miskawayh: *al-Ḥikma al-ḫālida.* al-Qāhira, 1952. — Ref. to | page | . | line | .

Cyranis

= Hermes Trismegistos: *Cyranides,* I. Ed. Maryse Waegeman: *Amulet and Alphabet: Magical Amulets in the First Book of Cyranides.* Amsterdam, 1987.

➢ *Kitāb Ǧiranīs.*

¶ Isabel Toral-Niehoff: *Kitāb Ǧiranīs. Die arabische Übersetzung der ersten Kyranis des Hermes Trismegistos und die griechischen Parallelen, herausgegeben, übersetzt und kommentiert.* Quellen und Forschungen zur antiken Welt, 43. München: Utz, 2004. — References from: Ullmann, *WGAÜ, Suppl.*

Diosc. Mat. med.

➢ *Versio Stephani* (sc. Iṣṭifān ibn Basīl): *Kitāb al-Ḥašāʾiš fī hayūlā l-ṭibb*

¶ Standard references are to the quotations in Ibn al-Bayṭār: *al-Ǧāmiʿ.*

¶ Occasional references
a) to ed. Dubler & Terés,
b) from Ullmann, *WGAÜ,* | page | (quoting ‹*versio A*›).

➢ *Versio Melitenensis* (sc. Abū Sālim al-Malaṭī)

¶ References from: Ullmann, *WGAÜ,* quoting mss. Paris: BnF, 4947; Istanbul: Topkapı Sarayı, Ahmet III, 2127 (‹*versio B*›).

➢ *Versio Mihrān* (sc. Mihrān ibn Manṣūr ibn Mihrān)

¶ References from: Ullmann, *WGAÜ Suppl.,* quoting mss. Mašhad, Istanbul, Tehran (*v. WGAÜ Suppl.* 23f., ‹*versio C*›).

➢ *Vetus translatio*

¶ References from: Ullmann Unters. = Manfred Ullmann, *Untersuchungen zur arabischen Überlieferung der* Materia medica *des Dioskurides,* mit Beiträgen von Rainer Degen. Wiesbaden 2009, 171–318 ('Glossar zur Vetus translatio'), quoting ms. Istanbul: Aya Sofya, 3704 (*olim* Topkapı Sarayı, Ahmet III, 2147).

Galen Alim. fac.

Correction of *GALex,* II, p. xiii:
References from *WGAÜ* are to ed. Kühn | vol. |, | page | . | line | .

Galen Diff. febr.

= *De differentiis febrium libri*. In: *Claudii Galeni Opera omnia*. Ed. C. G. Kühn. T. VII, 4. Lipsiae 1824 [repr. Hildesheim 1965], pp. 273–405. — Ref. to | vol. |, | page | . | line | .

➢ *K. Aṣnāf al-ḥummayāt.*

¶ Ed. Matthias Wernhard: *Über die Arten der Fieber in der arabischen Version des Ḥunain ibn Isḥāq*. Diss. München 2004. URL: <http://edoc.ub.uni-muenchen.de/archive/00006399/01/Wernhard_Matthias.pdf>. — References from: Ullmann, *WGAÜ, Suppl.*

Galen In Progn.

= *In Hippocratis Prognosticum commentarii.* In: *Claudii Galeni Opera omnia*. Ed. C. G. Kühn. T. XVIII, 1. Lipsiae 1829 [repr. Hildesheim 1965], pp. 1–317. — Ref. to | vol. |, | page | . | line | .

➢ *Tafsīr k. Buqrāṭ fī Taqdimat al-maʿrifa.*

¶ Ms. Dublin: Chester Beatty, 3127. — References from: Ullmann, *WGAÜ, Suppl.*

Galen Loc. aff.

= Galenus: *De locis affectis.* In: *Claudii Galeni Opera omnia*. Ed. C. G. Kühn. T. VIII, 1. Lipsiae 1824 [repr. Hildesheim 1965], pp. 1–451. — Ref. to | vol. |, | page | . | line | .

➢ *K. al-Aʿḍāʾ al-ālima.*

¶ Ms. London: Wellcome Library, Or. 14a; cf. Ivan Garofalo: 'La traduzione araba del *De locis affectis* di Galeno'. In: *Studi Classici e Orientali* 45 (1995) 13–63. — References from: Ullmann, *WGAÜ, Suppl.*

Galen Nat. fac.

= Galen: *De facultatibus naturalibus.* In: *Claudii Galeni Opera omnia.* Ed. C. G. Kühn. T. II, 1. Lipsiae 1821 [repr. Hildesheim 1965], pp. 1–214. — Ref. to | vol. |, | page | . | line | .

➢ *K. al-Quwā l-ṭabīʿiyya.*

¶ Ms. Leiden, Univ., or. 1297. References from: Ullmann, *WGAÜ.*

Galen Puls. introd.

= Galenus: *De pulsibus ad eos qui introducunter (ad Teuthram)*. In: *Claudii Galeni Opera omnia*. Ed. C. G. Kühn. T. VIII, 2. Lipsiae 1824 [repr. Hildesheim 1965], pp. 453–92. — Ref. to | vol. |, | page | . | line | .

➢ *K. al-Nabḍ al-ṣaġīr (K. ilā Ṭūṯaran fī l-nabḍ li-l-mutaʿallimīn)*.

¶ Ed. Muḥammad Salīm Sālim: *Kitāb Ǧālīnūs ilā Ṭūṯaran fī l-nabḍ li-l-mutaʿallimīn*. [Cairo:] al-Hayʾa al-miṣriyya al-ʿāmma li-l-kitāb, 1985. — References from: Ullmann, *WGAÜ Suppl.*

Hippocr. Superf.

in vol. I, page / line references are to ed. Littré, as given in Lyons's Glossary.

Men. Mon.

= Menandri Comici *Sententiae* [*Μενάνδρου γνῶμαι μονόστιχοι*]. Ed. Siegfried Jäkel. Lipsiae 1964. (Bibliotheca scriptorum Graecorum et Romanorum Teubneriana.)

¶ Occasional references to:

Carlo Pernigotti: *Menandri Sententiae.* Studi e Testi per il Corpus dei Papiri Filosofici Greci e Latini, 15. Firenze: Leo S. Olschki, 2008.

¶ Manfred Ullmann: *Die arabische Überlieferung der sogenannten Menandersentenzen*. Wiesbaden 1961. (Abhandlungen für die Kunde des Morgenlandes XXXIV, 1) – Ref. to | *versio* [I / II) | , | number of monostichon | : | page | . | line | .

Ullmann Bem. = Manfred Ullmann: 'Bemerkungen zu den arabischen Übersetzungen der Menandersentenzen'. In: *Islam* 42 (1966), 79-88.

Paulus Aeg.

= Paulus Aegineta: *Pragmatica.* Ed. Iohan L. Heiberg. Corpus Medicorum Graecorum, 9. Lipsiae, Berolini: Teubner, 1921–4.

¶ Arabic excerpts, *v.* Peter Pormann: *The Oriental Tradition of Paul of Aegina's Pragmatica.* Studies in Ancient Medicine, vol. 29. Leiden, Boston: Brill, 2004. — References from: Ullmann *WGAÜ, Suppl.*

Philum. Ven.

= Philumenus: *De venenatis animalibus eorumque remediis.* Ed. Maximilianus Wellmann. Corpus medicorum Graecorum, 10, 1. Lipsiae, Berolini: Teubner, 1908.

¶ Arabic excerpts in: Ibn Sīnā, *al-Qānūn fī l-ṭibb, kitāb* 4, *fann* 6, *maqāla* 3. — References from: Ullmann, *WGAÜ*.

Plato Tim.

= Plato: *Timaeus*. Cf. *GALex*, II, p. xx.

➢ *Galen Comp. Tim.* (= *Ǧawāmiʿ Kitāb Ṭīmāwus fī ʿilm al-ṭabīʿī).*

¶ *Galeni Compendium Timaei Platonis aliorumque dialogorum synopsis quae extant fragmenta,* edd. Paulus Kraus & Richardus Walzer. Plato Arabus, 1. London: Warburg Institute, 1951. Repr. Nendeln / Liechtenstein: Kraus Reprint, 1973. — Ref. to | page | . | line | .

Theomn. Hippiatr.

= Theomnestus Nikopolitanus: *Hippiatrica*. [Greek fragments in:] *Corpus hippiatricorum Graecorum,* edd. Eugenius Oder & Carolus Hoppe. Lipsiae: Teubner, 1924–7; repr. Stuttgart 1971. — Ref. to Arabic version, | section | , |paragraph | .

➢ *Kitāb al-Bayṭara*.

¶ Ed. Susanne Saker: *Die Pferdeheilkunde des Theomnest von Nikopolis*. Wiesbaden: Harrassowitz, 2008. — Ref. to | page | . | line | .

Theophr. Princ.

= Theophrastus: *De principiis. Theophrasti de prima philosophia libellus.* Ref. to ed. Gutas (v. infra), giving | page | a/b | line | divisions as in ed. H. Usener (Bonnae 1890–91).

➢ *Maqālat Ṯāwufrasṭus fī Mā baʿd al-ṭabīʿa.*

¶ Dimitri Gutas: Theophrastus *On First Principles* (known as his *Metaphysics*), Greek text and medieval Arabic translation, ed. and transl. Philosophia Antiqua, vol. 119. Leiden, Boston: E. J. Brill, 2010. — Ref. to | page | . line |.

ADDITIONAL ABBREVIATIONS

Ullmann Unters. = Manfred Ullmann: *Untersuchungen zur arabischen Überlieferung der* Materia medica *des Dioskurides.* Mit Beiträgen von Rainer Degen. Wiesbaden: Harrassowitz, 2009.

WGAÜ Suppl. = Manfred Ullmann: *Wörterbuch zu den griechisch-arabischen Übersetzungen des 9. Jahrhunderts.*Supplement, Bd I: A-O; Bd II: Π-Ω. Wiesbaden 2006–7.

بشر

باشر III. bāšara

1. ἅπτομαι *med.* (*to apprehend, to perceive*) : ὥστε τῆς ὕλης ἂν εἶεν ἡμμένοι *Arist. Metaph. Λ 2, 1069b24* = ḥattā yūǧadū qad bāšarū l-māddata *1443.5.*

2. τηρέω (*to watch over s.th., observe*) = *in hend.* bāšara wa-raṣada : οἱ πάλαι τετηρηκότες (*sc.* περὶ τοὺς ἄλλους ἀστέρας) ἐκ πλείστων ἐτῶν Αἰγύπτιοι καὶ Βαβυλώνιοι *Arist. Cael. II 12, 292a8* = ahlu Miṣra wa-ahlu Bābila llaḏīna bāšarū ḏālika wa-raṣadūhu *versio B 271.4 Badawī.*

استبشر X. mustabširun *act. part.*

1. ἱλαρός (*cheerful, merry*) : αἱ δὲ ἕτεραι γυναῖκες αἱ ἐκεῖθεν παραγινόμεναι ἱλαραί τε καὶ γελῶσαι *Ceb Tab. 23.19* = fa-l-nisāʾu l-uḫaru llawātī yaʾtīna min hunāka ka-annahunna mustabširātun ḍāḥikātun *252.6.*

2. ἄπλαστος (*unaffected; un-made-up* [*without maquillage*]) : ἔτι τε ὡς ἄπλαστοί εἰσι καὶ οὐδαμῶς κεκαλλωπισμέναι καθάπερ αἱ ἄλλαι *Ceb. Tab. 17.21* = *in hend.* bāššun mustabširun : wa-ka-annahunna bāššātun mustabširātun lā yušbihna šayʾan mimmā fī ġayrihinna mina l-zīnati l-daġilati *246.13.*

بشرة bašaratun, *pl.* **bašarun**

1. σάρξ (*flesh*) : κοινῶς δὲ πᾶν ἔλαιον θερμαντικόν ἐστι καὶ μαλακτικὸν τῆς σαρκός *Diosc. Mat. med. I, 34.5* = wa-ǧamīʿu aṣnāfi l-zayti ḥārratun mulayyinatun li-l-bašarati *Ibn al-Bayṭār Ǧāmiʿ II, 176.12.*

2. εἶδος (*form; looks*) = bašaratu l-waǧhi : τά τε εἴδεα τῶν ἀνθρώπων εὔχροά τε καὶ ἀνθηρά ἐστι μᾶλλον (*post* μᾶλλον *add.* ἢ ἄλλῃ *ed.* : *om. V, Arab., Gal.*) *Hippocr. Aer. 32.17** = wa-bašaratu wuǧūhihim ḥasanatun layyinatun wa-alwānuhum nayyiratun muḍīʾatun *versio B 37.16.*

3. *sem. amplif.;* χρώς (*color of the skin, complexion*) = lawnu l-bašarati : καθαίρει δὲ τὸ ἄλευρον χρῶτα καὶ πελιώματα *Diosc. Mat.*

med. I, 184.8 = wa-daqīqu l-turmusi yunaqqī lawna l-bašarati wa-yuḏhibu āṯāra l-ḍarbi *versio A WGAÜ Suppl. II, 711*.

بشريّ bašariyyun

1. βρότειος (*mortal, human*) : Νῆστιν δὲ καὶ κρούνωμα βρότειον οἱονεὶ τὸ σπέρμα καὶ τὸ ὕδωρ *Ps.-Plut. Placita 287a15* = wa-yaʿnī bi-qawlihī nīsṭis wa-l-sayalāni l-bašariyyi l-rūḥa l-insāniyya wa-l-māʾa *7.25*.

بشارة bišāratun

1. ἀγγελία (*message, tidings*) : ἰδίᾳ δὲ τὸ ρ ἀπὸ τοῦ ἀριθμοῦ κρινέσθω ... ἔστι γὰρ ἀγγελία τὸ ρ (ἀγγελία τὸ ρ *L, Arab.* : ἀνγελία τὰ ἑκατόν *V* : <καὶ τὸ> 'ἀνγελία' [τὸ] ἑκατόν *Pack*) *Artem. Onirocr. 218.18** = fa-ammā ḥarfu l-rū (*sic leg.*) bi-ḫāṣṣatin fa-inna l-qaḍāʾa fīhi yuʾḫaḏu mina l-ʿadadi ... wa-ḏālika anna ḥarfa l-rū (*sic leg.*) yadullu bi-l-yūnāniyyati ʿalā bišāratin *398.12**.

بشع

بشاعة I. bašāʿatun *maṣdar*

1. ἀηδία (*nauseousness, distastefulness*) : γλαύκιον στύφει μετά τινος ἀηδίας *Galen Simpl. medic. XI, 857.4* = hāḏā l-nabātu fīhi qabḍun maʿa bašāʿatin *versio B WGAÜ, 75*.

2. αἶσχος (*ugliness, deformity*) : τὸ γὰρ γελοῖόν ἐστιν ἁμάρτημά τι καὶ αἶσχος *Arist. Poet. 5, 1449a35* = wa-ḏālika anna l-istihzāʾa huwa zalalun mā wa-bašāʿatun (bašāʿatun *cod., ʿAyyād, Badawī* : šanāʿatun *Margoliouth, Tkatsch*) *45.10 ʿAyyād, 95.5 Badawī, 12.7* Margoliouth, 228.17* Tkatsch*.

استبشع X. istabšaʿa

1. ἀηδῶς *adv.* (*with displeasure, sc.* ἀκούειν, *to hear*) : καὶ τὰ μὲν (*sc.* ἃ εὖ ἐποίησεν) ἡδέως ἀκούειν τὰ δ' (*sc.* ἃ ἔπαθεν εὖ) ἀηδῶς *Arist. Eth.*

Nic. IV 3, 1124b15 = wa-huwa yastaliḏḏu samāʿa l-faḍīlati wa-yastabšiʿu samāʿa mā ufḏila bihī ʿalayhi *265.4*.

بشع bašiʿun

1. λυπηρός (*unpleasant, distressing*) : καὶ ὅταν γε (*sc.* προσαποφαίνηται ἡ αἴσθησις) ὅτι λυπηρὸν ὥσπερ τὴν χολήν, τηνικαῦτα φεύγει *Them. In De an. 113.2* = wa-iḏā ḥakama (*sc.* al-ḥissu) bi-annahū bašiʿun ka-l-marāri (*cf. WGAÜ Suppl. II, 691*) fa-ḥīnaʾiḏin yahrubu minhu *206.8*.

2. αἰσχρός (*ugly, deformed*) : οἷον εὐθὺς τὸ γελοῖον πρόσωπον αἰσχρόν τι καὶ διεστραμμένον *Arist. Poet. 5, 1449a36* = *in hend.* baši ʿun qabīḥun : miṯālu ḏālika wağhu l-mustahzaʾi (mustahzaʾi *nos* : mustahziʾi *Ullmann*) huwa min sāʿatihī bašiʿun (bašiʿun *cod., ʿAyyād, Badawī* : šanīʿ *Margoliouth, Tkatsch*) qabīḥun wa-huwa munkarun *45.12 ʿAyyād, 95.6 Badawī, 12.8* Margoliouth, 228.18* Tkatsch, WGAÜ Suppl. II, 212*.

بشم

بشام bašāmun

1. ὀποβάλσαμον (*balsam tree*) : ἄλειψον ἐλαίῳ ὀποβαλσάμῳ *Cass. Bass. Geopon. XIV, 2.1* = ṭalayta ... bi-duhnin yuttaḫaḏu min šağarin yusammā bašām (*sic ed. pro* bašāman) *WGAÜ Suppl. I, 783*⊗.

بشنين

بشنين bišnīnun, bašnīnun

1. λωτὸς ὁ ἐν Αἰγύπτῳ *bot.* (*Egyptian lotus; v. Dietrich, Dioscurides Triumphans, p. 616*) : λωτὸς ὁ ἐν Αἰγύπτῳ γεννώμενος ἐν τῷ ὕδατι τῶν πεδίων ἐπικλυσθέντων *Diosc. Mat. med. II, 264.15* = bišnīnun ... lūṭūs allaḏī yakūnu bi-miṣra yanbutu fī l-māʾi iḏā aṭbaqa l-nīlu ʿalā arḍi miṣra *Ibn al-Bayṭār Ğāmiʿ I, 96.1*.

بصّ

بصّ I. baṣṣa

1. *sem. concentr.;* ἐξάπτομαι οὐ ζοφώδει φλογί (*to be kindled and burn with a non-dark flame*) = *in hend.* aḍāʾa wa-baṣṣa : ὀπός ... καὶ πρὸς λύχνον ἐξαπτόμενος οὐ ζοφώδει φλογί *Diosc. Mat. med. II, 220.11* = wa-iḏā dunniya mina l-sirāǧi aḍāʾa wa-baṣṣa *versio B WGAÜ Suppl. I, 436; Suppl. II, 617.4.*

بصّاص baṣṣāṣun

1. στίλβων *act. part.* (*glistening, glittering*) : στίβι δὲ κράτιστόν ἐστι τὸ στίλβον καὶ λαμπυρίζον ἐν τῇ θραύσει, πλακῶδες (*sic interpunx. Arab., Orib.* : λαμπυρίζον, ἐν *codd. graec., Wellmann*) *Diosc. Mat. med. III, 55.20* = al-kuḥlu aǧwaduhu l-baṣṣāṣu llaḏī kasruhū barrāqan yušbihu l-zuǧāǧa *versio B WGAÜ Suppl. I, 617*; πίσσα ... ἔστι δὲ καλὴ ἡ στίλβουσα καὶ λεία καὶ καθαρά *I, 70.17* = al-ziftu ... aǧwaduhu l-amlasu l-baṣṣāṣu l-ṣāfī *versio B WGAÜ Suppl. II, 337.*

بصبص

بصبص I. baṣbaṣa

1. σαίνω *c. acc.* (*to wag the tail at s.o.*) : κύων ... τοὺς μὲν διδόντας σαίνων τοὺς δὲ μὴ διδόντας ὑλακτῶν (*v. Overwien, Die Sprüche des Kynikers Diogenes, 108*) *Diogenes Laertius VI 60, 273 Long* ≈ ubaṣbiṣu li-l-aḫyāri wa-ahli l-faḍli wa-anbaḥu wa-aʿaḍḍu man kāna bi-ḫilāfi ḏālika *Ibn Durayd, Kitāb Muǧtanā, 51.19 Hyderabad ed. (= WGAÜ Suppl. II, 261).*

بصر

بصر I. baṣura

1. *transl.* ὁράω (*to see, look*) *and its derivatives*

1.1 ὁράω (*to see, look*) : διὸ καὶ ἀπὸ τῶν ἰσχυρῶν χρωμάτων μεταβάλλοντες οὐχ ὁρῶσι *Arist. Gener. anim. V 1, 780a10* = wa-li-ḏālika llaḏīna yatanaqqalūna mina l-alwāni l-aqwā fa-l-abyaḍi lā yabṣurūna *177.20* ↤ ἐχῖνον δὲ πλανώμενον, ὡς εἶδεν αὐτήν (*sc.* ἀλώπεκα) *Arist. Rhet. II 20, 1393b27* = fa-baṣura bihī (*sc.* al-ṯaʿlabi) l-qunfuḏu wa-huwa hāʾimun mutaḥayyirun *135.19* ↤ οὕτως γὰρ ἂν ὁ μὲν δρῶν ὁρῴη, τὸ δὲ χειριζόμενον οὐχ ὁρῷτο *Hippocr. Off. med. 31.9* = fa-innahū iḏā kāna l-amru ʿalā hāḏā kāna l-muʿāliğu yabṣuru wa-l-fatā (*fort. leg.* al-šayʾu? *ed.*) llaḏī yuʿāliğuhū lā yarāhu aḥadun *2.6*.

1.2 ὅραμα (*that which is seen, a sight*) = mā yubṣaru ilayhi : ἄλυποι γάρ εἰσιν αἵ τε μαθηματικαὶ καὶ τῶν κατὰ τὰς αἰσθήσεις αἱ διὰ τῆς ὀσφρήσεως, καὶ ἀκροάματα δὲ καὶ ὁράματα πολλὰ καὶ μνῆμαι καὶ ἐλπίδες *Arist. Eth. Nic. X 3, 1173b18* = min ağli anna l-laḏḏāti l-taʿlīmiyyata laysa fīhā ḥuznun wa-lā llatī takūnu bi-l-ḥissi wa-l-šammi wa-l-samāʿi, wa-mā yubṣaru ilayhi yakūnu, iḏā kāna kaṯīratan (taḏkiratan *coni. Badawī*) wa-rağāʾan, miṯla hāḏihī *537.8** (*text is corrupt in this passage*).

1.3 *sem.; def.; transl. the word* ὤψ (*eye*) *in the def. of* νυκτάλωψ (*nightblind*) = allaḏī lā yabṣuru/yubṣiru bi-l-layli : τὸ μὲν γὰρ γλαύκωμα γίγνεται μᾶλλον τοῖς γλαυκοῖς, οἱ δὲ νυκτάλωπες καλούμενοι τοῖς μελανοφθάλμοις *Arist. Gener. anim. V 1, 780a16* = fa-inna l-dāʾa llaḏī yusammā šuhūlatan yaʿriḍu li-šahali l-ʿuyūni akṯara, fa-ammā l-dāʾu llaḏī yaʿriḍu li-l-laḏīna lā yabṣurū bi-l-layli fa-huwa yaʿriḍu li-sūdi l-ʿuyūni *178.3* (*cf. below,* abṣara 3).

2. *transl.* βλέπω (*to see; to perceive*) *and its compounds*

2.1 βλέπω (*to see; to perceive*) **(a)** *abs.* : εἰσὶ γάρ τινες οἳ καθεύδοντες ἀνίστανται καὶ πορεύονται βλέποντες ὥσπερ (*post* ὥσπερ *add.* οἱ *Sb, Arab.*) ἐγρηγορότες *Arist. Gener. anim. V 1, 779a17** = wa-mina l-nāsi man huwa nāʾimun yaqūmu wa-yamšī wa-huwa yabṣuru miṯla mā yafʿalu l-sāhiru *175.17* ↤ ἵνα ταῖς χερσὶν ἢ τοῖς ποσὶ ψηλαφῶν ὥσπερ βλέπῃ *Artem. Onirocr. 35.8* = fa-yaṣīru ilā an yağussa bi-yadayhi aw bi-riğlayhi fa-ka-annahū yabṣuru bihā *66.5* **(b)** *in hend.* baṣura wa-aḥassa bi- : καὶ πεῖσαι τοὺς ἀνθρώπους, ὡς ἔστι δαίμων ἀφθίτῳ θάλλων βίῳ, ὃς ταῦτ' (ταῦτ' *ed.* : πάντ' *ut vid. Arab.*) ἀκούει καὶ βλέπει *Ps.-Plut. Placita 298a26** = wa-aqnaʿa l-nāsa bi-anna ḏāmun bāqin (*sic ed. pro* bāqiyan) abadan yasmaʿu wa-yabṣuru wa-yuḥissu bi-ğamīʿi l-ašyāʾi *13.5*⊗.

2.2 ἐπιβλέπω (*to look closely*) : τὰς δ' ἅμα λεγομένας δήλας εἶναι ἐπιβλέψασιν *Arist. Rhet. II 21, 1394b15* = min qibali annahū ḥīna yuqālu fa-huwa ẓāhirun min sāʿatihī li-llaḏīna yabṣurūna *138.9*.

3. θεωρέω (*to observe, theorize*) : ὥσπερ ὁ καθεύδων γεωμέτρης τοῦ ἐγρηγορότος πορρωτέρω καὶ οὗτος τοῦ θεωροῦντος *Arist. Gener. anim. II 1, 735a11* = miṯla l-massāḥi l-nāʾimi fa-innahū yuqālu innahū yabʿudu mina l-massāḥi l-mustayqiẓi wa-huwa ayḍan yabʿudu mina llaḏī yabṣuru *59.14* ⟼ δι᾽ ὃ γὰρ ἐπιτυγχάνουσιν οἵ τε διὰ συνήθειαν καὶ οἱ ἀπὸ ταὐτομάτου τὴν αἰτίαν θεωρεῖν ἐνδέχεται *Arist. Rhet. I 1, 1354a10* = wa-li-ḏālika qad yanǧaḥu llaḏīna yafʿalūna hāḏā bi-l-iʿtiyādi wa-llaḏīna yastaṭīʿūna an yabṣurū l-ʿillata fīhi min tilqāʾi anfusihim *1.13*; φανερὸν ὅτι ταύτας ἐστὶ λαβεῖν τοῦ συλλογίσασθαι δυναμένου καὶ τοῦ θεωρῆσαι περὶ τὰ ἤθη καὶ τὰς ἀρετὰς καὶ τρίτον τοῦ περὶ τὰ πάθη *I 2, 1356a22* = fa-huwa maʿlūmun annahū innamā yaqdiru ʿalā tanāwuli hāḏihi llaḏī yastaṭīʿu an yafʿala l-salǧasata wa-llaḏī yabṣuru maḏāhiba l-aḫlāqi wa-l-faḍāʾili wa-l-ṯāliṯatu maʿrifatu l-ālāmi *9.4*; οὐδὲ ῥητορικὴ τὸ καθ᾽ ἕκαστον ἔνδοξον θεωρήσει, οἷον Σωκράτει ἢ Ἱππίᾳ *I 2, 1356b33* = wa-laysat ayḍan ṣifatu l-rīṭūriyyati annahā llatī tabṣuru l-maḥmūdāti ʿinda kulli wāḥidin mina l-nāsi miṯla Suqrāṭīs aw Īfiyās *11.6*.

4. γιγνώσκων *act. part.* (*he who comprehends*) = allaḏī yabṣuru : ὅταν γὰρ γιγνώσκοντι ἐπεμβάλλῃ, διαλύει τὸ σαφὲς τῷ (τῷ *ed.* : τὸ *ut intell. Arab.*) ἐπισκοτεῖν *Arist. Rhet. III 3, 1406a34** = fa-iḏā tuzuyyida fīhi aw nuqiṣa minhu šayʾun ʿinda llaḏī yabṣuru tabayyana lahū ḏālika l-ġāmiḍu wāḍiḥan *182.15*.

بصر **I. baṣarun** *maṣdar → listed below after the verbal forms*

باصر **I. bāṣirun** *act. part.*

1. *transl.* ὁράω (*to see*) *and its derivatives*

1.1 ὁρῶν *act. part.* (*seeing*) : ἤτοι μὴ κινουμένου τοῦ ὁρῶντος ἢ λανθάνοντος αὐτὸν ὅτι κινεῖται, τότε ὡς κινούμενον ὁρᾷ τὸ ὁρώμενον *Alex. An. mant. [Vis.] 147.9* = <wa-> kāna l-bāṣiru <lā> yataḥarraku aw lā <yuḥissu bi-an> yataḥarraka fa-innā narā ḥīnaʾiḏin l-mubṣara ka-annahū yataḥarraku *161.155*.

1.2 ὁρατικός (*having the power of sight*) : εἴ γε καὶ αὐτὴ διαφανὴς ἔκκειται, τῇ τροπῇ τῇ ὑπὸ τῶν χρωμάτων, ὑφ᾽ ὧν τρεπομένη πως ὁμοιοτρόπως τῷ ἐκτὸς διαφανεῖ, ὁρατική τε καὶ αἰσθητικὴ ψυχὴ γίνεται *Alex. An. mant. [Vis.] 142.20* = iḏ kānat hiya ayḍan mušiffatan wa-tataḥarraku bi-l-taġayyuri llaḏi yakūnu mina l-alwāni fa-iḏā taġayyarat ḍarban mina l-taġayyuri ḫadamat l-nafsa l-ḥassāsata l-bāṣirata ʿalā miṯāli ḫidmati l-mušiffi l-ḫāriǧi *149.25* ⟼ πάλιν τοίνυν, ἐπειδὴ τὸ ἔργον ἑκάστης δυνάμεως περί τι ὑποκείμενον θεωρεῖται, καὶ οὐ πάσης περὶ ἅπασαν ὕλην ἐστὶν ἡ ἐνέργεια, ἀλλὰ τῇ μὲν ὁρατικῇ περὶ τὸ ὁρατόν *Them. In De an. 49.25* = innahū lammā kāna fiʿlu kulli wāḥidatin mina l-quwā innamā yūǧadu fī mawḍūʿihā wa-laysa yakūnu fiʿlu kulli quwwatin <...> (*lac. coni. Lyons*) fiʿlu l-quwwati l-bāṣirati yakūnu fī l-mubṣari *67.6*; καλεῖν μὲν ἁπτικὸν προσήκει, ὥσπερ ἀκουστικὸν καὶ ὁρατικὸν καὶ ὀσφραντικόν *76.37* = fa-qad yanbaġī an yusammā lāmisan ka-mā yuqālu sāmiʿun wa-bāṣirun wa-šāmmun *129.5*.

1.3 ὀπτικός (*pertaining to sight*) : τὸ μαλακὸν νεῦρον, ὃ δὴ καὶ ὀπτικὸν ὀνομάζεται *Galen Loc. aff. VIII, 219.14* = tilka l-ʿaṣabatu l-layyinatu llatī tusammā ʿaṣabatan bāṣiratan *WGAÜ Suppl. I, 785.13* ⟼ ὑπὸ ἀσθενείας γινομένης τοῦ ὀπτικοῦ πνεύματος *Paulus Aeg. III, 22.35* = fa-yakūnu ḏālika min ḍuʿfi l-rūḥi l-bāṣiri *WGAÜ Suppl. I, 785.16*.

1.4 *sem. amplif.*; τὸ ὁρατικόν (*the power of sight*) = al-quwwatu l-bāṣiratu : Δημόκριτος Ἐπίκουρος κατὰ εἰδώλων εἴσκρισιν οἴονται τὸ ὁρατικὸν συμβαίνειν *Ps.-Plut. Placita 403a3* = Ḏīmūqrīṭūs wa-Abīqūrus yarayāni anna l-quwwata l-bāṣirata takūnu bi-taḫayyulātin tutaṣawwaru *56.11*; Ἵππαρχος ἀκτῖνάς φησιν ... πρὸς τὸ ὁρατικὸν ἀποδιδόναι *404a6* = wa-ammā Ibbarḫus fa-yarā anna l-šuʿāʿāti ... tuʾaddī ḏālika ilā l-quwwati l-bāṣirati *56.17*.

مبصور I. mabṣūrun *pass. part.*

1. *sem. amplif.; added to provide the implied object of* ὁράω (*to see*) = ἡ δὲ εὐαισθησία ἐκ τῶν τοῦ σώματος μερῶν (*sc.* γίνεται) οἷον ἐάν τις ὀφθαλμοῖς ὁρᾷ *Ps.-Arist. Div. 27a16* = wa-l-iḥsāsu l-ṣaḥīḥu yatimmu bi-an takūna l-aʿḍāʾu salīmatan fa-yudriku l-baṣaru mabṣūrātihī *versio T 49.6*.

أبصر IV. abṣara

1. *transl.* ὁράω (*to see*) *and its derivatives and compounds*

1.1 ὁράω (*to see*) : τοῦ γὰρ χρόνου, ἐν ᾧ τις ὁρᾷ, τούτου ἐν ᾡτινιοῦν μορίῳ καὶ τῷ τυχόντι τοῦτο ὁρᾷ *Alex. An. mant.* [*Vis.*] *143.31* = wa-ḏālika anna l-zamāna llaḏī fīhi yubṣiru l-insānu šayʾan qad yubṣiruhū fī ayyi ǧuzʾini ttafaqa minhu *153.63* ⟼ ὁ γὰρ ὁρῶν στάδιον οὐ καὶ τὰ ἐντὸς ὄψεται μεγέθη, ἀλλὰ ... ὁ δυνάμενος ἰδεῖν στιγμὴν ... καὶ τῶν μειζόνων ἕξει αἴσθησιν *Arist. Cael. I 11, 281a20, 22* = wa-huwa anna man abṣara šayʾan min ġalwatin lā yastaṭīʿu an yubṣira mā dūnahū fī l-ʿiẓami min aqalli min ġalwatin, lākin ... man qawiya <ʿalā> (*nos*) an yubṣira nuqṭatan ... qawiya ʿalā an yubṣira akbara mina l-nuqṭati *versio B 206.7, 9*; sim.versio A 103b 1, 2* ↦ καὶ ὁρατὸν τὸ δυνατὸν ὁρᾶσθαι *Arist. Metaph. Θ 8, 1049b15* = wa-l-mubṣaru huwa llaḏī lahū quwwatun an yubṣara *1177.6*; οὐ γὰρ ἵνα ὄψιν ἔχωσιν ὁρῶσι τὰ ζῷα ἀλλ' ὅπως ὁρῶσιν ὄψιν ἔχουσιν (ἀλλὰ πῶς ὁρῶσιν ὃ οὐκ ἔχουσιν *ut intell. Arab. ut vid.*) *Θ 8, 1050a10-11** = fa-inna l-ḥayawāna lā yubṣiru li-yakūna lahū baṣarun bal kayfa yubṣiru mā laysa lahā *1186.8* ↦ ἄν τις δύνηται τὸ ὅμοιον ὁρᾶν *Arist. Rhet. II 20, 1394a5* = iḏā kāna l-marʾu yubṣiru l-šabīha wa-l-mušākila *136.7*; τὸ μὲν «ἰδὼν» οὐ κοινόν, τὸ δ' «αἰσθόμενος» κοινόν *III 5, 1407b20* = fa-inna qawlaka abṣartu laysa ʿāmman wa-ammā qawluka aḥsastu fa-ʿāmmun *188.4* ↦ ἰδεῖν δὲ ἀπὸ γῆς πλοῖα διὰ θαλάσσης πλέοντα καὶ εὐπλοοῦντα ἀγαθὸν πᾶσι *Artem. Onirocr. 140.19* = fa-in raʾā l-insānu ka-annahū ʿalā šāṭiʾi l-baḥri wa-annahū yubṣiru safīnatan tasīru fī l-baḥri sayran raqīqan fa-inna ḏālika dalīlu ḫayrin li-ǧamīʿi l-nāsi *253.6* ↦ τίς γὰρ οὐκ ὁρᾷ τὸ σῶμα καὶ τὴν ψυχὴν ἁπάντων τῶν ὑπὸ τοῖς ἄρκτοις <ἀνθρώπων> ἐναντιώτατα διακείμενα τοῖς ἐγγὺς τῆς διακεκαυμένης ζώνης; *Galen An. virt. 64.13* = fa-man tarāhu lā yubṣiru anna l-nāsa llaḏīna yaskunūna l-ǧirbiyāʾa hum ḍiddu l-nāsi llaḏīna yaskunūna qarīban min mawḍiʿi l-iḥtirāqi fī abdānihim wa-anfusihim? *33.2* ↦ καμπύλας δὲ γραμμὰς καθ' ὕδατος βλέπομεν γινομένας *Ps.-Plut. Placita 372a22* = wa-ammā l-ašyāʾu llatī narāhā ʿalā ḫuṭūṭin munḥaniyatin fa-hiya mā nubṣiruhū fī l-māʾi *42.6*; ὁρᾷ δὲ οὐδέν, ἀλλὰ δοκεῖ μόνον *402a27* = wa-huwa lā yubṣiru šayʾan min ḏālika lakinnahū yaẓunnu ẓannan faqaṭ *56.4*; βλέπεται γὰρ ταῖς ἀληθείαις, ὅτι ἐστὶ σκότος *406a2* = fa-innahū qad tubṣiru šayʾan taʿlamu annahū ẓalāmun *57.13*; *sim. 402a32* = *56.6.*

1.2 ὁρατός (*seen, visible*) : διὸ καὶ δυσόρατα ἢ ὁρατὰ καθ' αὑτά, ὅσοις ὁμόχρουν τὸ περιέχον *Alex. An. mant.* [*Vis.*] *146.3* = wa-li-ḏālika ṣārati l-ašyāʾu l-šabīhatu fī l-lawni bi-l-muḥīṭi yaṣʿubu idrākuhā bi-l-baṣari aw takūnu lā tubṣaru bi-ḏātihā *159.132* ↦ τὰ μὲν γὰρ γλαυκὰ δι' ὀλιγότητα τοῦ ὑγροῦ κινεῖται μᾶλλον ὑπὸ τοῦ φωτὸς καὶ τῶν ὁρατῶν ᾗ ὑγρὸν καὶ ᾗ διαφανές *Arist. Gener. anim. V 1, 780a3* = li-anna l-šuhla li-qillati l-ruṭūbati tataḥarraku ḥarakatan akṯara mina l-ḍawʾi wa-l-ašyāʾi llatī tubṣaru li-anna qillata l-ruṭūbati takūnu ṣāfiyata l-lawni min qibali l-ḍawʾi *177.14*.

1.3 ὁρατικός (*able to see*) : πόρρωθεν δ' ἔσται ὁρατικὸν *Arist. Gener. anim. V 1, 780b26* = fa-aṣḥābu hāḏihi l-ṣifati yubṣirūna min buʿdin kaṯīrin *179.15*; τὰ δ' ἐντὸς ἔχοντα τὰ ὄμματα ἐν κοίλῳ κείμενα ὁρατικὰ τῶν πόρρωθεν *V 1, 781a1* = wa-l-ʿaynu l-ġāʾiratu tubṣiru mā baʿuda ʿanhā *179.22*.

1.4 συνοράω (*to be able to see*) : οἵ οὐ δύνανται διὰ πολλῶν συνορᾶν *Arist. Rhet. I 2, 1357a4* = allaḏīna lā yastaṭīʿūna an yubṣirū l-umūra ʿan marātiba kaṯīratin *11.15*.

2. *transl.* βλέπω (*to see*) *and its compounds*

2.1 βλέπω (*to see*) : ὅταν δέ <τις> οἴηται βλέπειν (*sc.* τὴν ψυχὴν) τὰ μὴ βλεπόμενα *Galen An. virt. 48.16* = fa-ammā iḏā huwa waǧadahā (*sc.* al-nafsa) taẓunnu annahā tubṣiru mā laysa yubṣiruhū *21.23*.

2.2 ἐμβλέπω (*to look [specifically] at [s.th.]*) : ὥσπερ κατὰ τὴν ὄψιν οἱ ἐμβλέποντες *Arist. Eth. Nic. X 4, 1175a 9* = miṯla llaḏīna yubṣirūna l-baʿīda bi-ḥissi l-baṣari *545.10*.

3. *sem.; def.;* νυκτάλωψ (*night blindness*) *Arist. Gener. anim. V 1, 780a16* = al-dāʾu llaḏī yaʿriḍu li-llaḏīna lā yubṣirūna/yabṣurūna bi-l-layli *178.3* (*cf. above,* baṣura 1.3).

4. *sem.*; *def.*; ἔμφασις (*appearance in a smooth surface, reflection*) = al-tamṯīlu llaḏī yubṣaru : περὶ κατοπτρικῶν ἐμφάσεων *Ps.-Plut. Placita 405a1-2* = fī l-tamāṯīli llatī tubṣaru fī l-marāyā *56.22*.

إبصار **IV. ibṣārun** *maṣdar*

1. *transl.* ὁράω (*to see*) *and its derivatives*

1.1 ὁράω (*to see*) **(a)** *abs.* : πῶς κατὰ Ἀριστοτέλη τὸ ὁρᾶν γίνεται *Alex. An. mant. [Vis.] 141.29* = kayfa yakūnu l-ibṣāru ʿalā maḏhabi Arisṭāṭālīs *147.2*; οὕτως δὲ καὶ τὸ ὁρᾶν πασχούσης τῆς ὄψεως γίνεσθαι *141.31* = ka-ḏālika l-ibṣāru bi-nfiʿāli l-ʿayni *147.5*; διὰ τοῦτο δὴ καὶ ἀχρόνως δείκνυσιν ὁ Ἀριστοτέλης γινόμενον τὸ ὁρᾶν *143.30* = wa-li-ḏālika yubayyinu Arisṭū anna l-ibṣāra yaḥduṯu bi-lā zamānin *153.62*; *sim. 147.16 = 161.145* ⤚ τῇ γὰρ τοῦ ὀφθαλμοῦ ἀρετῇ εὖ ὁρῶμεν *Arist Eth. Nic. II 6, 1106a19* = li-anna faḍīlata l-ʿayni l-ibṣāru *169.14* **(b)** τὸ ὁρᾶν = *in hend.* al-muʿāyanatu wa-l-ibṣāru : ἔνια γὰρ εἰ ἑωρῶμεν οὐκ ἂν ἐζητοῦμεν, οὐχ ὡς εἰδότες τῷ ὁρᾶν, ἀλλ' ὡς ἔχοντες τὸ καθόλου ἐκ τοῦ ὁρᾶν *Arist. An. post. I 31, 88a13-14* = wa-ḏālika anna baʿḍa l-ašyāʾi law kunnā nuʿāyinuhā la-mā kunnā nabḥaṯu, wa-laysa ḏālika min qibali annā kunnā nuḥaṣṣilu ʿilman bi-l-muʿāyanati wa-l-ibṣāri lākin min qibali annā kunnā nuḥaṣṣilu l-kulliyya mina l-muʿāyanati wa-l-ibṣāri *419.1-2*.

1.2 ὅρασις (*seeing, the act of sight*) : ἡ μὲν γὰρ τῆς ὄψεως ἐνέργεια ὅρασις λέγεται *Them. In De an. 84.17* = fa-inna fiʿla l-baṣari yuqālu lahū ibṣārun *146.4*.

1.3 ὄψις (*sight, power of seeing*) : ὥστε τὸ μὲν κοῖλον ἄνω γίνεσθαι, τὸ δὲ κυρτὸν κάτω πρὸς τὴν ἡμετέραν ὄψιν *Ps.-Plut. Placita 354a8* = fa-yaṣīru muqaʿʿaruhū ila fawqu wa-maḥdūdun bihī ilā asfala mimmā yalī ibṣāranā *34.20*; ἄλλοι δὲ ἀνάκλασιν (*sc.* τὸν κομήτην εἶναι) τῆς ἡμετέρας ὄψεως εἰς τὸν ἥλιον παραπλησίαν ταῖς κατοπτρικαῖς ἐμφάσεσιν *366a11* = wa-āḫarūna yarawna annahu (*sc.* kawkaba l-ḏuʾābati) nʿikāsu šuʿāʿi ibṣārinā ʿani l-šamsi qarīban mimmā yurā fī l-marāyā *39.21*.

2. ἀνάβλεψις (*seeing*) : εἰ μή τις καὶ τὴν ἀνάβλεψιν καὶ τὴν ἁφὴν γενέσεις φησίν *Arist. Phys. VII 3, 247b21 (textus alter)* = allāhumma illā an yaqūla qāʾilun inna l-ibṣāra wa-l-lamsa takawwunun *762.13*.

مبصر **IV. mubṣirun** *act. part.*

1. *transl.* ὁράω (*to see*) *and its derivatives*

1.1 ὁρῶν *act. part.* (*seeing*) : ὁ γὰρ μεταξὺ ἀὴρ καθὸ συμβάλλει ἀλλήλοις τὰ χρώματα, τοῦτο δέ ἐστι καθὸ τέμνουσιν ἄλληλα, αὐτῶν τὰ διαγώνια ὁρώντων, ἅμα δόξει τὰ ἐναντία χρώματα ἀναδέχεσθαι *Alex. An. mant.* [*Vis.*] *147.21* = wa-ḏālika anna l-hawāʾa fī-mā baynahumā yuẓannu bihī annahū yaqbalu l-alwāna l-mutaḍāddata ʿinda talāqī l-alwāni aʿnī ʿinda taqāṭuʿi šuʿāʿāti mubṣirī (mubṣirī *corr. Gätje* : baṣarī *ms.*) l-mutaqābilīna *161.149*.

1.2 ὀπτικός (*of sight, pertaining to sight*) : πάλιν αὖ δυνάμεις αὐτὴν ἔχειν λέγομεν ὀπτικὴν ἀκουστικὴν ὀσφρητικὴν γευστικὴν ἁπτικήν *Galen An. virt. 35.2* = qad naqūlu ayḍan <inna lahā> (*add. Biesterfeldt Ǧālīnūs, p. 134*) quwwatan mubṣiratan wa-sāmiʿatan wa-šāmmatan wa-ḏawwāqatan wa-lāmisatan *11.14*; οὐδὲν αὐτῆς τῆς ὀπτικῆς δυνάμεως πεπονθυίας *49.9* = min ġayri an yakūna fī l-rūḥi l-mubṣiri šayʾun mina l-alami *22.14*; τὸ δ' ἀνθ' ἑνὸς τρία βλέπειν αὐτῆς τῆς ὀπτικῆς δυνάμεώς ἐστι μέγιστον πάθος *49.10* = wa-ammā mā yaʿriḍu fī l-baṣari min ruʾyati l-wāḥidi ṯalāṯatan fa-innahū dalīlun ʿalā alamin ʿaẓīmin fī l-quwwati l-mubṣirati *22.15*.

! 2. *transl.* (ἐν)θεάομαι (*to behold, view*), *misunderstood as being the derivation of* ἐνθεαστικός (*inspired*) : Πλάτων καὶ οἱ Στωικοὶ τὴν μαντικὴν εἰσάγουσι κατὰ τὸ ἔνθεον ὅπερ ἐστὶν ἐνθεαστικόν *Ps.-Plut. Placita 415a12* = inna Aflāṭūn wa-aṣḥāba l-Riwāqi yaqūlūna bi-lkahānati min qibali l-ǧawhari l-ilāhiyyi l-ḫāmisi llaḏī huwa mubṣirun *63.4*.

مبصر IV. mubṣarun *pass. part.*

1. *transl.* ὁράω (*to see*) *and its derivatives*

1.1 ὁρώμενος *pass. part.* (*seen, visible*) : καὶ σώζει τὴν ἀπὸ τοῦ ὁρωμένου εἰκόνα καὶ σκιάν *Alex. An. mant.* [*Vis.*] *142.28* = wa-taḥfaẓu ṣūrata l-mubṣari wa-ẓillahū *149.30*; τὸ δὲ φῶς καὶ τὰ εἴδη τῶν ὁρωμένων *143.27* = fa-ammā l-ḍawʾu wa-ṣuwaru l-mubṣarāti *151.60*; ἀλλ' οὐ πρὸς τὰ ὁρώμενα (τὰ ὁρώμενα *Arab., cf. Bruns, note 19* : τῷ ὁρωμένῳ *codd., ed.*) ἐκπεμπομένου τινὸς ἀπὸ τῆς ὄψεως *145.19** = min ġayri an yakūna šayʾun yaḫruǧu mina l-ʿayni ilā l-mubṣarāti *157.116*; *sim. 141.34* = *147.8* (*v. infra* 1.2); *147.9-10* = *161.156* (*v. supra* bāṣirun 1.1) *etc.* ⟼ ἔξωθεν γὰρ καὶ οὐκ ἐν τῷ αἰσθανομένῳ ... τὸ ὁρώμενον *Alex. qu. III 3* [*Sens.*] *85.7* = aʿnī anna l-mubṣara lā yakūnu fī dāḫili baṣari l-mubṣiri ... lākinnahū yakūnu ḫāriǧan minhu *182.113* ⟼ οὐθὲν γὰρ διαφέρει κινεῖν τὴν ὄψιν ἢ (ἢ *om. Arab. versionis B*) τὸ ὁρώμενον *Arist. Cael. II 8, 290a24* = wa-lā yunkaru (*sic leg. cum mss.*) an yakūna l-baṣaru (*sic leg.* : li-l-baṣar *mss.*) yuḥarriku l-mubṣara *versio B 261.1**; wa-lā farqa bayna an yakūna ḏālika min ǧihati l-baṣari aw min ǧihati l-mubṣari *versio A 87a13* ⟼ πάντα γὰρ τὰ ὁρώμενα, ὅσα μήτε ὑπὸ τύχης μήτε ὑπὸ ἀνάγκης μήτε ἐστὶ θεῖα μήτε τοιαύτην αἰτίαν ἔχει, φυσικὰ λέγεται *Ps.-Plut. Placita 274a27* = fa-inna kulla l-mubṣarāti llatī lam takun bi-ttifāqin wa-lā bi-ḍarūratin wa-lam takun ilāhiyyatan wa-lam takun lahā ʿillatun miṯla hāḏihī yuqālu innahā ṭabīʿiyyatun *2.15*.

1.2 ὁρατός (*seen, visible*) **(a)** *abs.* : ἀλλὰ τοῦ μεταξὺ τῆς τε ὄψεως καὶ τοῦ ὁρωμένου διαφανοῦς ἀλλοιουμένου πως ὑπὸ τοῦ ὁρατοῦ καὶ τὸ εἶδος τὸ ἀπὸ τοῦ ὁρατοῦ τῇ ὄψει διαγγέλλοντος *Alex. An. mant.* [*Vis.*] *141.35* = lākin bi-an yastaḥīla l-mušiffu llaḏī fī-mā bayna l-ʿayni wa-l-šayʾi l-mubṣari ʿani l-mubṣari bi-ḍarbin mina l-istiḥālati wa-yuʾaddiya ilā l-ʿayni ṣūrata l-mubṣari *147.8*; ἤτοι τοῦ φωτὸς ἀπελθόντος ἢ τῶν φωτιζόντων ἢ τῶν ὁρατῶν *145.16* = ʿinda tamaḥḥī l-ḍawʾi wa-l-aǧsāmi llatī tufīdu l-ḍawʾa awi l-mubṣarāti *157.113* ⟼ *Arist. Metaph. Θ 8, 1049b15* = *1177.5* (*v. supra* abṣara 1.1) ⟼ περὶ ἥν (*sc.* τὴν ἀόριστον δυάδα) ἐστι τὸ ὑλικὸν πλῆθος καὶ ὁ ὁρατὸς κόσμος (καὶ ὁ ὁρατὸς κόσμος *add. Arab.* : ἔστι δὲ καὶ ὁρατὸς ὁ κόσμος *(A)B C* : *om. E, Stob., Diels*) *Ps.-Plut. Placita 302a10** = wa-fīhā (*sc.* alṯāniyati llatī lā ḥadda lahā) l-kaṯratu l-ʿunṣuriyyatu wa-l-ʿālamu l-mubṣaru *14.23*; Πλάτων ὁρατὸν τὸν κόσμον γεγονέναι πρὸς παράδειγμα τοῦ νοητοῦ κόσμου *334a10* = wa-ammā Aflāṭūn fa-innahū yarā anna l-ʿālama l-mubṣara ʿumila ʿalā miṯāli l-ʿālami l-ʿaqliyyi *26.19*; Εἰ ὁρατὸν τὸ σκότος. Οἱ Στωικοὶ ὁρατὸν εἶναι τὸ σκότος *405a26-27* = hali l-ẓulmatu mubṣaratun? al-riwāqiyyūna yaqūlūna inna l-ẓulmata mubṣaratun *57.11-12*; *sim. 334a12 = 26.20*; *406a13 = 57.18* ⟼ *Them. In De an. 49.25 = 67.6* (*v. supra* bāṣir 1.2) ⟼ καθάπερ εἴ τις τῷ ἀοράτῳ τὸ ὁρατόν *Theophr. Princ. 9a23* = ka-mā law qāla qāʾilun fī šayʾin mina l-ašyāʾi innahū mubṣarun min ṭarīqi annahū ġayru mubṣarin *204.12* **(b)** *sem.; etym.; transl.* ὁρατός (*seen*) *in* ἀόρατος (*unseen*) = ġayru mubṣarin *Theophr. Princ. 9a23 : see the immediately preceding entry.*

2. θεωρητός (*that can be observed, contemplated*) *pass. part. of* θεωρέω : Ἐπίκουρος ἀνθρωποειδεῖς μὲν τοὺς θεούς, λόγῳ δὲ πάντας θεωρητοὺς διὰ τὴν λεπτομέρειαν τῆς τῶν εἰδώλων φύσεως *Ps.-Plut. Placita 306a14-15* = wa-ammā Abīqūrus fa-innahū yarā anna l-ālihata fī ṣūrati l-nāsi wa-annahum mubṣarūna bi-l-ʿaqli li-laṭāfati ṭabīʿati ǧawāhirihim *15.15*.

3. δεῖξις (*displaying, making visible*) = taṣyīrun mubṣaran : ἰδέα ... εἰκονίζουσα δὲ τὰς ἀμόρφους ὕλας καὶ αἰτία γινομένη τῆς τούτων δείξεως *Ps.-Plut. Placita 308a19* = lākinnahā (*sc.* al-ṣūrata) tuʿṭī l-ʿanāṣira llatī lā ṣūrata lahā taṣawwuran wa-takūnu ʿillatan li-taṣyīrihā mubṣaratan *16.16*.

تبصر **V. tabaṣṣurun** *maṣdar*

1. *sem. amplif.*, κρίνω (*to choose by distinguishing*) = tabaṣṣurun bi-l-tafriqa : κακῶς κρίνειν ἐστὶν τὸ βέλτιον καὶ τὸ χεῖρον *Arist. Phys. VIII 3, 254a31-32*= innamā huwa min fiʿli man lā tabaṣṣura lahū bi-l-tafriqati bayna l-ašrafi wa-l-aḫassi *829.16*.

بصر **baṣarun**

1. *transl.* ὁράω (*to see*) *in its sundry morphologies and their derivatives and compounds*

1.1 *transl.* ὁράω (*to see*) *and its derivatives and compounds*

1.1.1 ὁράω (*to see*) **(a)** *abs.* : οἷον τὸ φρονεῖν καὶ ὁρᾶν *Arist. Eth. Nic. I 6, 1096b17* = bi-manzilati l-fahmi wa-l-baṣari *127.12* ⟼ οὐ γὰρ καθ’ ὁτιοῦν μέρος ἄρρεν οὐδὲ θῆλυ, ὥσπερ οὐδ’ ὁρῶν καὶ ἀκοῦον *Arist. Gener. anim. IV 1, 766b6* = wa-lā yakūnu ḏālika (*sc.* al-ḏakaru wa-l-unṯā) bi-ḫtilāfi ayyimā yakūnu mina l-aʿḍāʾi li-anna li-kulli ʿuḍwin ʿamalan ḫāṣṣan miṯla mā yunsabu l-baṣaru ilā l-ʿayni wa-l-samʿu ilā l-uḏuni *141.9*; οὐ μόνον δὲ τὰ εἰρημένα αἴτια τοῦ ἀμβλὺ ἢ ὀξὺ ὁρᾶν *V 1, 780a26* = wa-laysa l-ašyāʾu llatī waṣafnā ʿilala ḥiddati wa-ḍuʿfi l-baṣari (*sic ed. pro* ḥiddati l-baṣari wa-ḍuʿfihī) faqaṭ *178.11*⊗; καὶ γὰρ διὰ τοῦθ’ οἱ γέροντες οὐκ ὀξὺ ὁρῶσιν *V 1, 780a31* = wa-li-hāḏihi l-ʿillati lā yakūnu baṣaru l-šuyūḫi ḥāddan *178.16* ⟛ ὁρῶν τε γὰρ εἶναί φαμεν καὶ τὸ δυνάμει (*post* δυνάμει *add.* ῥητῶς *codd., secl. Jaeger : om.* A^{b}, Al^{p}, *Arab.*) ὁρῶν καὶ τὸ ἐντελεχείᾳ *Arist. Metaph. Δ 7, 1017b3-4** = fa-inna baʿḍahā huwiyyātun bi-l-baṣari fa-innahā tarā wa-baʿḍahā fa-inna lahā quwan tarā *555.14* ⟛ οἷον τὸ ἀκριβῶς ὁρᾶν αἱρετώτερον τοῦ ὀσφραίνεσθαι *Arist. Rhet. I 7, 1364a38* = ka-mā anna ṣiḥḥata l-baṣari āṯaru min ṣiḥḥati l-istinšāqi *35.23* ⟛ ὀξὺ ὁρᾶν τοῖς ὀφθαλμοῖς ἀγαθὸν πᾶσιν ἐπίσης *Artem. Onirocr. 32.9* = ḥiddatu l-baṣari fī l-manāmi maḥmūdun li-ǧamīʿi l-nāsi bi-l-sawiyyati *61.6*; καὶ τὰ τοῦ ἰδόντος ὄμματα, ὅτι τοῦ ὁρᾶν καὶ αὐτή ἐστιν αἰτία *163.7* = wa-yadullu ayḍan ʿalā ʿaynay ṣāḥibi l-ruʾyā wa-ḏālika annahā ayḍan ʿillatun li-l-baṣari *293.5*; οὔτε γὰρ τῷ ὁρῶντί φησί τις ἀναβλέψεις *221.1* = li-anna man kāna lahū baṣarun fa-laysa yaqūlu lahū l-nāsu tuʿṭā baṣaran *404.9*; *etc.* ⟛ ὁρῶμεν δὴ κατὰ γραμμὰς ἢ κατ’ εὐθείας ἢ κατὰ καμπύλας ἢ κατ’ ἀνακλωμένας *Ps.-Plut.Placita 372a14* = wa-baṣarunā yakūnu immā ʿalā ḫuṭūṭin mustaqīmatin wa-immā ʿalā ḫuṭūṭin munḥaniyatin wa-immā ʿalā ḫuṭūṭin munʿakisatin *42.1*; ἐπὶ τοῦ πῶς ὁρῶμεν *405a25* = kayfa yakūnu l-baṣaru? *57.10*; Χρύσιππος κατὰ τὴν συνέντασιν τοῦ μεταξὺ ἀέρος ὁρᾶν ἡμᾶς *406a5* = wa-ammā Ḫurūsībus fa-yarā anna l-baṣara yakūnu bi-mušārakati l-hawāʾi l-munbasiṭi l-mutawassiṭi bayna l-bāṣiri wa-mubṣari *57.14*; *etc.* **(b)** *sem. metathesis*; *pass. / act. transformation;* ὁρῶμαι = waqaʿa l-baṣaru ʿalā : ὄφις ἐξαίφνης ὀφθεὶς χλωρότητα ἐποίησεν *Hippocr. Humor. IX : 14* = iḏā waqaʿa l-baṣaru ʿalā ḥayyatin baġtatan ḥadaṯa fī l-lawni ṣufratun *21.7.*

1.1.2 ὅρασις (*seeing, the act of sight*) : δοκεῖ γὰρ ἡ μὲν ὅρασις καθ’ ὁντινοῦν χρόνον τελεία εἶναι *Arist. Eth. Nic. X 4, 1174a14* = fa-qad yuẓannu anna l-baṣara fī waqtin mā nāfiḏun *539.11*; οὐδὲ γὰρ ὁράσεώς ἐστι γένεσις *X 4, 1174b12* = fa-innahū laysa kawnun li-l-baṣari *543.2* ⟛ οἱ Στωικοὶ πέντε τὰς εἰδικὰς αἰσθήσεις, ὅρασιν ἀκοὴν ὄσφρησιν γεῦσιν ἁφήν *Ps.-Plut. Placita 399a3* = al-riwāqiyyūna yarawna anna l-ḥawāssa l-ḫāṣṣata ḫamsuni l-baṣaru wa-l-samʿu wa-l-šammu wa-l-ḏawqu wa-l-lamsu *54.2*; οἷον ἐπειδὰν δι' ὄψεως θεωρῶμεν τὸ λευκόν, ἔστι πάθος τὸ ἐγγεγενημένον διὰ τῆς ὁράσεως ἐν τῇ ψυχῇ *401a20* = miṯla mā annā iḏā ra'aynā l-abyaḍa bi-a'yuninā kāna baṣarunā lahū ta'ṯīran fī l-nafsi yaṣīru ilayhi bi-l-baṣari *55.13*; περὶ ὁράσεως, πῶς ὁρῶμεν *403a1* = fī l-baṣari wa-kayfa nanẓuru *56.10*; *etc.*

1.1.3 ὁρατός (*seen, visible*) **(a)** *sem. amplif.* mudrakun bi-ḥissi l-baṣari : χρῶμά ἐστι ποιότης σώματος ὁρατή *Ps.-Plut. Placita 313a3* = al-lawnu huwa kayfiyyatun li-l-ǧismi mudrakatun bi-ḥissi l-baṣari *18.12* **(b)** *sem. amplif.* wāqi'un taḥta l-baṣari: μάλιστα γὰρ τοῦτο (*sc.* τὸ λευκὸν) χρῶμα καὶ μάλιστα ὁρατὸν *Alex. qu. I 2 [Color] 6.29* = fa-inna l-bayāḍa ... huwa afḍalu l-alwāni fa-ṣāra li-ḏālika wāqi'an taḥta l-baṣari akṯara min sā'iri l-alwani *82*; ἔστι δὲ τῶν ἁπλῶν σωμάτων μάλιστα μὲν τὸ πῦρ ὁρατόν *7.1* = wa-naqūlu ayḍan inna l-nāra wāqi'atun taḥta l-baṣari min bayni l-aǧrāmi l-mabsūṭati *88* **(c)** *sem. amplif.* ὁρατός in δυσόρατος (*seen with difficulty*) = idrākun bi-l-baṣari : διὸ καὶ δυσόρατα ἢ ὁρατὰ καθ' αὑτά, ὅσοις ὁμόχρουν τὸ περιέχον *Alex. An. mant.* [*Vis.*] *146.3* = wa-li-ḏālika ṣārati l-ašyā'u l-šabīhatu fī l-lawni bi-l-muḥīṭi yaṣ'ubu idrākuhā bi-l-baṣari aw takūnu lā tubṣaru bi-ḏātihā *159.132*.

1.1.4 ὁρατικός (*having the power of sight; the power itself*) : διὰ τῆς κινήσεως τῆς γινομένης ὑπὸ τῶν ἐκείνοις ὄντων χρωμάτων ἐν αὐτῷ, διακονεῖσθαι τοῖς τῶν ζῴων ὁρατικοῖς *Alex. qu. I 2 [Color] 6.13* = fa-iḏā taḥarraka mina l-alwāni qabila ba'ḍahā wa-addāhu ilā baṣari l-ḥayawāni *64*; διάκονον γίνεται ταῖς ὁρατικαῖς αἰσθήσεσιν *6.21* = yu'addīhā ilā ḥissi l-baṣari *71* ⟼ οἱ Στωικοὶ ἐξ ὀκτὼ μερῶν φασι συνεστάναι, πέντε μὲν τῶν αἰσθητικῶν ὁρατικοῦ ἀκουστικοῦ ὀσφραντικοῦ γευστικοῦ ἁπτικοῦ *Ps.-Plut. Placita 390a7* = wa-ammā aṣḥābu l-riwāqi fa-innahum yarawna anna aǧzā'a l-nafsi ṯamāniyatun: ḫamsun minhā l-ḥawāssu wa-hiya l-baṣaru wa-l-sam'u wa-l-šammu wa-l-ḏawqu wa-l-lamsu *51.12*.

1.1.5 *sem.; etym.;* ὁράω in εἰσοράω (*to look steadily or sharply at*) = aḥadda l-baṣara: ἐσορῶντι δὲ κλέπτεταί οἱ ἡ αὐγή *Hippocr. Nat. hom. 220.7* = iḏā aḥadda l-baṣara ḫtabasa l-ḍaw'u *36.8*.

1.2 *transl. derivatives and compounds of* ὄπωπα, *2nd perf. of* ὁράω (*to see*)

1.2.1 ὄψις (*vision, power of seeing*) **(a)** *abs.*; ὅτι δὲ ἡ ὄψις καὶ ἡ κόρη, διαφανὴς οὖσα *Alex. An. mant.* [*Vis.*] *145.16* = anna l-baṣara wa-l-ḥadaqata lammā kānat mušiffatan *157.114*; τὰ δὲ λαμπρότερα (*sc.* τῶν χρωμάτων) μᾶλλον καὶ σφοδρότερον κινεῖ τὴν ὄψιν *145.32* = wa-minhā (*sc.* al-alwāni) mā hiya akṯaru išrāqan wa-tuḥarriku l-baṣara taḥrīkan ašadda *159.125*; παρὰ δὴ τὰς τοιαύτας διαφορὰς τῶν ὁρωμένων σχημάτων ἡ ὄψις ἀντιλαμβάνεται *146.1* = fa-bi-ḥasabi hāḏihi l-iḫtilāfāti yudriku l-baṣaru l-aškāla l-mubṣara *159.130* ↤ ἡ μὲν γὰρ ὄψις ἡ τοῦ ἐλάττονος ὑπερέχει *Arist. Cael. I 11, 281a26* = wa-ḏālika anna l-baṣara iḏā adraka aṣġara mā yumkinuhū idrākuhū lam yatamakkan min idrāki mā huwa aṣġaru minhu *versio A 104a2*; ἡ γὰρ ὄψις ἀποτεινομένη μακρὰν ἑλίσσεται διὰ τὴν ἀσθένειαν *II 8, 290a17* = wa-ḏālika anna l-baṣara iḏā na'ā kaṯīran wa-mtadda ltawā (*sic leg. cum mss.*) li-ḍuʿfihī (*sic leg. cum mss.*) wa-dāra *versio B 260.10**; wa-ḏālika anna l-baṣara iḏā mtadda kaṯīran ḍaʿufa wa-ḍṭaraba *versio A 86b15*; οἱ μὲν γὰρ πλάνητες ἐγγύς εἰσιν, ὥστ' ἐγκρατὴς οὖσα πρὸς αὐτοὺς ἀφικνεῖται ἡ ὄψις *II 8, 290a21* = fa-li-ḥāli qurbihā (*sc.* al-kawākibi l-mutaḥayyirati) (minhā *add. ed., delendum*) yanāluhā l-baṣaru wa-yabluġu ilayhā bulūġan qawiyyan *versio B 260.15**; fa-li-aǧli qurbihā mā yudrikuhā l-baṣaru idrākan ṣaḥīḥan wa-yantahī ilayhā *versio A 87a5*; *etc.* ↤ νωδόν τε γὰρ λέγομεν οὐ τὸ μὴ ἔχον ὀδόντας, καὶ τυφλὸν οὐ τὸ μὴ ἔχον ὄψιν *Arist. Cat. 10, 12a32* = fa-innā innamā naqūlu adrada lā li-man lam takun lahū asnānun wa-naqūlu aʿmā lā li-man lam yakun lahū baṣarun *65.2*; στέρησις δὲ καὶ ἕξις λέγεται μὲν περὶ ταὐτόν τι, οἷον ἡ ὄψις καὶ ἡ τυφλότης περὶ ὀφθαλμόν *10, 12a27* = fa-ammā l-ʿadamu wa-l-malakatu fa-innahumā fī šay'in wāḥidin bi-ʿaynihī yuqālāni, miṯālu ḏālika l-baṣaru wa-l-ʿamā fī l-ʿayni *64.20* ↤ διαφέρει δὲ ἡ ὄψις ἁφῆς καθαρειότητι *Arist. Eth. Nic. X 5, 1176a1* = wa-yanfaṣilu l-baṣaru mina l-lamsi bi-l-bahā'i *551.2*; *etc.* ↤ ὅπερ ἐμφαίνεται κατὰ τὴν ὄψιν μιγνυμένων καὶ συνδυαζομένων *Arist. Gener. anim. I 23, 731a13* = wa-ḏālika bayyinun li-l-baṣari iḏā kāna fī l-ǧimāʿi *48.9* ↤ ἐνδέχεται γὰρ τῷ αὐτῷ κατὰ μὲν τὴν ὄψιν μέλι φαίνεσθαι τῇ δὲ γεύσει μή *Arist. Metaph. Γ 6, 1011a26* = fa-innahū yumkinu an yaẓhara l-šay'u l-wāḥidu bi-l-baṣari annahū ʿasalun wa-bi-l-ḏawqi annahū laysa bi-ʿasalin *442.5*; ὁμοίως δὲ καὶ τινός ἐστιν ἡ ὄψις ὄψις, οὐχ οὗ ἐστὶν ὄψις *Δ 15, 1021a33-1021b1* = wa-miṯla ḏālika in kāna l-baṣaru baṣaran li-šay'in mā fa-laysa huwa baṣaran li-llaḏī huwa *611.3-4*; *Θ 8, 1050a10-11* = *1186.8* (*v. supra* abṣara 1.1) ↤ τὴν ὄψιν προτερεῖν τῆς ἀκοῆς *Arist. Meteor. II 9, 369b9* = wa-l-baṣaru yasbiqu l-samʿa wa-yuḥissu li-waqtihī *844* ↤ καὶ ἡ μὲν ἐπιφάνεια πρὸς τὸ φῶς, τὸ δὲ φῶς πρὸς τὴν ὄψιν *Arist. Phys. VII 2, 245a24 (textus alter)* = wa-l-basīṭu yalī l-ḍaw'a wa-l-ḍaw'u yalī l-baṣara *751.11* ↤ καὶ γὰρ ὄψις ὀσφρήσεως (*sc.* αἱρετωτέρα) *Arist. Rhet. I 7, 1364a38* = li-anna l-baṣara ayḍan āṯaru mina l-istinšāqi *35.24*; ἀκοὴν καὶ ὄψιν μετὰ λόγου (*sic interpunx. Arab.*) δὲ ὅσα ἐκ τοῦ πεισθῆναι ἐπιθυμοῦσιν *I 11, 1370a25** = fa-ammā l-samʿu wa-l-baṣaru fa-innamā yarkunāni ilā l-šahwati maʿa kalmāniyyatin manṭiqiyyatin *55.22* ⟼ ἀμαυρωτικὸν ὄψεως γίνεται *Diosc. Mat. med. I, 215.12* = aẓlamati l-baṣara *vetus transl. Ullmann Unters., 183* ⟼ ἀλλ' ἅμα τῇ ὄψει καὶ τὴν αἴσθησιν τῆς ἁφῆς προσπαραλαμβάνοντες *Galen Ther. Pis. 221.6* = iḏā raʾaynā šayʾan bi-l-baṣari mimmā nurīdu taǧribatahū nudannīhi ilā abdāninā *107b2*; τῆς ὄψεως, οἶμαι, διαπεμπούσης τῇ φύσει ... *254.5* = li-anna l-baṣara awrada ʿalā l-ṭabīʿati ... *118a3* ⟼ γλυκὺ ἐς τὴν ὄψιν καὶ ἐν χρώμασι καὶ ἐν ἄλλῃσι μίξεσι *Hippocr. Alim. 144.1* = ḥulwun fī l-baṣari wa-fī l-ḏihni wa-fī l-lawni wa-fī sāʾiri l-aḫlāṭi *11.7* ⟼ ἃ καὶ τῇ ὄψει καὶ τῇ ἁφῇ καὶ τῇ ἀκοῇ καὶ τῇ ῥινὶ καὶ τῇ γλώσσῃ καὶ τῇ γνώμῃ ἔστιν αἰσθέσθαι *Hippocr. Off. med. 30.5* = al-ašyāʾu llatī yumkinu an tuḥassa bi-l-baṣari wa-bi-l-lamsi wa-bi-l-samʿi wa-bi-l-anfi wa-bi-l-lisāni wa-bi-l-ʿaqli *1.6* ⟼ Πλάτων φλόγα (*sc.* τὸ χρῶμα) ἀπὸ τῶν σωμάτων, σύμμετρα μόρια ἔχουσαν πρὸς τὴν ὄψιν *Ps.-Plut. Placita 313a10* = wa-ammā Aflāṭūn fa-innahū kāna yarā anna l-lawna huwa ltihābun fī l-aǧsāmi lahū aǧzāʾun mušārikatun li-l-baṣari *18.17*; κάμπτεται γὰρ ἡ ὄψις βίᾳ διὰ τὴν πυκνοτέραν τοῦ ὕδατος ὕλην *372a23* = wa-ḏālika anna l-baṣara yanḥanī li-takāṯufi ʿunṣuri l-māʾi *42.6*; μεταξὺ τῆς σελήνης ἤ τινος ἄλλου ἄστρου καὶ τῆς ὄψεως ἀὴρ παχὺς καὶ ὀμιχλώδης (*sic leg. pro* ὁμιχλώδης *ed.*) ἵσταται *384a4** = in yakun bayna l-qamari wa-l-baṣari aw bayna l-baṣari wa-kawkabin āḫara hawāʾun ġalīẓun min ǧinsi l-ḍabābi *48.24-25*; *etc.* ⟼ ἀλλὰ καθ' ὃν ἥ τε τάξις ὁμοῦ καὶ ἡ διαφορὰ τῶν κινήσεων ὑπ' ὄψιν *Ptol. Hypoth. 72.1* = lākin bi-an yaʿmala ḏālika bi-nawʿin yuwaqqiʿu taḥta l-baṣari niẓāma l-ḥarakāti wa-fuṣūlahā *17.4* ⟼ καὶ ὥσπερ ἐπὶ τῆς ὄψεως τὰ μὲν χρῆται βλεφάροις ὥσπερ περιφράγμασι καὶ ἐλύτροις *Them. In De an. 69.30* = wa-ka-mā anna fī l-baṣari baʿḍa l-ḥayawāni yastaʿmilu l-aǧfāna bi-manzilati l-ḥuǧubi wa-l-waqāʾi *114.4; 68.37 = 112.5* (*v. infra* baṣarun 1.3); *84.16 = 146.4.* (*v. supra* ibṣārun 1.2) **(b)** *sem. amplif.* ḥissu l-baṣari : *Arist. Eth. Nic. X 4, 1175a8 = 545.10* (*v. supra* abṣara 2.2) ⟼ οἷον τὸ (*sc.* γένος) τῶν ἀσπαλάκων· τοῦτο γὰρ ὄψιν οὐκ ἔχει *Arist. Hist. anim. IV 8, 533a3* = miṯla ǧinsi l-ḫuldi fa-innahū laysa li-hāḏā l-ḥayawāni ḥissu l-baṣari *183.6* ⟼ ὥσπερ ἡ κόρη τῆς ὄψεως (*sc.* τὸ πρῶτον αἰσθητήριον) *Arist Part. anim. II, 8 653b25* = ka-mā naqūlu inna ḥadaqata l-ʿayni awwalu ḥissi l-baṣari *40.17* **(c)** *sem. amplif.* ālatu l-baṣari : τοῦ μὲν οὖν τὰς διαφορὰς (*sc.* τοῦ ἀκούειν καὶ ὀσφραίνεσθαι) κρίνειν καλῶς τὸ αἰσθητήριον αἴτιον, ὥσπερ ἐπὶ τῆς ὄψεως *Arist. Gener. anim. V 2, 781a19* = fa-iḏā kānat ālatu hāḏayni l-ḥissayni ǧayyidata l-ḫilqati takūnu taqḏī ʿalā fuṣūli l-kalāmi llaḏī yusmaʿu wa-l-aǧsādi allatī tušammu bi-qaḏāʾin šāfin (*sic. ed. pro* šāfin) ka-mā ḏakarnā ḥāla ālati l-baṣari *180.10*⊗.

1.2.2 ἡ ὀπτική (*sc.* θεωρία) (*the study of vision, optics*) = ʿilmu l-baṣari : ὁμοίως δὲ καὶ περὶ ὧν ἡ ὀπτικὴ πραγματεύεται καὶ ἡ ἐν τοῖς μαθήμασιν ἁρμονική *Arist. Metaph. B 2, 997b20* = wa-ka-ḏālika naqūlu fī l-ašyāʾi llatī yastaʿmiluhā l-ubṭīqā yaʿnī ʿilma l-baṣari wa-llatī yastaʿmiluhā ʿilmu taʾlīfi l-luḥūni l-taʿlīmiyyi *205.3*.

1.2.3 ὀπωπή (*poet. for* ὄψις; *sight, vision*) : καὶ φαέων ἀμβλεῖα ἄφαρ λάμψειεν ὀπωπή τῷ καὶ ἀρχομένης οὐκ ἀλέγοι φθίσιος *Galen Ther. Pis., Androm. 43* = wa-huwa nāfiʿun ayḍan min ġašāwati l-baṣari wa-min kawni l-māʾi fī l-ʿayni fī btidāʾi ḥudūṯihī *129a10*.

1.2.4.1 *sem.; etym.*; ἀμβλυώττω (*to be short-sighted, have weak sight*) = ḍaʿufa baṣaruhū, ḍuʿfu l-baṣari : τὸ δὲ ἀμβλυώττειν ἔνδειαν ἀργυρίου <καὶ ἀπραξίαν σημαίνει· ἀργυρίου> (*lac. suppl. Arab., cf. Brown III, 176-7* : δηλοῖ, ἐπειδὴ *V, ed. Pack* : *om. L*) μέν, ὅτι καὶ τὰ ὄμματα ψήφους ἔχει· ἀπραξίαν δέ, ὅτι οἱ ἀμβλυώττοντες ἧττον τὰ πρὸ ποδῶν ὁρῶσι *Artem. Onirocr. 32.10-11** = wa-ammā ḍuʿfu l-baṣari fa-yadullu ʿalā annahū sa-yakūnu muḥtāǧan ilā l-māli wa-annahū yaṣīru fī ʿuṭlatin, wa-ḏālika anna l-māla bi-manzilati l-ʿayni, wa-ammā l-ʿuṭlatu fa-yadullu ʿalayhā li-anna man ḍaʿufa baṣaruhū lam yadri mā bayna yadayhi illā bi-mašaqqatin *61.7-9* ↦ πρὸς τοὺς ... ἀμβλυωποῦντας ... ἁρμόζει *Diosc. Mat. med. I, 229.12* = wāfaqa ... ḍuʿfa l-baṣari *WGAÜ, 715.2*.

1.2.4.2 *sem.; etym.*; ἀμβλυωπία (*dim-sightedness*) **(a)** ḍuʿfu l-baṣari: βοηθεῖ ἀμβλυωπίαις *Diosc. Mat. med. I, 216.10* = nafaʿa min ḍuʿfi l-baṣari *WGAÜ, 714.23*; *II, 60.5 = vetus transl. Ullmann Unters., 183* ↦ ὁ δὲ ἱέραξ ἑψηθεῖς μετὰ μύρου σουσίνου ἀμβλυωπίας ἰᾶται *Galen Ther. Pis. 243.1* = wa-ammā l-bāzī fa-iḏā ṭubiḫa bi-duhni l-sawsani yanfaʿu min ḍuʿfi l-baṣari *114a15*; κεφαλαίας γοῦν τὰς χρονίας καὶ τὰ σκοτώματα ἰᾶσθαι πέφυκε καὶ δυσηκοΐας καὶ ἀμβλυωπίας παύειν *271.4* = wa-qad yusakkinu l-ṣudāʿa l-muzmina wa-yubriʾu mina l-dawarāni l-šadīdi wa-l-ṣamami wa-yanfaʿu min ḍuʿfi l-baṣari *123b9* **(b)** ġašāwatu l-baṣari: καὶ ἀμβλυωπίας δέ ἐστιν ἀνασκευαστικόν *Diosc. Mat. med. I, 38.6* = wa-yanfaʿu ġašāwata l-baṣari *al-Ḥāwī XX, 460.12*; *II, 97.19 = WGAÜ, 715.ult.* **(c)** ẓulmatu l-baṣari : *Diosc. Mat. med. I, 216.10 = vetus transl. Ullmann Unters., 182* **(d)** kadaru l-baṣari wakalāluhū : καὶ ἀμβλυωπίας δέ ἐστιν ἀνασκευαστικόν *Diosc. Mat. med. I, 38.6* = wa-yanfaʿu min kadari l-baṣari wa-kalālihī *al-Ḥāwī XXI, 397.4.*

1.2.4.3 *sem.; etym.;* ἀμβλυωπής, -ός (*dimming the sight*) = aẓlama l-baṣara : ὤκιμον βιβρωσκόμενον πολὺ ἀμβλυωπές ἐστιν *Diosc. Mat. med. I, 210.15* = bādarūǧun: al-iktāru minhu yuẓlimu l-baṣara *versio B WGAÜ Suppl. I, 102.9* = *sim. vetus transl. Ullmann Unters., 182*; *I, 181.5* = *WGAÜ Suppl. I, 102.12*; *etc.*

1.2.5 *sem.; etym.*; εὐωπός (*seeing well*) = yubṣiru baṣaran ǧayyidan: τὰ μὲν γὰρ ἐξόφθαλμα οὐκ εὐωπὰ πόρρωθεν *Arist. Gener. anim. V 1, 780b36* = fa-inna l-ʿayna l-nātiʾata (*sic leg.;* al-bāʾinata *ed.*) lā tubṣiru mā baʿuda ʿanhā baṣaran ǧayyidan *179.21**.

1.2.6.1 *sem.; etym.*; ὀξυωπής, -ός (*sharp-sighted*) = ḥāddu l-baṣari : τὰ μὲν γλαυκὰ (*sc.* τῶν ὀμμάτων) μὴ εἶναι ὀξυωπὰ τῆς ἡμέρας *Arist. Gener. anim. V 1, 779b35* = lā takūnu l-ʿuyūnu l-šuhlu ḥāddata l-baṣari fī l-nahāri *177.13* ⟼ ἔστι δὲ καὶ ὀξυωπὲς ἐσθιόμενον ὠμὸν καὶ ταριχευτόν *Diosc. Mat. med. II, 58.9* = idā ukila mamlūḥan aw ġayra mamlūḥin aḥadda l-baṣara *versio A* = wa-yuḥiddu l-baṣara akluhū *versio B WGAÜ Suppl. I, 781.7.*

1.2.6.2 *sem. methathesis*; *superlative / positive transformation*: ὀξυωπέστατος (*most sharp-sighted*) = ḥiddatu baṣarin : τούτων οἱ ἐντὸς (*sc.* ὀφθαλμοὶ) μάλιστα ὀξυωπέστατοι <ἐπὶ> (*Arab.* : *om. codd.*) παντὸς ζῴου *Galen An. virt. 56.13-14** = wa-l-ġāʾiratu minhā (*sc.* al-ʿaynayni) tadullu ʿalā ḥiddati baṣarin fī ǧamīʿi l-ḥayawāni *27.21.*

1.2.6.3 *sem.; etym.;* ὀξυωπία (*sharp-sightedness*) = ḥiddatu l-baṣari : μετὰ ... μέλιτος ἐὰν χρίσῃς τοὺς ὀφθαλμούς, ὀξυωπίαν μὲν παρέξεις *Cyranis I, 17* = idā uhidā ... ʿasal wa-ǧuʿila quṭūran li-ḥiddati l-baṣari nafaʿa min dālika *WGAÜ, 465.8.*

1.2.7 *sem.*; *def.*; νυκτάλωψ (*nightblindness*) = al-dāʾu lladī yamnaʿu mina l-baṣari fī l-layli : ὁ δὲ νυκτάλωψ ὑγρότητος πλεονασμός *Arist. Gener. anim. V 1, 780a20* = fa-ammā l-dāʾu lladī yamnaʿu mina l-baṣari fī l-layli fa-huwa yakūnu min katrati l-ruṭūbati *178.6.*

1.2.8 ὀφθαλμός (*eye*) : μηθὲν τῶν ἡμῶν ἐν ὀφθαλμοῖς φαινομένων *Arist. Cael. II 4, 287b17* = lā fī šayʾin mimmā yaqaʿu taḥta l-baṣari *versio B 245.10* ⟼ ἀποκαθαίρει ἀχλῦς τὰς ἐν ὀφθαλμοῖς *Diosc. Mat. med. I, 211.6* = taǧlū iẓlāma l-baṣari *vetus transl. Ullmann Unters., 183* ⟼ οἷον ἐάν τις ὀφθαλμοῖς ὁρᾷ *Ps.-Arist. Div. 27a16* = fa-yudriku l-baṣaru mabṣūrātihī *versio T 49.6* ⟼ διὰ τί, ἐὰν ἀφροδισιάζῃ ὁ ἄνθρωπος, οἱ ὀφθαλμοὶ ἀσθενοῦσι μάλιστα *Ps.-Arist. Probl. phys. IV 32, 880* *b8* = mā bālu aṣḥābi l-ǧimāʿi taḍʿufu abṣaruhum? *V 30, 298.5* ↤ Μητρόδωρος (*sc.* τοὺς Διοσκούρους) τῶν ὁρώντων ὀφθαλμῶν μετὰ δέους καὶ καταπλήξεως εἶναι στιλβηδόνας *Ps.-Plut.Placita 347a7* = wa-ammā Miṭrūḏurus fa-innahū yarā annahā (*sc.* al-kawākiba llatī tusammā Diyusqūrū) stināratun taẓharu (taẓharu *secl. Gutas, p. 120*) li-l-baṣari l-maḥsūsi ʿalā sabīli l-bahtati *32.4*.

1.3 ὄμμα (*eye*) : καὶ τοῖς χρωμένοις πλείοσιν ἀφροδισίοις ἐνδιδόασι τὰ ὄμματα φανερῶς *Arist. Gener. anim. II 7, 747a16* = wa-iḏā kāna l-insānu kaṯīra l-ǧimāʿi kāna baṣaruhū ḍaʿīfan *90.22* ↤ διὰ τί καὶ οἱ ἀφροδισιάζοντες ... τὰ ὄμματα πρὸς ὀξυωπίαν βλάπτονται *Ps.-Arist. Probl. phys. IV 3, 876b25* = mā bālu aṣḥābi l-ǧimāʿi wa-mudminīhi taʾlamu abṣāruhum *V 3, 256.32* ↤ τὸ δὲ (*sc.* ἀόρατον) καὶ διὰ τὸ βλάπτειν τὴν ὄψιν ὡς τὰ λίαν στιλπνὰ καὶ ἀνταυγοῦντα τοῖς ὄμμασιν *Them. In De an. 68.38* = wa-minhu mā ġayru marʾiyyin min qibali annahū ayḍan yankī l-baṣara miṯla l-ašyāʾi llatī lahā barīqun šadīdun wa-lamʿun yaḫtaṭifu l-abṣāra *112.6*.

2. *transl.* βλέπω (*to see*) *and its compounds*

2.1 βλέπω (*to see*) : ἐν μὲν οὖν τῷ γήρᾳ καὶ ταῖς νόσοις διὰ ταύτας τὰς αἰτίας οὐκ ὀξὺ βλέπουσι *Arist. Gener. anim. V 1, 780b1* = fa-li-hāḏihi l-ʿilali lā yakūnu l-baṣaru ḥāddan fī l-amrāḍi wa-fī kibari l-sinni *178.20* ↤ τρίτος τρόπος τοῦ βλέπειν τὰ ἀνακλώμενα *Ps.-Plut. Placita 372a26* = wa-l-ǧihatu l-ṯāliṯatu min ǧihāti l-baṣari takūnu bi-l-inʿikāsi *42.8*.

2.2 ἀναβλέπω (*to recover one's sight*) = yuʿṭā baṣaran : *Artem. Onirocr. 221.1* = *404.10* (*v. supra* baṣarun 1.1.1).

3. θεωρέω (*to observe*) : βλέποντες δὲ τοὺς ἀστέρας ἀεὶ θέοντας αἰτίους τε τοῦ θεωρεῖν ἡμᾶς ἥλιον καὶ σελήνην θεοὺς προσηγόρευσαν *Ps.-Plut. Placita 296a9* = wa-lammā raʾaw l-kawākiba tataḥarraku dāʾiman wa-tasīru wa-anna l-šamsa wa-l-qamara ʿillatu baṣarinā sammūhā l-ālihata *11.21*.

4. *transl. derivatives of* δέρκομαι (*to see clearly*) *in compound words*

4.1 *sem., etym.;* ὀξυδερκία (*sharp-sightedness*) = ḥiddatu l-baṣari **(a)** *abs.* : ἁρμόζει δὲ εἰς τὰ πρὸς ὀξυδερκίαν ὀφθαλμικὰ καὶ μαλάγματα *Diosc. Mat. med. I, 18.8* = ǧayyidatun fī adwiyati l-ʿayni llatī yuzādu bihā ḥiddatu l-baṣari *al-Ḥāwī XXI, 4.3* **(b)** ὀξυδερκίαν ποιεῖ = aḥadda l-baṣara : εὔχροιάν τε καὶ ὀξυδερκίαν καὶ ὄρεξιν ποιεῖ *Diosc. Mat. med. I, 106.24* = wa-ḥassana l-lawna wa-aḥadda l-baṣara waanhaḍa l-šahwata *al-Ḥāwī XXI, 281.4* ⟼ τὸ τοῦ χερσαίου κροκοδείλου (*sc.* αἷμα) ποιητικὸν ὀξυδορκίας ἐστίν *Galen Simpl. medic. X, 263.2* = dam al-ḥarāḏīni yuḥiddu l-baṣara *WGAÜ, 463.4* **(c)** πρὸς ὀξυδερκίαν *Diosc. Mat. med. I, 34.14* = yağlū l-baṣara wa-yuḥidduhū *vetus transl. Ullmann Unters., 182* **(d)** *sem. metathesis; affirm. / neg. conceptual transformation* τὸ δὲ παλαιὸν (*sc.* ἔλαιον) θερμαντικώτερον καὶ διαφορητικώτερον, πρὸς ὀξυδερκίαν τε ὑπάλειμμα *Diosc. Mat. med. I, 34.14* = wa-l-ʿatīqu (*sc.* minhu) ašaddu isḫānan wa-taḥlīlan wa-yuktaḥalu bihī li-ẓulmati l-baṣari *al-Ḥāwī XX, 556.2*.

4.2 *sem., etym.;* ὀξυδερκής ([*becoming*] *sharp-sighted*) **(a)** aḥadda l-baṣara : ἡ χολὴ ... ὡς ὀξυδερκές *Galen Simpl. medic. X,279.6* = al-marāratu ... annahā tuḥiddu l-baṣara wa-tağlūhu *WGAÜ, 462.21* ⟼ ὁ δὲ χυλὸς τῆς ῥίζης καὶ τῆς πόας ὀξυδερκής *Diosc. Mat. med. II, 87.3* = wa-māʾu l-aṣli minhu wa-ġayri l-aṣli ... iḏā ktuḥila bihī aḥadda l-baṣara *WGAÜ, 462.-2* **(b)** ğalā l-baṣara : *Diosc. Mat. med. I, 228.6* = *vetus transl. Ullmann Unters., 182*.

4.3 *sem. metathesis; affirm. / neg. conceptual transformation* ὀξυδερκέστατος (*best in promoting sharp-sightedness*) = yanfaʿu min ḍuʿfi l-baṣari (*beneficial for weak sight*) : τὸ δὲ τῆς ἀσπίδος γῆρας τριφθὲν μετὰ μέλιτος καὶ ὑπαλειφόμενον ὀξυδερκέστατόν ἐστιν *Galen Ther. Pis. 242.5* = wa-ammā ğildu l-afʿā llatī tusammā bi-asbīs fa-iḏā suḥiqa bi-l-ʿasali yanfaʿu min ḍuʿfi l-baṣari *114a5*.

5. *medic.; used in the transl. of* ὑπόχυσις (*cataract*) *and its derivatives*

5.1 *sem.; def.;* ὑπόχυσις (*cataract*) **(a)** al-māʾu l-musātiru l-baṣara : παραπλήσιον εἶναι δόξει τῷ μὴ βλέπειν διὰ λήμην ἢ ὑπόχυσιν *Galen An. virt. 49.8* = fa-innahū yušbihu mā yaʿriḍu fī l-ʿayni mina l-qaḏā awi l-māʾi l-musātiri l-baṣara wa-l-māniʿi lahū mina l-naẓari *22.13* **(b)** nuzūlu l-māʾi fī l-baṣari : ποιεῖ δὲ καὶ πρὸς ἀρχομένας ὑποχύσεις *Cyranis I, 11* = nāfiʿun li-nuzūli l-māʾi fī l-baṣari *WGAÜ, 716.10*.

5.2 *paraphr.* ὑποχέομαι *pass.* (*to suffer from cataract*) = kāna ḍaʿīfa l-baṣari : οὔτε γὰρ τῷ ὁρῶντί φησί τις ἀναβλέψεις ἀλλ' <ὡς> εἰκὸς τῷ ὑποκεχυμένῳ *Artem. Onirocr. 221.2* = li-anna man kāna lahū baṣarun fa-laysa yaqūlu lahū l-nāsu tuʿṭā baṣaran bal innamā yaqūlūna<hū> li-man kāna ḍaʿīfa l-baṣari *404.10*.

6. *used in the transl. of* ἀχλύς (*film in the eyes*) *and its derivatives*

6.1 ἀχλύς (*film in the eyes*) **(a)** ẓulmatu l-baṣari : ἀποκαθαίρει ἀχλῦς *Diosc. Mat. med. I, 211.6* = yağlū ẓulmata l-baṣari *versio A WGAÜ Suppl. I, 205.13* **(b)** ġašāwatu l-baṣari : καὶ ἀχλῦς δὲ ὀφθαλμῶν *Cass. Bass. Geopon. XII, 25.5* = qad aṣābathu fī baṣarihī ġašāwatun *WGAÜ Suppl. I, 205.15.*

6.2 ἀχλυώδης (*dim [of sight]*) = *in hend.* aʿšā l-baṣara wa-aṯqalahū : νότοι βαρυήκοοι, ἀχλυώδεες *Hippocr. Humor. XIV : 1* = al-rīḥu l-ǧanūbiyyatu tuṯqilu l-samʿa wa-tuʿšī l-baṣara wa-tuṯqiluhū *29.4.*

7. *used in the transl. of* τυφλός (*blind*) *and its derivatives*

7.1 τυφλός (*blind*) = ḏahaba baṣaruhū : λόγος δέ τις ἔχει ὡς καὶ ὁ ποιητὴς Ὅμηρος τυφλὸς ἦν *Artem. Onirocr. 33.24* = wa-qad yušākilu ḏālika baʿḍa l-mušākalati amru Ūmīrus al-šāʿiri wa-anna baṣarahū ḏahaba *64.1*; τούτου ὁ πατὴρ τυφλὸς ἤδη ἐγεγόνει *34.3* = wa-kāna qad ḏahaba baṣaru abīhi qabla ḏālika *64.5*; καὶ τυφλὸς μὲν οὐκ ἐγένετο *35.11* = fa-lam yaḏhab baṣaruhū *66.8*; *sim. 34.24* = *65.11*; *35.5* = *66.2-3*; *etc.*

7.2 τυφλοῦμαι (*to be or become blind*) = ḏahaba baṣaruhū, ḏahābu l-baṣari : οἷον [δέ] ἐστι καί τὸ τετυφλῶσθαι τέκνοις ὄλεθρον καὶ οὐχὶ τῷ ἰδόντι σημαῖνον *Artem. Onirocr. 7.23* = wa-min hāḏā l-ǧinsi ayḍan insanun raʾā fī manāmihī anna baṣarahū ḏāhibun fa-dalla ḏālika ʿalā mawti wuldihī lā ʿalā mawtihī *16.4*; οἷον ἔδοξέ τις χρύσεα ὄμματα ἔχειν· ἐτυφλώθη διὰ τὸ μὴ ἴδιον ὀμμάτων εἶναι τὸ χρυσίον *12.22* = fa-miṯla insānin raʾā fī manāmihī ka-anna ʿaynayhi min ḏahabin fa-ʿaraḍa lahū ḏahābu l-baṣari *26.5.*

8. *sem.; expr.; used in the transl. of* φαίνομαι (*come to light, appear*) *and its derivatives* = waqaʿa taḥta l-baṣari

8.1 φαίνομαι (*appear, be seen*) : μηθὲν τῶν ἡμῖν ἐν ὀφθαλμοῖς φαινομένων *Arist. Cael. II 4, 287b17* = lā fī šayʾin mimmā yaqaʿu taḥta l-baṣari *versio B 245.10.*

8.2 φαντασία (*appearance*) : διὰ τῆς τῶν ἄστρων φαντασίας οὐ μόνον φανερὸν ὅτι περιφερής (*sc.* ἡ γῆ) *Arist. Cael. II 14, 297b31* = al-dalīlu ʿalā stidārati l-arḍi wa-annahā falakiyyatun wuqūʿu l-kawākibi taḥta l-baṣari *versio B 301.15.*

8.3 φανερός (*visible, evident*) = *in hend.* ġayru ḫafiyyin wāqiʿun taḥta l-abṣāri : ἀνάγκη τὸ ἄνω εἶναι τὸν ἀφανῆ πόλον· εἰ γὰρ ἔσται ὁ φανερός ... *Arist. Cael. II 2, 285b21* = kāna l-falaku l-aʿlā lā maḥālata huwa llaḏī yaḫfā ʿannā fa-lā narāhu, fa-in kāna l-mawḍiʿu l-aʿlā ġayra ḫafiyyin wa-kāna wāqiʿan taḥta abṣārinā ... *versio B 233.12.*

9. *meton.*; φῶς (*light*) : συνέβη καὶ τούτου τὸν πατέρα ἀποθανεῖν, ὃς καὶ τοῦ ζῆν καὶ τοῦ φωτὸς αἴτιος ἦν, ὥσπερ καὶ ἡ κεφαλὴ (*post*

κεφαλὴ *add.* τοῦ παντὸς σώματος *L V* : *om. Arab.,* secl. Hercher) *Artem. Onirocr. 7.22** = wa-ʿaraḍa li-hāḏā l-insāni an māta abūhu llaḏī huwa sababu ḥayātihī wa-baṣarihī ka-mā anna l-raʾsa huwa sababun li-ḏālika *16.3.*

10. *meton.*; αἴσθησις (*sense perception*) : ἀναγκαῖον εἶναι τὸ σχῆμα σφαιροειδὲς αὐτῆς (*sc.* τῆς γῆς) ... διὰ τῶν φαινομένων κατὰ τὴν αἴσθησιν *Arist. Cael. II 14, 297b24* = inna l-dalīla ʿalā šakli stidārati l-arḍi bi-l-ašyāʾi l-wāqiʿati taḥta l-baṣari *versio B 301.5* ⟼ ἀκριβοῖ τὰς αἰσθήσεις *Diosc. Mat. med. I, 187.1-2* = aḥadda l-baṣara *vetus transl. Ullmann Unters., 182.*

11. *meton..*; κόρη (*pupil of the eye*) : καὶ τὰ ταῖς κόραις ἐπισκοτοῦντα ἀποκαθαίρει *Diosc. Mat. med. I, 20.9* = wa-yaǧlū ẓulmata l-baṣari *al-Ḥāwī XX, 495.3*; *sim. I 62.9 = XXI, 314.1*; *I 92.9 = XX, 315.2*; ποιοῦν πρὸς τὰ ἐπισκοτοῦντα ταῖς κόραις *I, 36.19* = wa-yaǧlū ẓulmata l-baṣari *vetus transl. Ullmann Unters., 182*; *etc.*

بصري **baṣariyyun**

1. ὁρατικός (*having the power of sight*) : καὶ ὁρατικὸν τὸ ὁρᾶν *Arist. Metaph. Θ 8, 1049b15* = wa-l-baṣariyyu huwa llaḏī lahū quwwatun an yarā *1177.5.*

2. ὄψις (*sight; power of seeing*) : συνεκτεινομένου (*sc.* τοῦ φωτὸς) τῷ πυρώδει τῆς ὄψεως *Ps.-Plut. Placita 404a14* = fa-yalqā (*sc.* al-ḍawʾu) l-ḍiyāʾa l-nāriyya l-baṣariyya *56.21.*

3. ὀφθαλμός (*eye*) : Πλάτων κατὰ συναύγειαν (*sc.* τὸ ὁρατικὸν συμβαίνειν), τοῦ μὲν ἐκ τῶν ὀφθαλμῶν φωτὸς ἐπὶ ποσὸν ἀπορρέοντος εἰς τὸν ὁμογενῆ ἀέρα *Ps.-Plut. Placita 404a8* = wa-ammā Aflāṭūn fa-yarā anna l-baṣara yakūnu bi-štirāki l-ḍawʾi l-baṣariyyi bi-l-ḍawʾi l-hawāʾiyyi wa-sayalānihī fīhi bi-l-muǧānasati llatī baynahumā *56.18.*

بصير **baṣīrun**

1. *transl.* ὁράω (*to see*) *and its derivatives and compounds*

1.1 ὁρῶν *act. part.* (*seeing*) : λέγω δὲ τοῦτο ὅτι τοῦδε μὲν τοῦ ἀνθρώπου τοῦ ἤδη ὄντος κατ' ἐνέργειαν καὶ τοῦ σίτου καὶ τοῦ ὁρῶντος πρότερον τῷ χρόνῳ ἡ ὕλη καὶ τὸ σπέρμα καὶ τὸ ὁρατικόν (ὁρατόν *Arab., cf. Bouyges, Notice, p. clxxi*), ἃ δυνάμει μέν ἐστιν ἄνθρωπος καὶ σῖτος καὶ ὁρῶν, ἐνεργείᾳ δ' οὔπω *Arist. Metaph. Θ 8, 1049b22**

= ka-qawlī innahū ammā fī hāḏā l-insāni llaḏī qad kāna bi-l-fiʿli wa-l-ḥinṭati wa-llaḏī yubṣiru fa-inna l-ʿunṣura qablahū bi-l-zamāni, wa-l-zarʿu ayḍan wa-l-mubṣaru ilayhi llaḏī huwa ammā bi-l-quwwati fa-insānun wa-ḥinṭatun wa-baṣīrun, wa-ammā bi-l-fiʿli fa-laysat qablu *1177.10.*

1.2 ὁρατικός (*having the power of sight*) : ἀλλ' οὐ κατὰ πᾶν γε αὐτὸ θῆλυ καὶ ἄρρεν ἐστὶν ἀλλὰ κατά τινα δύναμιν καὶ κατά τι μόριον, ὥσπερ καὶ ὁρατικὸν καὶ πορευτικόν, ὅπερ καὶ φαίνεται κατὰ τὴν αἴσθησιν *Arist. Gener. anim. I 2, 716a30* = wa-lākin laysa l-unṯā wa-l-ḏakaru muttafiqayni ʿalā kulli ḥālin bal baynahumā ḫtilāfun bi-l-quwwati wa-bi-ʿuḍwin mina l-aʿḍāʾi ka-mā yuqālu l-baṣīru wa-l-sayyāru wa-ḏālika ẓāhirun bayyinun li-l-ḥissi *5.2.*

1.3 *sem. concentr.*; ὄψιν ἔχω (*to have sight*) : ὅταν γὰρ ἤδη πεφυκὸς ᾖ ἔχειν ὄψιν, τότε ἢ τυφλὸν ἢ ἔχον ὄψιν ῥηθήσεται *Arist. Cat. 10, 13a10* = aʿnī annahū iḏā ṣāra fī ḥaddin mimmā min šaʾnihī an yakūna lahū baṣarun fa-ḥīnaʾiḏin yuqālu lahū aʿmā aw baṣīrun *67.7*; τὸ γὰρ ὄψιν ἔχειν Σωκράτη τῷ τυφλὸν εἶναι Σωκράτη ἀντίκειται ὡς στέρησις καὶ ἕξις *10, 13b22* = fa-inna Suqrāṭ baṣīrun muqābilun li-Suqrāṭ aʿmā taqābula l-ʿadami wa-l-malakati *69.1*; μὴ ὄντος δὲ ὅλως τοῦ Σωκράτους καὶ οὕτω ψευδῆ ἀμφότερα, καὶ τὸ ὄψιν αὐτὸν ἔχειν καὶ τὸ τυφλὸν εἶναι *10, 13b26-27* = wa-matā lam yakun ayḍan Suqrāṭ aṣlan, fa-ʿalā hāḏā l-waǧhi ayḍani l-amrāni ǧamīʿan kāḏibāni aʿnī annahū baṣīrun wa-annahū aʿmā *69.5.*

2. εἰδώς (*knowing*), *act. part. of* οἶδα (*to have seen, to know*) : τὸν εἰδότα ἐμποδίζουσι *Arist. Soph. el. I 8, 169b29* = wa-l-baṣīru bihī qad yubṭiʾu ʿani l-ǧawābi *852.13 / fol. 341a.*

3. ἔμπειρος (*knowledgeable, experienced*) : αὐτός τε γὰρ ἦν ἔμπειρος οἰωνῶν *Galen Simpl. medic. XII, 314.16* = wa-kāna raǧulan baṣīran bi-l-takahhuni *WGAÜ Suppl. I, 348.7.*

4. *in hend.*; ἐπιμελής (*careful, attentive*) = baṣīrun nāfiḏun : καὶ τοὺς ῥαθύμους· ἐπιμελοῦς γὰρ τὸ ἐπεξελθεῖν *Arist. Rhet. I 12, 1372 b30* = wa-ḏawū l-kasali wa-l-tarāḫī ḫāṣṣatan li-anna stiḫrāǧa l-ḥukmi innamā huwa li-l-raǧuli l-baṣīri l-nāfiḏi *64.10.*

بصيرة **baṣīratun**

1. *sem. amplif.*; προσλαμβάνω (*to gain additionally, i.e., insight; in context*) : τῇ γὰρ ἐπὶ τὸν βασιλέα γενομένῃ ὑγιεινῇ καταστάσει τὴν πίστιν τῆς ὠφελείας ἡ ἀντίδοτος μᾶλλον προσείληφεν *Galen Ther. Pis. 217.3* = wa-ḏālika annahum lammā raʾaw l-malika qadi ntafaʿa bihī (*sc.* al-maʿǧūni) tazayyadū fīhi baṣīratan wa-waṯiqū bi-manfaʿatihī *106a10*.

باصور **bāṣūrun,** *pl.* **bawāṣīru** → bāsūrun *s. r.* b-s-r.

بوصير **būṣīrun**

1. φλόμος *bot.* (*mullein*) : ἄρκτιον τὸ μὲν τῷ φλόμῳ παραπλήσιον *Galen Simpl. medic. XI, 837.4* = arqaṭiyūn ... aḥaduhumā šabīhun bi-l-būṣīri *versio B WGAÜ, 736* (*and see Ullmann ad loc.*).

بصق

بصاق **buṣāqun** (*see also above s.v.* buzāqun, *II 230-231*)

1. *transl.* πτύω (*to spit*) *and its derivatives*

1.1 *in hend.;* πτύω (*to spit out*) = nafaṯa bi-l-buṣāqi : κώλυσις ἐπὶ (*sic interpunx. Arab.*) τοῖσι (τοῖσι *Arab. ut vid.* : τοῖσι δὲ δὴ *M, ed.*) αἱματώδεα πτύουσιν ὥρη, πλευρῖτις, χολή *Hippocr. Humor. 20:16** = manʿun fī man yanfuṯu bi-l-buṣāqi šayʾan damawiyyani l-waqtu wa-ḏātu l-ǧanbi wa-l-marāru *35.11*.

1.2 πτύσμα (*sputum*) : ἢν τὸ πτύσμα, ὅ τι ἂν ἀποβήσσωσι, βαρὺ ὄζῃ ἐπὶ τοὺς ἄνθρακας ἐπιχεόμενον ... θανατῶδες *Hippocr. Aphor. V.11* = iḏā ... kāna ma yaqḏifuhū bi-l-suʿāli mina l-buṣāqi (*sic. leg. pro* al-bḍāq *ed.*) munkara l-rāʾiḥati iḏā ulqiya ʿalā l-ǧamri ... fa-tilka min ʿalāmāti l-mawti *41.14**.

1.3 πτύαλον *or* πτύελον (*saliva, sputum*) : δύναμιν δὲ ἔχει (τὸ βδέλλιον) θερμαντικήν ... ἐνεθὲν πτυέλῳ ἀσίτου *Diosc. Mat. med. I, 61.6* = li-l-muqli quwwatun musḫinatun ... maḥlūlan bi-buṣāqi insānin ṣāʾimin *versio B WGAÜ Suppl. II, 223.2* ⟝ ἀποκρίσιες κατὰ φύσιν, κοιλίης, οὔρων, ἱδρῶτος, πτυάλου *Hippocr. Alim. 142.8* = inna l-marḫaḏa (*nos* : al-mrḫḏ *ed.*) l-ṭabīʿiyya huwa l-baṭnu wa-l-bawlu wa-l-ʿaraqu wa-l-buṣāqu *5.9** ⟝ τό τε γὰρ πτύαλον ἐνισχόμενον πυκνὸν τὸ πνεῦμα ποιεῖ, τό τε πνεῦμα ... ἐπιγλισχραίνει τὸ πτύαλον *Hippocr. Diaet. acut. 43.16, 18* = wa-ḏālika anna l-buṣāqa iḏā ḥtabasa ǧaʿala l-tanaffusa mutawātiran, wa-l-tanaffusu ayḍan ... yazīdu fī luzūǧati l-buṣāqi *10.4-5; 42.16 = 9.4* ⟼ πτυάλου, βηχός, μύξης (βηχός, μύξης *A, Arab.* : μύξης, βηχός *M, ed.*) *Hippocr. Humor. 2:6** = al-buṣāqu wa-l-suʿālu wa-l-muḫāṭu *3.12;* ἢ πτύαλον, ἢ ῥίς, ἢ δάκρυον *4:13* = aw buṣāqun aw anfun aw dumūʿun *7.9; 4:12 = 7.8* (*v. supra* anfun 1, *I 560-61*); *etc.* ⟼ πτύελον δὲ χρὴ ἐπὶ πᾶσι τοῖσιν ἀλγήμασι *Hippocr. Prognost. XIV, 210.12* = fa-ammā l-buṣāqu fa-yanbaġī fī ǧamīʿi l-ʿilali *217.16; XIV, 211.13 = 218.14 etc.*

1.4 πτυελισμός (*salivation*) = nafṯu l-buṣāqi : ἢν μὲν ὁ πόνος ἐν ἀρχῇσι ἐγκέηται καὶ ἡ δύσπνοια καὶ ἡ βὴξ καὶ ὁ πτυελισμὸς διατελῇ ἔχων *Hippocr. Prognost. XVII, 215.14* = fa-in kāna l-alamu yaḥduṯu munḏu awwali l-amri wa-sūʾu l-tanaffusi wa-l-suʿālu wa-nafṯu l-buṣāqi lā yazālu bāqiyan *221.17;* προσγενέσθαι (προσγενέσθαι *G, GalL, Lat., Arab.* : προγίγνεσθαι *X* : γίνεσθαι *v* : προγενέσθαι *codd. cett., ed.*) δὲ ἀνάγκη καὶ πόνον καὶ δύσπνοιαν καὶ πτυελισμὸν πρὸ τῆς τοῦ πύου πτύσεως (πτύσεως *CsN, GalL (PV), Arab.* : ῥήξιος *codd. cett., ed.*) *XVII, 216.3** = wa-lā budda qabla nafṯi l-middati an yatazayyada l-alamu wa-sūʾu l-tanaffusi wa-nafṯu l-buṣāqi *222.4.*

2. σίελον (*saliva*) : τούτῳ τοιγαροῦν τῷ σιέλῳ καὶ αἱ τροφαὶ τῶν παίδων τοὺς λειχῆνας ἰῶνται *Galen Simpl. medic. XII, 288.16* = wa-hāḏā l-buṣāqu huwa llaḏī tastaʿmiluhū ẓiʾaratu l-aṭfāli fī qūbāʾi l-aṭfāli fa-yaqlaʿūnahā bihī *WGAÜ, 607.*

3. *interpr.;* τὰ ὑγρά (*fluids; in context, of the lungs and mouth, relating to coughing*) : τὰ ... ὑγρὰ λεπτοποιοῦσαι *Diosc. Mat. med. I, 6.11* = yudiqqu l-buṣāqa *vetus transl. Ullmann Unters., 183.*

بصل

بصل basalun

1. κρόμμυον *or* κρόμυον (*onion*) : τούτων (*sc.* τῶν φυτῶν) γὰρ γίγνεται ... ἔνια ... τῷ παραβλαστάνειν, οἷον τὸ τῶν κρομμύων γένος *Arist. Gener. anim. III 11, 761b29* = fa-inna baʿḍa l-šaǧari yakūnu ... min furūʿin miṯla l-baṣali *128.18* ⟼ κρόμμυα δὲ καὶ σκόροδα ἐσθίειν μὲν πονηρόν *Artem. Onirocr. 74.10* = fa-ammā l-baṣalu wa-l-ṯūmu (*nos* : wa-l-tūmu *ed.*) fa-inna aklahumā (aklahumā *corr. e* kilayhimā *in* *cod. Fahd*) fī l-manāmi raḍī'un *136.14**; *74.14* = *137.4*; κρομμύοις δὲ ἐστεφανῶσθαι δοκεῖν τὸν μὲν ἰδόντα ὠφελεῖ *86.15* = fa-ammā man ra'ā ka-annahū yukallalu bi-iklīlin min baṣalin fa-inna ḏālika li-ṣāḥibi l-ru'yā ǧayyidun *160.1* ⟼ μετὰ δὲ κρομύου καὶ ἁλὸς καὶ μέλιτος πρὸς κυνόδηκτα καὶ ἀνθρωπόδηκτα ποιεῖ *Diosc. Mat. med. I, 114.7* = wa-iḏā ḫuliṭa bihī ʿasalun wa-milḥun wa-baṣalun kāna ṣāliḥan li-ʿaḍḍati l-kalbi wa-ʿaḍḍati l-insāni *Ibn al-Bayṭār Ǧāmiʿ I, 174.1*; κρόμυον *I, 216.3* = krbydn' (*sic cod.*) wa-huwa l-baṣalu *vetus transl. Ullmann Unters., 183* ⟼ καθάπερ κρόμμυά τε καὶ σκόροδα καὶ κάρδαμα καὶ πράσα *Galen Diff. febr. VII, 285.5* = miṯla l-baṣali wa-l-ṯūmi wa-l-ḥurfi wa-l-kurrāṯi *WGAÜ Suppl. I, 597.*

بصل الزيز **baṣalu l-zīzi**

1. βολβός *bot.* (*bulb*) : περὶ βολβοῦ ἡμέρου *Galen Simpl. medic. XI, 851.11* = al-qawlu fī bulbūs wa-yudʿā bi-l-ʿarabiyyati l-ḥadaqa wa-huwa baṣalu l-zīzi *versio A* = ḏikru baṣali l-zīzi *versio B WGAÜ, 165;* περὶ βολβοῦ ἐμετικοῦ *XI, 852.1* = ḏikru baṣali l-zīzi llaḏī yuhayyiǧu l-qay'a *versio B WGAÜ, 165.*

بصل الفأر **baṣalu l-fa'ri**

1. σκίλλα *bot.* (*squill, sea onion*) : σκίλλα γεωργοῖς μὲν ἀφορίας ἐστὶ σημαντικὴ διὰ τὸ μηδὲν ἐδώδιμον ἔχειν *Artem. Onirocr. 225.10* = baṣalu l-fa'ri fī l-ru'yā yadullu fī l-akarati ʿalā qaḥṭihim wa-ḏālika annahū šay'un lā yu'kalu *414.3;* ἀσφόδελος τῇ σκίλλῃ κατὰ τὰ αὐτὰ καὶ ὡσαύτως ἀποβαίνει *225.17* = fa-ammā l-asfūdīlūs fa-inna dalā'ila-hū miṯla dalā'ili baṣali l-fa'ri *414.10* ⟼ σκίλλα δύναμιν ἔχει δριμεῖαν πυρωτικήν *Diosc. Mat. med. I, 237.15* = al-isqīlu wa-mina l-nāsi man yusammīhi baṣala l-fa'ri wa-lahū quwwatun ḥāddatun muḥriqatun *versio A WGAÜ Suppl. II, 294* ⟼ σκίλλα τμητικῆς ἱκανῶς ἐστι δυνάμεως *Galen Simpl. medic. XII, 125.4* = ḏikru l-ʿunṣuli quwwatu hāḏā l-baṣali l-maʿrūfi bi-baṣali l-fa'ri quwwatun qaṭṭāʿatun taqṭīʿan balīġan *WGAÜ Suppl. II, 293* ⟼ αὐτίκα δὲ σκίλλην τριχοειδέσιν ἄμμιγα φλοιοῖς σταιτὶ περιπλάσσας θάλπε κατὰ φλογιῆς *Galen Ther. Pis. Androm. 107* = ṯumma yu'ḫaḏu min baṣali l-fa'ri wa-qišrihī wa-lubbisa ʿalayhi ʿaǧīnan wa-yušwā *129b14.*

بضع

مباضعة III. mubāḍaʿatun *maṣdar*

1. μίξις (*sexual intercourse*) : οὔτε γὰρ τῷ ἀνδρὶ ἡ ἐπιθυμίη τῆς μίξιος γίγνεται (πολλή *add. codd. graec. : om. Arab.*) *Hippocr. Aer. 70.21** = li-annahā (*sc.* l-ṭabīʿata) lā tuhayyiǧu šahwata l-riǧāli ilā l-mubāḍaʿati *145.15*.

2. συνουσία (*sexual intercourse*) : ἡ κεδρία ... περιχρισθεῖσα δὲ αἰδοίῳ πρὸ τῆς συνουσίας ἀτόκιόν ἐστι *Diosc. Mat. med. I, 77.7* = wa-iḏā taǧammala (*nos* : tḥml *Ullmann*) bihi (*sc.* al-qaṭirāni) l-imraʾatu qabla l-mubāḍaʿati manaʿa mina l-ḥabali *versio C WGAÜ Suppl. II, 393**; συνουσίαν παρορμᾶν *II, 138.12 and 139.14* = yuhayyiǧu l-mubāḍaʿata *vetus transl. Ullmann Unters., 183*.

3. *transl. derivatives of* Ἀφροδίτη (*Venus*)

3.1 ἀφροδισιασμός (*sexual intercourse*) : παῖς οὐ ποδαγριᾷ πρὸ τοῦ ἀφροδισιασμοῦ (ἀφροδισιασμοῦ *MC´* : ἀφροδισιάζειν *V, Urb.*) *Hippocr. Aphor. VI.30* = al-ġulāmu lā yuṣībuhu l-niqrisu qabla an yabtadiʾa fī l-mubāḍaʿati *56.9*.

3.2 τὰ ἀφροδίσια (*sexual activities*) : πάντες δὲ οἱ ἄρτοι οἱ ἄνευ ζύμης γινόμενοι ἐνεργητικώτατοί εἰσι πρὸς τὰ ἀφροδίσια *Cass. Bass. Geopon. II, 33.4* = fa-innahū yaqūmu maqāma l-ḫamīri maʿa mā fī ḏālika mina l-manfaʿati fī l-mubāḍaʿati *WGAÜ Suppl. I, 202* ⟝ ὡς ἀφροδίσια συνιστάντα *Diosc. Mat. med. II, 137.5* = yuhayyiǧu l-mubāḍaʿata *vetus transl. Ullmann Unters., 183*.

4. ὄρεξις (*desire*) : τὸ σκίμβρον ... ὀρέξεώς ἐστιν ἐνεργητικὸν καὶ οὔρων κινητικόν *Cass Bass. Geopon. XII, 35.1* = fī amri l-ḫardali l-barriyyi innahā tusḫinu maʿidata ākilihā wa-maṯānatahū wa-tunaššiṭuhū li-l-mubāḍaʿati *WGAÜ Suppl. I, 791*.

بضعة biḍʿatun (*also* baḍʿatun, buḍʿatun)

1. *transl.* σάρξ (*flesh*) and its compounds

1.1 σάρξ (*flesh, piece of flesh*) **(a)** *abs.* : ἀποτίκτει μὲν γὰρ ἡ ἄρκτος ἅπασι τοῖς γεννωμένοις ὁμοίως ζώοις. ἔστι δὲ σὰρξ μόνη γεννωμένη ἄπλαστός τε καὶ ἀδιάρθρωτος, μορφὴν μὲν οὐδεμίαν ἔχουσα *Galen Ther. Pis. 255.1* = wa-mina l-dubbi l-unṯā fa-innahā talidu ḥayawānan ka-l-biḍʿati lā yastabīnu fīhi šayʾun min aʿḍāʾihī wa-lā ṣūratu ḥayawānin *118a12* **(b)** *in hend.* biḍʿatu laḥmin : ἔτεκε σάρκα ἣν καλοῦσι μύλην *Arist. Gener. anim. IV 7, 775b33* = waladat biḍʿata laḥmin yusammā mūlī *166.13*.

1.2 *sem.; etym.;* εὔσαρκος (*well-fleshed, i.e., fleshy, plump*) = *in hend.* ǧayyidu l-biḍʿati kaṯīru l-laḥmi : ταῖς γὰρ εὐσάρκοις (*sc.* γυναιξὶ) πορεύεται εἰς τὴν τροφὴν τοῦ σώματος τὸ πολὺ τῆς ἐκκρίσεως *Arist. Hist. anim. VII 2, 583a9* = fa-inna l-marʾata iḏā kānat ǧayyidata l-biḍʿati kaṯīrata l-laḥmi tafnā kaṯratu l-ruṭūbati llatī taḫruǧu mina l-ǧasadi fī kaṯrati ḏālika l-laḥmi *467.1*.

2. *sem. amplif.;* ἡ καλουμένη μύλη (*hard formation in a woman's womb*) = al-biḍʿatu llatī tusammā mūlī : τότε γίγνεται ἡ καλουμένη μύλη ἐν ταῖς γυναιξὶν εὐλόγως ἢ μάλιστα ἢ μόναις *Arist. Gener. anim. IV 7, 776a13** = ḥīnaʾiḏin takūnu l-biḍʿatu llatī tusammā mūlī fī arḥāmi l-nisāʾi wa-bi-ḥaqqin yaʿriḍu lahunna faqaṭ hāḏā l-ʿaraḍu *167.5*.

مبضع **mibḍaʿun**

1. ὄνυξ (*scalpel*) : τὸ δὲ ὀποβάλσαμον λεγόμενον ὀπίζεται ... ἐντεμνομένου σιδηροῖς ὄνυξι τοῦ δένδρου *Diosc. Mat med. I, 24.10* = fa-ammā labanu l-balasāni fa-yuʾḫaḏu ... ʿinda mā yušaqqu sāqu l-šaǧarati bi-mibḍaʿin ḥadīdin *versio C WGAÜ Suppl. I, 777* = bi-mibḍaʿin ḥadīdin *vetus transl. Ullmann Unters., 183*.

بطّ

بطّ **I. baṭṭa**

1. τέμνω (*to cut, lance*) : κἂν εἴ τις διὰ τὸ μαχαίριον οἴοιτο τὸ ὕδωρ ἐξεληλυθέναι μόνον τοῖς ὑδρωπιῶσιν, ἀλλ' οὐ διὰ τὸ ὑγιαίνειν οὗ ἕνεκα τὸ μαχαίριον ἔτεμεν *Arist. Gener. anim. V 8, 789b13* = šabīhun bi-qawli l-qāʾili inna l-māʾa llaḏī yaḫruǧu min aṣḥābi l-ḥabani innamā yaḫruǧu li-ḥāli l-ḥadīdati llatī tabuṭṭu wa-laysa li-ḥāli l-ṣiḥḥati *197.6* ⟼ τοῦτο (*sc.* τὸ πύον) κομίσασθαι βουλόμενος ὁ θεραπεύων ἔτεμε τὸν παῖδα *Galen Anat. admin. II, 632.11* = fa-arāda l-ṭabību l-mutawallī [kāna] (*secl. nos*) l-ʿilāǧihī an yuḫriǧa tilka l-middata fa-baṭṭa l-ġulāma *WGAÜ Suppl. II, 445* ⟼ ὁκόσοι ἔμπυοι ἢ ὑδρωπικοὶ καίονται ἢ τέμνονται (*sic Urb., Arab.* : τέμνονται ἢ καίονται *codd. cett., ed.*) *Hippocr. Aphor. VI:27** = man kuwiya aw buṭṭa mina l-mutaqayyiḥīna awi l-mustasqīna *56.4*; *sim. VII:44* = 63.16.*

بطّ[1] **I. baṭṭun** *maṣdar*

1. *transl.* τέμνω (*to cut, to lance*) *and derivatives*

1.1 τέμνειν (*to cut, to lance*) **(a)** *abs.* : τί δεῖ λέγειν, ὡς οὐδ' ἀποσκήμματα τέμνειν *Galen Anat. admin. II, 340.6* = wa-lastu aḥtāǧu an aqūla innahum lā yaltamisūna baṭṭa l-ḫurāǧi[1] *132.10* Garofalo* **(b)** *in hend.*; baṭṭun wa-qaṭʿun, qaṭʿun wa-baṭṭun : τοὺς μὲν (*sc.* μῦς) εὐλαβῶς, τοὺς δ' ἀφειδῶς τέμνειν *Galen Anat. admin. II, 229.12* = kāna baṭṭuhū wa-qaṭʿuhū li-baʿḍi l-ʿaḍali bi-tawaqqufin wa-ḥaḏarin wa-tawaqqin šadīdin wa-li-baʿḍihī bi-lā raḥmatin *WGAÜ, 670.8* ⟼ ἡ δὲ χειρουργικὴ διὰ τοῦ τέμνειν καὶ καίειν ὑγιάζει *Ps.-Arist. Div. 9a14* = wa-ammā l-ālātu fa-bi-an yustaʿmala fīhā l-qaṭʿu wa-l-baṭṭu wa-l-kayyu (*sic leg. pro* wa-l-kayyu wa-l-baṭṭu *ed.*) *versio T 54.20*.*

1.2 τομή (*incision, lancing*) : πρὸς ... συρίγγων καὶ κόλπων καὶ ἀποστημάτων τομάς *Galen Anat. admin. II, 283.16* = fī baṭṭi l-nawāṣīri wa-l-qurūḥi l-ḏāhibati taḥta l-ǧildi wa-l-dubaylāti *WGAÜ Suppl. II, 470.6* ⟼ καὶ μετ' αὐτὸ πῦον συναγαγών, ἐδεήθη καὶ τομῆς *Galen Ther. Pis. 213.1* = wa-ǧamaʿa middatan kaṯīratan ḥattā ḥtāǧa ilā baṭṭihī *104b6;* σὺ μέν, ὡς χρηστὸς πατήρ, ὀκνηρότερον εἶχες πρὸς τὴν τομήν *219.11* = wa-išfāquka kāna min baṭṭi l-aṭibbāʾi iyyāhu *106b17.*

2. *transl.* χειρουργία (*surgery*) *and its derivatives*

2.1 χειρουργία (*surgery*) **(a)** *in hend.* baṭṭun wa-qaṭʿun, qaṭʿun wa-baṭṭun : ἕτερα δὲ μυρία διὰ τὰς ἀρτηρίας τε καὶ τὰς φλέβας, ἃς οὐδ' ἄχρι τοσούτου γιγνώσκουσιν ἔνιοι τῶν ἰατρῶν, ὡς φυλάττεσθαι κατὰ τὰς χειρουργίας τιτρώσκειν αὐτάς *Galen Anat. admin. II, 343.3* = fa-inna qawman mina l-aṭibbāʾi qad balaġa min ǧahlihim bi-amri l-širyānāti wa-l-ʿurūqi annahum lā yaʿrifūna mawāḍiʿahā li-yatawaqqawhā fī mawāḍiʿi l- baṭṭi wa-l-qaṭʿi *WGAÜ, 761.15* ⟼ πρὸς τὰς ἐν ταῖς χειρουργίαις αἱμοῤῥαγίας *Galen Simpl. medic. XII, 376.3* = fī mudāwāti nfiǧāri l-dami l-ʿāriḍi ʿinda l-qaṭʿi wa-l-baṭṭi *WGAÜ, 761.11* **(b)** *in hend.* baṭṭun wa-šaqqun : καὶ κατ' αὐτὰς δὲ τὰς χειρουργίας,

---

[1] Galen uses ἀπόσκημμα in a sense related to ἀπόστημα, abscess; see the references, s.v., in R.J. Durling, *A Dictionary of Medical Terms in Galen*, Leiden 1993. Neither LSJ nor Durling record this meaning. The Arabic translators clearly understood it as ἀπόστημα, translating it with one of the common words used to render ἀπόστημα, *ḫurāǧ*.

ὅσας ἑκάστοτε ποιούμεθα *Galen Anat. admin. II, 386.7* = fī l-baṭṭi wa-l-šaqqi llaḏī naf‘aluhū dā’iman *WGAÜ Suppl. II, 680.13.*

2.2 ἡ χειρουργική (*sc.* τέχνη) (*surgery*) : τῆς ἰατρικῆς ἐστιν εἴδη πέντε· ἡ μὲν φαρμακευτική, ἡ δὲ χειρουργική *Ps.-Arist. Div. 9a10* = li-l-ṭibbi anwā‘un ḫamsatun minhu bi-l-‘aqāqīri wa-minhu bi-l-baṭṭi *versio Q 36.3.*

3. *in hend.;* κουρά (*shearing, cropping*) = baṭṭun aw qaṭ‘un : τὸ ἔλαιον ... τὰς ἐπὶ τῇ κουρᾷ γινομένας ἑλκώσεις αὐτῶν ἀπουλοῖ *Diosc. Mat. med. I, 77.21* = wa-yaḫtimu (*sc.* al-duhnu) l-qurūḥa fīhim min baṭṭin aw qaṭ‘in *versio B WGAÜ Suppl. I, 586.9.*

^{2}**بطّ baṭṭun** *coll.,* **baṭṭatun** *nom. unit.*

1. *transl.* χήν (*goose*) *and its derivatives*

1.1 χήν (*goose*) **(a)** *abs.* : χῆνας ἐπιλεκτέον τοὺς μεγίστους καὶ λευκοτάτους *Cass. Bass. Geopon. XIV, 22.1* = afḍalu mā ttuḫiḏa mina l-baṭṭi a‘ẓamuhunna wa-l-bīḍu minhunna *WGAÜ Suppl. II, 684.6;* δεῖ δὲ σημειοῦσθαι ἑκάστης χηνὸς τὰ ᾠὰ διὰ χαρακτήρων τινῶν *XIV, 22.9* = wa-mina l-wāǧibi an yumayyaza bayḍu kulli baṭṭatin *WGAÜ Suppl. II, 684.8* ⟼ μεταξὺ δέ πως τῆς τῶν γεράνων τε καὶ χηνῶν ἡ τῶν καλουμένων ὀτίδων ἢ ὠτίδων ἐστίν *Galen Alim. fac. VI, 703.9* = wa-fī-mā bayna laḥmi l-karākiyyi wa-laḥmi l-baṭṭi laḥmu l-ṭayri llaḏī yuqālu lahū bi-l-yūnāniyyati ’ūṭis wa-hwa l-tadruǧu *WGAÜ, 763.21* ⟼ ἡ δὲ τῶν χηνῶν κόπρος ἄχρηστός ἐστι διὰ πολλὴν δριμύτητα *Galen Simpl. medic. XII,305.2* = fa-ammā zubūlu l-baṭṭi fa-lasnā nasta‘miluhā li-faḍli ḥiddatihā *WGAÜ, 763.24* **(b)** *in hend.;* iwazzun wa-baṭṭun : τὸ μὲν τῶν χηνῶν ὄνομα σύνηθές ἐστι καὶ τοῖς παλαιοῖς *Galen Alim. fac. VI, 702.11* = ammā smu l-iwazzi wa-l-baṭṭi fa-smun qad ǧarā bi-l-‘ādati fī kalāmi qudamā’i l-yūnāniyyīna *WGAÜ, 763.18.*

1.2 χήνειος (*of a goose*) : ἁρμόζει δὲ (*sc.* τὸ βαλάνινον ἔλαιον) καὶ ὠταλγίαις ... μετὰ χηνείου στέατος ἐγχεόμενον *Diosc. Mat. med. I, 38.11* = wa-yuwāfiqu (*sc.* duhnu l-bāni) waǧa‘a l-āḏāni ... iḏā ḫuliṭa bi-šaḥmi al-baṭṭi wa-quṭira fīhā *Ibn al-Bayṭār Ǧāmi‘ II, 112.14, sim. al-Ḥāwī 20, 160.11;* καὶ τὰ πυρίκαυτα δὲ ἕλκη (ἕλκη *codd., Arab.* : *secl. Wellmann*) ... ἰᾶται (*sc.* ὁ λίβανος) σὺν στέατι χηνείῳ ἢ χοιρείῳ *I, 62.15** = iḏā ḫuliṭa (*sc.* al-kunduru) bi-šaḥmi al-baṭṭi aw šahmi l-ḫinzīri abra’a l-qurūḥa l-‘āriḍata min iḥrāqi l-nāri *Ibn al-Bayṭār Ǧāmi‘ IV, 84.3, sim. al-Ḥāwī 21, 315.1* ⟼ τὸ χήνειον στέαρ *Galen Simpl. medic. XII, 326.1* = šaḥmu l-baṭṭi *WGAÜ, 764.*

2. νῆττα (*duck*) **(a)** *abs.* : σκληροτέρα τούτων ἐστὶ ... ἡ (*sc.* σὰρξ) τῆς νήττης *Galen Alim. fac. VI, 700.16* = wa-aṣlabu laḥman min hāḏihī ... al-baṭṭatu llatī yuqālu lahā l-ḫašinsāru *WGAÜ, 435ult.* **(b)** baṭṭu l-māʾi : αἷμα χηνὸς ... καὶ νήσσης ἀντιδότοις χρησίμως μείγνυται *Diosc. Mat. med. I, 160.19* = damu l-iwazzi ... wa-damu baṭṭi l-māʾi yuntafaʿu bihī fī aḫlāṭi l-adwiyati l-maʿǧūnati *Ibn al-Bayṭār Ǧāmiʿ II, 96.23.*

بطء

بطؤ I. **baṭuʾa**

1. τὸ ἠρέμα (*what [comes about] gently, slowly*) = mā yabṭuʾu : τὸ δὲ ἠρέμα καὶ κατὰ σμικρὸν ἀναίσθητον *Plato Tim. 64D2* = wa-ammā mā yabṭuʾu wa-yabdū qalīlan qalīlan fa-ġayru maḥsūsin *Galen Comp. Tim. 19.13.*

بُطْءٌ I. **buṭʾun** *maṣdar*

1. σχολαίως *adv.* (*tardily*) : πρὸς εὐπάθειαν δὲ σχολαίως *Arist. Eth. Nic. IX 11, 1171b24* = wa-ammā fī an yuṣṭanaʿa l-maʿrūfu ilayhi fa-yanbaġī an yakūna buṭʾun (buṭʾun *cod., Ullmann NE I, 66* : baṭīʾan *Dunlop, Akasoy / Fidora* : baṭarun *Badawī*) *525.6*.*

بطّأ II. **baṭṭaʾa**

1. *sem.; etym.; morph.; transl.* δυσ- (*mis-, hard to ...; negating or diminishing the positive sense of a word*) *in* δυσέγερτος (*hard to wake*) *and* δυσαπόκριτος (*hard to receive an answer from*) : ὑπνώδεις τε διὰ παντός εἰσι καὶ δυσέγερτοι καὶ δυσαπόκριτοι *Paulus Aeg. III, 9.1* = wa-yubaṭṭiʾūna bi-l-intibāhi wa-l-ǧawābi *WGAÜ, 209.22.*

أبطأ IV. **abṭaʾa** *abs.*

1. ὑστερίζω (*to lag behind, come later*) : ὅσων ἢ ἅμα λεγομένων ἡ γνῶσις γίνεται ... ἢ μικρὸν ὑστερίζει ἡ διάνοια *Arist. Rhet. III 10, 1410b25* = mimmā iḏā qīla yakūnu maʿrūfan min sāʿatihī ... wa-lākin yubṭiʾu fīhi l-fikru qalīlan *199.18.*

2. ἐγχρονίζω (*to delay, linger*) = *in hend.* abṭaʾa wa-labiṯa : καίτοι οὐ πάνυ πορίμη ἐστὶν ἡ ἀπὸ τοῦ γλυκέος οἴνου φῦσα, ἀλλ' ἐγχρονίζει περὶ ὑποχόνδρια (ὑποχόνδρια *MV, Arab.* : ὑποχόνδριον *A Gal., ed.*) *Hippocr. Diaet. acut. 58.5** = ʿalā anna l-nafḫata l-ḥādiṯata ʿani l-šarābi l-ḥulwi laysa nḥidāruhā bi-l-sarīʿi lākinnahā qad tubṭiʾu wa-talbaṯu fī l-mawāḍiʿi llatī dūna l-šarāsīfi *30.17* (*cf. also WGAÜ, 772-3, WGAÜ Suppl. II, 707, s.v.* χρονίζω).

3. βραδέως *adv.* (*slowly*) : καὶ γένεια δὲ βραδέως ἀνιόντα προκαλεῖται *Galen Simpl. medic. XI, 806.17* = wa-qad yusriʿu nabāta liḥyatin mā (li-man *coni. Ullmann*) abṭaʾa nabātu liḥyatihī *versio A*; wa-huwa ayḍan yunbitu l-liḥyata iḏā abṭaʾat fī l-ḫurūǧi *versio B WGAÜ, 169.21-23.*

! 4. ἀργός, ἐνειλημένος τὰς χεῖρας (*of babies, not working and with swaddled hands*) = abṭaʾati l-tarbiyatu (*to take a long time to be brought up*) : τῷδε γὰρ (*sc.* χειροτέχνῃ) σχολὴν προαγορεύει· ἀργὰ γὰρ τὰ βρέφη καὶ ἐνειλημένα τὰς χεῖρας τυγχάνει *Artem. Onirocr. 21.16* = fa-inna hādhihi l-ruʾyā tadullu ʿalā tarbīṯi ʿamalin (tarbīṯi ʿamalin *nos* : tartībi ʿamalin *ed.*) wa-ʿawāʾiqa taʿūqu fīhi wa-ḏālika anna l-mawlūdīna tubṭiʾu tarbiyatuhum *41.15** (*where the transl. misunderstood* ἀργός *as 'slow' rather than 'idle', ignored the meaning of* ἐνειλημένος *and guessed the sense as* abṭaʾati l-tarbiyatu).

أبطأ **IV. abṭaʾa** *c.* ʿan

1. ἐμποδίζω (*to hinder*) = *sem. metathesis; act. / med. transformation* abtaʾa ʿan : οἱ δὲ σοφιστικοὶ ἔλεγχοι ... οὐ ποιοῦσι δῆλον· (*sic interpunx. Arab.*) εἰ ἀγνοεῖ καὶ γὰρ τὸν εἰδότα ἐμποδίζουσι τούτοις τοῖς λόγοις *Arist. Soph. el. I 8, 169b29** = wa-ammā l-sūfisṭāʾiyyūna fī tahǧīnihimi l-kalāma ... fa-laysū yaǧʿalūna ḏālika l-qawla wāḍiḥan bayyinan, fa-l-ǧāhilu bihī lā yuʿṭī ǧawāban wa-l-baṣīru bihī qad yubṭiʾu ʿani l-ǧawābi *vetus transl. 852.13 / fol. 341a.*

ابطاء **IV. ibṭāʾun** *maṣdar*

1. *transl.* βραδύς (*slow*) *and its derivatives and compounds*

1.1 βραδύς (*slow*) **(a)** *abs.* : οἷον ... ἐναντία ἐστὶν τὸ δὲ βαρὺ τῷ κούφῳ καὶ τὸ ταχὺ τῷ βραδεῖ *Ps.-Arist. Div. 35a3* = ka-ḍiddi l-razānati li-l-ḫiffati wa-l-ʿaǧalati li-l-ibṭāʾi *versio Q 33.20* **(b)** *sem.; etym.; transl.* βραδύς *in* βραδέως *adv.* (*slowly*) = bi-ibṭāʾin (*v. supra* bi- 24, *II 27*) :

βαδίζειν δὲ καὶ αὔξεσθαι καὶ πάντα τὰ τοιαῦτα μεταβάλλει (τοιαῦτα μεταβάλλει *Arab.* : τοιαῦτα. μεταβάλλειν *ed.*) μὲν οὖν εἰς τὴν ἡδονὴν ταχέως καὶ βραδέως ἔστιν *Arist. Eth. Nic. X 3, 1173b3** = wa-ammā l-mašyu wa-l-nušūʾu wa-ǧamīʿu mā kāna miṯla hāḏihī fa-yumkinu an yataġayyara ilā l-laḏḏati bi-surʿatin wa-ibṭāʾin *535.13* **(c)** *sem.; etym.; transl.* βραδύς *in* βραδυπεψία (*slow digestion*) = ibṭāʾun fī l-haḍmi : ἀτὰρ οὖν καὶ ἀπεψίαι προηγοῦνται πολλαὶ καὶ βραδυπεψίαι καὶ ὀξυρεγμίαι *Galen De crisibus IX, 661.11* = wa-yataqaddamuhā tuḫamun kaṯīratun wa-ibṭāʾun fī l-haḍmi wa-ǧušāʾun ḥāmiḍun *WGAÜ, 169.20.*

1.2 βραδύτερος *comp.* (*slower*) = *sem. metathesis; comp. / positive transformation* : τὰ δε σχήματα οὐκ αἴτια τοῦ φέρεσθαι ἁπλῶς ἢ κάτω ἢ ἄνω, ἀλλὰ τοῦ θᾶττον ἢ βραδύτερον *Arist. Cael. IV 6, 313a15* = inna l-aškāla laysat ʿillata sulūki baʿḍi l-aǧrāmi ilā fawqu wa-baʿḍihā ilā asfalu, lākinnahā ʿillatu surʿati sulūkihā wa-ibṭāʾihī *385.8 Badawī* ⟼ τὰ δὲ βραδύτερον πλαδῶντα καὶ ἧσσον βραδυτέρην σημαίνει τὴν κρίσιν *Hippocr. Diaet. acut. 41.4* = wa-man kāna l-ifrāṭu (*sc.* ifrāṭu l-ruṭūbati) ʿalayhi abṭaʾa wa-aqalla dalla ḏālika ʿalā ibṭāʾi buḥrānihī *7.1.*

1.3 βραδυτής (*slowness*) : πάσῃ (*sc.* κινήσει) γὰρ οἰκεῖον εἶναι δοκεῖ τάχος καὶ βραδυτής *Arist. Eth. Nic. X 3, 1173a32* = fa-qad yuẓannu anna li-kulli wāḥidin min ǧamīʿi l-ašyāʾi surʿatan ḫāṣṣiyyatan wa-ibṭāʾan *535.10* ⟼ διὰ γὰρ τὸ εἶναι αὐτῶν (*sc.* τῶν ὄφεων) προμήκη τὴν φύσιν ... ἐψύχετ᾽ ἂν ἡ γονὴ διὰ τὴν βραδυτῆτα *Arist. Gener. anim. I 7, 718a22* = wa-min aǧli anna ḫilqatahā (*sc.* al-ḥayyāti) min qibali l-ṭibāʿi mustaṭīlatun ... baruda l-zarʿu li-ḥāli ibṭāʾi ḫurūǧihī *10.16* ⟼ διὸ οὐκ εἴδη κινήσεως οὐδὲ διαφοραὶ τάχος καὶ βραδυτής *Arist. Phys. V 4, 228b29* = wa-li-ḏālika ṣāra l-surʿatu wa-l-ibṭāʾu laysā nawʿayni wa-lā faṣlayni li-l-ḥarakati *569.15*; *228b27* = *569.13* ⟼ πρὸς δὲ τὰς ἀποδημίας πολλὴν προαγορεύουσιν ἀσφάλειαν (παρολκὰς δὲ *add. ed.* : *om. Arab.*) καὶ βραδύτητας ἐργάζονται *Artem. Onirocr. 121.8** = wa-ayḍan fa-innahā tadullu fī l-musāfiri ʿalā ǧūdati safarihī wa-ibṭāʾihī *220.13; 212.3* = *384.7.*

2. ἄνεσις (*remission, deceleration*) : ἡ γὰρ ἄνεσις ἑκάστου γίνεται δι᾽ ἀδυναμίαν, ἡ δ᾽ ἀδυναμία παρὰ φύσιν *Arist. Cael. II 6, 288b13* = wa-ḏālika anna ibṭāʾa kulli šayʾin mina l-ašyāʾi yakūnu min aǧli ḍuʿfihī, wa-l-ḍuʿfu huwa amrun ḫāriǧun ʿani l-ṭabʿi *versio A 71b2.*

3. κατοχή (*holding back*) : τοῖς δὲ λοιποῖς (*sc.* τῶν ἀνθρώπων) ἐμπόδια καὶ κατοχὰς σημαίνουσι (*sc.* οἱ μαλακοὶ τῶν ἰχθύων) *Artem.*

Onirocr. 131.6 = fa-ammā fī sāʾiri l-nāsi fa-innahā (*sc.* al-samaka l-layyina l-qišri) tadullu ʿalā taʿaqqudi umūrihim wa-ibṭāʾihā *236.14.*

4. *in hend.;* ἀτονία (*sluggishness, laziness*) : al-ibṭāʾ wa-l-raḫāwa : καὶ ἐν ταῖς πράξεσιν ἀτονίας πολλὰς προαγορεύουσι (*sc.* οἱ μαλακοὶ τῶν ἰχθύων) *Artem. Onirocr. 131. 7* = wa-tadullu (*sc.* al-samaku l-layyinu l-qišri) ayḍan ʿalā ibṭāʾi l-aʿmāli wa-raḫāwatihā *236.15.*

5. *in hend.;* βαρύς (*lumbering, moving heavily*) = ḏū tawānin wa-ibṭāʾin : νωθροὺς δὲ καὶ βαρεῖς καὶ δυσκινήτους ἡ τῆς κράσεως ψυχρότης (*sc.* ἐργάζεται) *Galen An. virt. 64.1* = wa-burūdatu l-mizāği tağʿaluhum (*sc.* al-nāsa) kasālā ḏawī tawānin (*corr. Biesterfeldt Ǧālīnūs, 136*) wa-ibṭāʾin wa-ʿasira ḥarakatin *32.12**.

6. *sem.; etym.; transl.* σχολή (*leisure, ease*) *in* σχολαίως (*leisurely*) = *in hend.* bi-anātin wa-ibṭāʾin : τοῖς ... καρκίνοις καὶ τοῖς ἄλλοις ὅσοις ἐνδέχεται σχολαίως ποιεῖσθαι τὴν λῆψιν *Arist. Part. anim. IV 11, 691 b21* = li-l-sarāṭīni wa-ğamīʿi l-ḥayawāni llaḏī yušbihu (*sic leg. pro* yšhh *ed.*) an taʾḫuḏa mā taʾḫuḏu bi-anātin wa-ibṭāʾin *142.14**.

7. ὀψέ *adv.* (*late, after a long time*) **(a)** *in expr.* baʿda ibṭāʾin : τοῖς δ' ἐπὶ ξένης οὖσι τὴν εἰς οἶκον ἀνακομιδὴν προαγορεύει ὀψὲ καὶ παρὰ προσδοκίαν *Artem. Onirocr. 45.19* = wa-ammā man kāna fī bilādi ġurbatin fa-inna hāḏihi l-ruʾyā tadullu ʿalā annahū yarğiʿu ilā bilādihī baʿda ibṭāʾin wa-ʿalā ġayri ṭamaʿin *85.12* **(b)** *in hend.* bi-ibṭāʾin wa-baʿda zamānin kaṯīrin, *vel sim.* : ὀψὲ γὰρ παύεται (*sc.* ὁ ἐγκέφαλος) τῆς ψυχρότητος καὶ τῆς ὑγρότητος *Arist. Gener. anim. II 6, 744a22* = min ağli anna l-burūdata wa-l-ruṭūbata llatī fīhi (*sc.* al-dimāġi) lā tukaffu illā bi-ibṭāʾin wa-baʿda zamānin kaṯīrin *83.17;* ὀψὲ μὲν οὖν διὰ τὸ πλῆθος τῆς περὶ τὸν ἐγκέφαλον πέψεως τελειοῦται τὰ ὄμματα *744b1* = fa-ḫilqatu l-ʿaynayni tatimmu baʿda zamānin kaṯīrin li-ḥāli ibṭāʾi nuḍūği kaṯrati l-ruṭūbati llatī tuḥīṭu bi-l-dimāġi *84.6.*

8. *sem.; etym.; morph.; transl. the alpha privative* (*un-, in-*) *in* ἀθυμία (*lack of anger, nonchalance*) = ibṭāʾu l-ġaḍabi : ἐκ ὀξυθυμίας τε καὶ ἀθυμίας *Galen Ars medica I, 356.2* = wa-min surʿati l-ġaḍabi wa-ibṭāʾihī *WGAÜ, 76.14.*

بطيء **baṭīʾun**

1. *transl.* βραδύς (*slow*) *and its derivatives and compounds*

1.1 βραδύς (*slow*) : καὶ κίνησις δὲ βραδεῖα τοῦ μεγαλοψύχου δοκεῖ εἶναι *Arist. Eth. Nic. IV 3, 1125a13* = wa-yuẓannu ayḍan bi-l-kabīri l-nafsi annahū baṭīʾu l-ḥarakati *267.12* ⟼ τὸ ... ἰσχῦον ... βραδεῖαν ποιεῖ τὴν κίνησιν *Arist. Gener. anim. V 7, 787a18* = al-qawiyyu ... ḥarraka ḥarakatan baṭīʾatan *194.16* ⟼ τὸ γὰρ βραδὺ καὶ ταχὺ χρόνῳ ὥρισται, ταχὺ μὲν τὸ ἐν ὀλίγῳ πολὺ κινούμενον, βραδὺ δὲ τὸ ἐν πολλῷ ὀλίγον *Arist. Phys. IV 10, 218b14-16* = wa-ḏālika anna l-sarīʿa wa-l-baṭīʾa innamā yuḥaddadāni bi-l-zamāni fa-l-sarīʿu huwa mā kāna kaṯīran fī qaṣīrin wa-l-baṭīʾu huwa mā kāna yasīran fī ṭawīlin *412.11-13* ⟼ ὅταν ᾗ κάτωθεν ὀμφαλοῦ τὸ στρέφον, βραδύς, μαλθακὸς ὁ στρόφος *Hippocr. Humor. 3:11* = iḏā kāna l-šayʾu l-mumaġġiṣu asfala l-surrati wa-l-maġaṣu ḥīnaʾiḏin yakūnu baṭīʾan layyinan *5.9* ⟼ οὐ ταὐτὸν οὖν τὸ ὀξὺ τῷ ταχεῖ, οὐδὲ τὸ βραδὺ τῷ βαρεῖ ..., ἀλλ' ὅτι συμβαίνει τοῦ μὲν ὀξέος ταχεῖαν εἶναι τὴν κίνησιν, τοῦ δὲ ἀμβλέος ἢ τοῦ βαρέος βραδεῖαν *Them. In De an. 66.10-12* = wa-laysa l-ḥāddu huwa l-sarīʿa wa-lā l-ṯaqīlu huwa l-baṭīʾa ... lākinna ḏālika li-annahū yaʿriḍu li-l-ḥāddi an takūna ḥarakatuhū sarīʿatan wa-li-l-kālli awi l-ṯaqīli an takūna ḥarakatuhū baṭīʾatan *106.6-8*.

1.2 βραδύτερος *comp.* (*slower*) = *sem. metathesis; comp. / positive transformation* : ἂν ἀπολύοιντο ... βραδύτερον *Arist. Cael. I 5, 272a27* = kāna ftirāquhumā baṭīʾan *versio B*; kāna ftirāquhumā wa-tabāʿuduhumā baṭīʾan *versio C 153.15 Badawī* ; βραδύτερον γὰρ ἂν ἐκινεῖτο τὸ πλεῖον πῦρ ἄνω καὶ ἡ πλείων γῆ κάτω *I 8, 277b2* = la-kānat ḥarakatu l-nāri l-ʿaẓīmati tasluku ilā fawqu sulūkan baṭīʾan, wa-la-kānat ḥarakatu l-arḍi l-ʿaẓīmati tasluku ilā asfalu sulūkan baṭīʾan *versio B 285.7 Badawī ; sim. 277b7 = 185.14* ; τοῦ μὲν (*sc.* ἄστρου) θᾶττον κινουμένου τοῦ δὲ βραδύτερον *II 6, 288b9* = baʿḍu l-kawākibi kāna yakūnu ... yataḥarraku ḥarakatan sarīʿatan, wa-baʿḍuhā yakūnu ... yataḥarraku ḥarakatan baṭīʾatan *251.6*; *sim. II 10, 291b1 = 267.11* ⟼ τοῖς δ' ὄρνισι καῖ τοῖς ᾠοτόκοις τῶν τετραπόδων δέχονται τὴν σπερματικὴν περίττωσιν, ὥστε βραδυτέραν εἶναι τὴν ἔξοδον ἢ τοῖς ἔχουσιν (ἔχουσιν *ut intell. Arab. ut vid.* : ἰχθύσιν *ed.*) *Arist. Gener. anim. I 4, 717b6** = fa-ammā aǧnāsu l-ṭayri wa-l-ḥayawāni llaḏī lahū arbaʿatu arǧulin wa-yalidu ḥayawānan fa-unṯayāhu qābilun (*sic ed. pro* qābilāni) li-faḍlati l-zarʿi wa-li-ḏālika yakūnu ḫurūǧuhū baṭīʾan mina l-ḥayawāni llaḏī <laysa> lahū makānun muwāfiqun li-qabūlihī *8.9*⊗ ⟼ καὶ ἀναγόμενα μὲν τὰ πλοῖα βραδύτερα τὰ ἀγαθὰ ποιεῖ *Artem. Onirocr. 140.22* = fa-ammā in raʾā (*sc.* al-insānu) l-sufuna ka-annahā muṣāʿida-tun dalla ʿalā ḫayrin baṭīʾin *253.10; 140.12 = 252.14* ⟼ ὁπόσοι δὲ βραδυτέρης προσθέσιος δέονται, στερεὴ τροφή *Hippocr. Alim. 147.6* = mani ḥtāǧa ilā ziyādatin baṭīʾatin fa-l-yalzami l-ġiḏāʾa l-yābisa *19.17* ⟼

ὅση δ' αὐτῆς (*sc.* τῆς φωνῆς) ταχεῖα, ὀξεῖαν (*sc.* θῶμεν), ὅση δὲ βραδυτέρα, βαρυτέραν *Plato Tim. 67B6* = inna l-ṣawta l-ḥādda yusammā l-ḫafīfa wa-l-ṣawta l-ṯaqīla yudʿā l-baṭīʾa *Galen Comp. Tim. 21.3.*

1.3 βραδέως *adv.* (*slowly*) : ἐάν τις ποιήσῃ τὰς μὲν ἀντικινουμένας ἀμφοτέρας φερομένας βραδέως *Arist. Cael. I 5, 272b6* = iḏā kāna l-mutaḥarrikāni bi-ḥarakatin muqābilatin yaslukāni sulūkan baṭīʾan *versio B;* iḏā kāna l-mutaḥarrikāni bi-l-ḥarakati l-mutaqābilati yataḥarrakāni ḥarakatan baṭīʾatan *versio C 154.9 Badawī* ⟼ ἔσω μὲν οὖν διακρίνεται (*sc.* τὸ θῆλυ) διὰ τὴν ψυχρότητα βραδέως *Arist. Gener. anim. IV 6, 775 a17* = fa-iḏā kānati l-unṯā dāḫilan fī l-raḥimi tanfaṣilu tafṣīlan baṭīʾan li-ḥāli l-bardi *164.18* ⟼ ἡ δὲ ἀχρὰς ... βραδέως πεπαινόμενον *Diosc. Mat. med. I, 109. 17* = wa-l-kummaṯrā baṭīʾu l-nuḍǧi *Ibn al-Bayṭār Ǧāmiʿ IV, 77.17, sim. al-Ḥāwī 21, 323.6.*

1.4 βράδιον *adv., comp.* (*more slowly*) = *sem. metathesis; comp. / positive transformation*: τὰ δὲ ἡψημένα (*sc.* κρέα) λιτῶς βράδιον τὰς αὐτὰς προαγορεύει ὠφελείας *Artem. Onirocr. 76.17* = fa-ammā l-laḥmu l-maṭbūḫu bi-ġayri abzārin (abzārin *Vajda 90, Rosenthal* : ʾnzʾr *ed.*) fa-innahū yadullu ʿalā manāfiʿa miṯla ḏālika illā annahā manāfiʿu baṭīʾatun *141.1**; ὅσα δὲ βράδιον ἢ ἧττον ἢ ἀτονώτερον *213.13* = ašyāʾ baṭīʾa qalīla ḍaʿīfa *387.5* .

1.5 *sem. etym.;* βραδυπορέω (*to proceed slowly*) = masīrun kāna baṭīʾan : διὰ τὸ βραδυπορεῖν τὸν ἥλιον τὴν ἡμέραν, ὁπόση νῦν ἐστιν ἡ δεκάμηνος *Ps.-Plut. Placita 427a20* = ʿalā ḥasabi masīri l-šamsi ... fa-innahū kāna baṭīʾan bi-miqdāri ʿašarati ašhurin fī hāḏā l-zamāni *71.1-2.*

1.6 *sem. amplif.;* βραδυτής (*slowness*) = ḥarakatun baṭīʾatun : διὰ δὲ βραδυτῆτα ἀπωθούμενον (*scil.* τὸ μεικτὸν) ὑπὸ τοῦ περιεστῶτος ἔξωθεν πνεύματος *Plato Tim. 76B6* = wa-li-anna ḥarakatahū (*sc.* al-muḫtaliṭi) baṭīʾatun yudāfiʿuhu l-hawāʾu l-muḥīṭu bihī min ḫāriǧin *Galen Comp. Tim. 25.12.*

2. *transl.* νωθής (*sluggish*) *and its derivatives*

2.1 νωθής (*sluggish*) : ἡ δὲ κίνησις αὐτοῦ νωθὴς ἰσχυρῶς ἐστι *Arist. Hist. anim. II 11, 503b8* = fa-ammā ḥarakatuhū fa-baṭīʾatun ǧiddan *72.12.*

2.2 νωθρός (*sluggish*) : τὸ δ' ἕτερον (*sc.* γένος τῶν φαλαγγίων) ... τὸ μὲν χρῶμα μέλαν ... καὶ τῇ κινήσει νωθρὸν *Arist. Hist. anim. IX 39, 622b32* = wa-ǧinsun āḫaru minhu (*sc.* mina l-laddāġi) aswadu l-lawni ... wa-huwa baṭīʾu l-ḥarakati *427.3.*

3. νωχελής (*slow-moving*) = baṭīʾu l-ḥarakati : σαλαμάνδρα εἶδός ἐστι σαύρας νωχελές, ποικίλον *Diosc. Mat. med. I, 140.15* = salāmandarā ... huwa ṣinfun min aṣnāfi ṣawrā baṭīʾu l-ḥarakati muḫtalifu l-lawni *WGAÜ, 441.*

4. ἀργός (*sluggish*) **(a)** *abs.* : διὸ μεταφέρων φαίη τις ἂν αὐτὴν ἀργὴν εἶναι φιλίαν *Arist. Eth. Nic. IX 5, 1167a11* = wa-min aǧli hāḏā yumkinu aḥadan an yanqula hāḏā l-isma wa-yaqūla innahā ṣadāqatun baṭīʾatun (buṭliyyatun *prop. Ullmann NE I, 66) 501.8* **(b)** *sem. amplif.;* baṭīʾu l-ḥarakati : μεγαλοψύχου δὲ ... καὶ ἀργὸν εἶναι καὶ μελλητήν *Arist. Eth. Nic. IV 3, 1124b24* = wa-min šaʾni l-kabīri l-nafsi ... ayḍan an yakūna baṭīʾa l-ḥarakati ḏā maṭlin *265.10.*

5. βαρύτερος *comp.* (*heavier;* [*moving*] *more heavily*) = *sem. amplif. and metathesis*; *comp.* / *positive transformation* **(a)** baṭīʾu l-ḥarakati : ἀχρούστεραί τε γὰρ ὡς ἐπὶ τὸ πολύ, καὶ βαρύτερον διάγουσι *Arist. Hist. anim. VII 4, 584a15* = annahā takūnu radīʾata l-lawni sayyiʾata l-ḥāli baṭīʾata l-ḥarakati *WGAÜ, 160.7* **(b)** baṭīʾu l-inḥidāri : ὁ δὲ Φλωρεντῖνός φησι ... τὸν δὲ ἐν τοῖς ἰπνοῖς ἠψημένον (*sc.* ἄρτον) βαρυτέραν τὴν πέψιν ποιεῖν *Cass. Bass. Geopon. II, 33.5* = ṯumma ḫubzu l-furni ... fa-huwa baṭīʾu l-inḥidāri ʿani l-maʿidati *WGAÜ Suppl. I, 212.20.*

6. *in hend.;* ὑπεκλείπων *part.* (*remittent, flagging at intervals*) = muntaqiṣun baṭīʾun : ὀρθοπνοίας ὀξείας σφυγμὸς ἀνώμαλος καὶ ἄτακτος καὶ ὑπεκλείπων *Galen Puls. introd. VIII, 849.2* = wa-ammā nabḍu aṣḥābi l-rabwi l-ḥāddi fa-hwa muḫtalifun ġayru muntaẓimin muntaqiṣun (munṭaqiṣun *prop. Ullmann* : munqabiḍun *ed.*) baṭīʾun *versio A WGAÜ Suppl. II, 531.10.*

7. *transl.* ὀψέ (*late*) *and its derivatives*

7.1 ὀψέ *adv.* (*late, after a long time*) = baṭīʿan : ἡβῶσί τε ὀψὲ ἐν ταύτῃ τῇ πόλει *Hippocr. Aer. 32.5* = inna ḥtilāma fityāni hāḏihi l-madīnati yakūnu baṭīʾan *versio A 33.6, sim. versio B 33.15.*

7.2 *in hend.;* ὀψιαίτατα *adv., superl.* (*after the longest amount of time*) = baṭīʾan wa-baʿda zamānin kaṯīrin : καὶ διὰ τὸ πλῆθος ὀψιαίτατα πήγνυται τὸ περὶ τὴν κεφαλὴν ὀστοῦν *Arist. Part. anim. II 7, 653a34* = wa-li-kaṯrati tilka l-burūdati wa-l-ruṭūbati lā yaṣlubu l-ʿaẓmu llaḏī yalī l-dimāġa illā baṭīʾan wa-baʿda zamānin kaṯīrin *39.21.*

8. *morph.; transl. prefixes negating or diminishing the sense of the word to which they are joined*

8.1 δυσ- (*mis-, hard to ...*); *in alphabetical order*:

8.1.1 δυσαλλοίωτος (*hard to alter*) = baṭīʾu l-istiḥālati : ξηρὴ τροφὴ εὐμετάβλητος μᾶλλον ἢ ὑγρή· ἡ δυσαλλοίωτος δυσεξανάλωτος *Hippocr. Alim. 147.2* = wa-l-ġiḏāʾu l-yābisu sarīʿu l-istiḥālati akṯara mina l-raṭbi wa-l-ġiḏāʾu l-baṭīʾu l-istiḥālati baṭīʾu l-infišāši *19.14.*

8.1.2 δυσέκτηκτος (*hard to exhaust and to melt*) = *in hend.* baṭīʾun fī l-ʿayāʾi wa-l-ḏawbi : μῦες στερεώτεροι δυσέκτηκτοι μᾶλλον (μᾶλλον *Arab.* : μᾶλλον τῶν ἄλλων *Littré* : τῶν ἄλλων *codd., Joly*) *Hippocr. Alim. 147.8** = al-ʿaḍalātu aṣlabu wa-abṭaʾu fī l-ʿayāʾi wa-l-ḏawbi *21.3.*

8.1.3 δυσεξανάλωτος (*hard to resolve*) = baṭīʾu l-infišāši; *see* 8.1.1 *above.*

8.1.4 δυσεπούλωτος (*hard to cicatrize*) = baṭīʾu l-ḫatmi : ἰᾶται δὲ τὰ δυσεπούλωτα τῶν ἑλκῶν *Galen. Simpl. medic. XI, 822.12* = wa-yubriʾu ayḍan al-qurūḥa l-baṭīʾata l-ḫatmi *versio A WGAÜ, 212.3.*

8.1.5 δύσπεπτος (*hard to digest*) **(a)** baṭīʾu l-inhiḍāmi : κίτρια (κίτρια *codd., Arab.* : †κίτρια† *Pack, sed v. Schmitt 39n7* : κινάρα *Hercher*) ... ὀδύνας σημαίνει καὶ (καὶ *codd., Arab.* : <ἔτι> καὶ *Pack*) ἀνεργασίας διὰ τὸ δύσπεπτον (διὰ τὸ δύσπεπτον *codd., Arab.* : *secl. Pack*) *Artem. Onirocr. 73.15** = al-utruǧǧu ... yadullu ʿalā waǧaʿin wa-baṭālatin li-annahū baṭīʾu l-inhiḍāmi (inhiḍām *nos; cf. Schmitt 91* : ihtiḍām *cod. f. 48r, ed.*) *135.8** ⟼ *Diosc. Mat. med. I, 114.2* = *vetus transl. Ullmann Unters., 183* **(b)** baṭiʾu l-istimrāʾi : κάρυα βασιλικά, ἃ ἔνιοι Περσικὰ καλοῦσιν, ἐσθιόμενα δύσπεπτα *Diosc. Mat. med. I, 114.2* = inna l-ǧawza ... llaḏī yusammā ǧawza l-maliki wa-yusammīhi āḫarūna l-fārisiyya fa-innahū iḏā nuḍiǧa kāna baṭīʾa l-istimrāʾi *al-Ḥāwī 20, 268.12 (sed vid. Dubler/Terés II, 118.7)* **(c)** baṭīʾu l-nuḍǧi : οὕτω δὲ καὶ ἡ ῥίζα δύσπεπτός τε καὶ φυσώδης ἐστί *Galen. Simpl. medic. XI, 861.10* = wa-aṣluhū ayḍan baṭīʾu l-nuḍǧi kaṯīru l-nafḫi *versio A WGAÜ, 213.15.*

8.1.6 δύστριπτος (*hard to grind*) = baṭīʾu l-inhiḍāmi : τὰ βόεια (*sc.* κρέα) <πόνους> (πόνους *Arab.* : πονηρά *coni. Hercher, cf. Pack 1976, p. 310*) διὰ τὸ δύστριπτον ... σημαίνει *Artem. Onirocr. 76.5** = inna laḥma l-baqari yadullu ʿalā taʿabin wa-ḏālika annahū baṭīʾu l-inhiḍāmi *140.3.*

8.2 *alpha privative* (*un-, in-*); *in alphabetical order*:

8.2.1 ἀνέψανος (*unfit for cooking or concoction*) = baṭīʾu l-nuḍǧi : ἀτέραμνα γὰρ καὶ ἀνέψανα (*sc.* τὰ ἁλμυρὰ ὕδατα) *Hippocr. Aer. 40.5* =

li-annahā (*sc.* al-miyāha l-māliḥata) ǧāsiʾatun baṭīʾatu l-nuḍǧi *versio A/B 67.6/15.*

8.2.2 ἀτέραμνος (*unsoftened, hard*) **(a)** baṭīʾu l-nuḍǧi : ὁκόσα δέ (*sc.* ὕδατα) ἐστιν ἁλυκὰ καὶ ἀτέραμνα καὶ σκληρὰ ... οὐκ ἀγαθά *Hippocr. Aer. 38.8* = inna kulla māʾin (*sic leg. pro* kulla mā *ed.*) kāna mina l-miyāhi māliḥan (fa-huwa *add. versio B*) baṭīʾa l-nuḍǧi ǧāsiʾan ... laysa bi-nāfiʿin *versio A/B 61.3/12*; 24.17 = versio A 77.6* **(b)** baṭīʾu l-taḥlīli : ταῦτα δὲ χρὴ ἐνθυμεῖσθαι (*sc.* τὸν ἰατρόν) ... τῶν ὑδάτων πέρι ὡς ἔχουσι ... πότερον ... χρέονται ... ἁλυκοῖσί τε καὶ ἀτεράμνοισι *Hippocr. Aer. 24.17* = yanbaġī an yunʿima (*sc.* al-ṭabību) l-naẓara fī ǧūdati l-miyāhi wa-radāʾatihā a- ... māliḥatun baṭīʾatu l-taḥlīli *versio B 7.14.*

8.2.2.1 ἀτεραμνότατος *superl.* (*most unsoftened, hardest*) = *sem. metathesis; superl. / positive transformation* baṭīʾu l-nuḍǧi : τούτοισι δὲ τὰ σκληρότατα καὶ ἀτεραμνότατα καὶ τὰ ὑφαλικά (*sc.* ὕδατα ξυμφέρει) *Hippocr. Aer. 38.23* = fa-inna l-miyāha l-ǧāsiʾata l-baṭīʾata l-nuḍǧi l-māliḥata lahū nāfiʿatun *versio A/B 67.1/8.*

أبطأ **abṭaʾu,** *elative*

1. *transl.* βραδύτερος (*slower*) *as adj., subst., and adv.*

1.1 βραδύτερος *comp. adj.* (*slower*) : καὶ γὰρ εἰ γίνεται ἀνώμαλος (*sc.* ἡ τοῦ οὐρανοῦ φορά), ἤτοι ὅλη μεταβάλλει καὶ ὁτὲ μὲν γίνεται θάττων ὁτὲ δὲ βραδυτέρα πάλιν, ἢ τὰ μέρη αὐτῆς *Arist. Cael. II 6, 288b8* = fa-in kānat ḥarakatu l-samāʾi ġayra mustawiyatin, fa-immā an yataġayyara kulluhā, fa-takūnu ḥarakatuhā marratan asraʿa wa-marratan abṭaʾa, wa-immā an takūna aǧzāʾuhā ʿalā hāḏihi l-ṣifati *versio A 71a4 = versio B 250.18 Badawī* ; τὸ μὲν (*sc.* ἄστρον) ἔσται θᾶττον τὸ δὲ βραδύτερον *II 8, 289b20* = kāna ... sulūku baʿḍihā (*sc.* al-kawākibi) asraʿa wa-baʿḍihā abṭaʾa *versio B 257.19 Badawī* ⟼ ἔτι δὲ μεταβολὴ μέν ἐστι θάττων καὶ βραδυτέρα, χρόνος δ᾽ οὐκ ἔστιν· τὸ γὰρ βραδὺ καὶ ταχὺ χρόνῳ ὥρισται, ταχὺ μὲν τὸ ἐν ὀλίγῳ πολὺ κινούμενον, βραδὺ δὲ τὸ ἐν πολλῷ ὀλίγον *Arist. Phys. IV 10, 218b14-16* = wa-ayḍan fa-inna kulla taġayyurin fa-qad yakūnu asraʿa wa-qad yakūnu abṭaʾa wa-laysa yakūnu l-zamānu hākaḏā wa-ḏālika anna l-sarīʿa wa-l-baṭīʾa innamā yuḥaddadāni bi-l-zamāni fa-l-sarīʿu huwa mā kāna kaṯīran fī qaṣīrin wa-l-baṭīʾu huwa mā kāna yasīran fī ṭawīlin *412.11-13; IV 14, 222b32 = 471.6; VI 2, 232b28-233a8 = 622.10-623.7; etc.* ⟼ ἄλευρα δὲ καὶ ἄλφιτα τὰ μὲν αὐτὰ τοῖς ἄρτοις σημαίνει, ἧττονα δὲ καὶ βραδύτερα (καὶ βραδύτερα *Arab., coni. Rosenthal 143b; cf. Pack 1967, p. 318* : καὶ βαρύτερα *codd., secl. Pack*) *Artem. Onirocr. 75.20** = fa-ammā l-daqīqu wa-l-ʿaṣīdatu fa-inna dalīlahumā yušbihu mā dalla ʿalayhi ḫubzu l-ḥinṭati illā anna llaḏī tadullu ʿalayhi yakūnu aqalla wa-abṭaʾa *139.12* ⟼ τοῦτο (*sc.* τὸ μέτωπον) δ' οἷς μὲν μέγα, βραδύτεροι, οἷς δὲ μικρόν, εὐκίνητοι *Galen An. virt. 55.14* = wa-man kāna hāḏā l-juzʾu minhu kabīran kāna abṭaʾa ḥarakatan wa-man ṣaġura hāḏā minhu kāna asraʿa ḥarakatan *27.4*.

1.2 τὸ βραδύτερον *subst.* (*the slower*) : λείπεται δὴ λέγειν ἐναλλὰξ εἶναι τῇ κινήσει τὸ θᾶττον καὶ τὸ βραδύτερον *Arist. Cael. II 6, 289a5* = fa-qad baqiya iḏan an naqūla inna ḥarakata l-samāʾi takūnu marratan šadīdatan wa-marratan mustarḫiyatan wa-takūnu hātāni l-ḥarakatāni tataʿāqabāni ʿalayhā, aʿnī an takūna l-samāʾu marratan asraʿa ḥarakatan wa-marratan abṭaʾa *versio B 254.2 Badawī*.

1.3 βραδύτερον *adv.* (*more slowly*) : κινουμένην ἐνδέχεται τὴν Α παρὰ κινουμένην τὴν Β βραδύτερον παρελθεῖν *Arist. Cael. I 5, 272b9* = qad yumkinu an yataḥarraka ḫaṭṭu ḥarfi A ilā ḫaṭṭi ḥarfi B wa-hwa mutaḥarrikun ayḍan fa-yaslukuhū sulūkan baṭīʾan abṭaʾa min sulūkihī ilā l-ḫaṭṭi l-sākini *versio B* = ... fa-yakūnu qaṭʿuhū lahū abṭaʾa min sulūkihī ilā l-ḫaṭṭi l-sākini *versio C 154.15 Badawī*; καὶ ἄνωθεν δὲ κάτω τὸ ὀλίγον οἰσθήσεται θᾶττον πῦρ, τὸ δὲ πολὺ βραδύτερον *IV 2, 308b21* = fa-inna l-nāra ... kullamā kānat aqalla kānat asraʿa sulūkan min fawqu ilā asfala, wa-kullamā kānat akṯara kāna abṭaʾa (sulūkan ... abṭaʾa *sic leg. cum mss.*) sulūkahā min fawqu ilā asfala *versio B* 362.6 *Badawī* ⟼ διὸ καὶ δοκοῦσι (*sc.* οἱ ὄφεις) βραδύτερον ἀπολύεσθαι τῶν ἰχθύων *Arist. Gener. anim. I 7, 718a32* = wa-li-ḏālika yuẓannu anna ftirāqahā (*sc.* al-ḥayyāti) yakūnu abṭaʾa min iftirāqi l-samaki *11.5* ⟼ πᾶν δὲ τὸ κινούμενον ἐνδέχεται καὶ θᾶττον κινεῖσθαι καὶ βραδύτερον *Arist. Phys. VI 2, 232b22* = wa-kāna kullu mutaḥarrikin fa-qad yumkinu an yataḥarraka asraʿa wa-abṭaʾa *622.4* ⟼ τὰ δὲ βραδύτερον πλαδῶντα καὶ ἧσσον βραδυτέρην σημαίνει τὴν κρίσιν *Hippocr. Diaet. acut. 41.4* = wa-man kāna l-ifrāṭu (*sc.* ifrāṭu l-ruṭūbati) ʿalayhi abṭaʾa wa-aqalla dalla ḏālika ʿalā ibṭāʾi buḥrānihī *7.1*.

2. νωθέστερος *comp. adj.* (*more sluggish*) : ὕδατος, διὰ τὸ νωθέστερον ἀέρος καὶ πυρὸς αὐτὸ εἶναι *Plato Tim. 86A5* = wa-ḏālika anna l-māʾa abṭaʾu ḥarakatan mina l-hawāʾi wa-l-nāri *Galen Comp. Tim.31.11*.

3. νωθέστατος *superl. adj.* (*most sluggish*) : τὸ δὲ γῆς, τετάρτως ὂν νωθέστατον τούτων *Plato Tim. 86A6* = al-arḍ wa-hwa l-rābiʿu fa-li-anna ḥarakatahū abṭaʾu min ǧamīʿihā *Galen Comp. Tim. 31.12*.

بطبط

بطباط baṭbāṭun

1. βρεττανική (*scurvy grass*) : βρεττανική·πόα ἐστὶν ἔχουσα φύλλα ὅμοια λαπάθῳ ἀγρίῳ *Diosc. Mat. med. II, 169.12* = birṭānīqī huwa l-bustāniyūn wa-qīla innahū l-baṭbāṭu wa-hwa ḥašīšatun lahā awrāqun ka-awrāqi l-ḥummāḍi l-barriyyi *versio B WGAÜ Suppl. I, 231* = *versio C Ullmann Unters., 351.9; v. supra* bustāniyyūn, *II 236.*

بطح

بطيحة baṭīḥatun, *pl.* **baṭāʾiḥu**

1. *transl.* ἕλος (*marsh*) *and its derivatives*

1.1 ἕλος (*marsh, swamp*) : ἥ τε δίαιτα τοῖσιν ἀνθρώποισιν ἐν τοῖσιν ἕλεσίν ἐστι *Hippocr. Aer. 60.4* = inna aġḏiyata hāʾulāʾi l-nāsi hiya min tilka l-baṭāʾiḥi *131.3.*

1.2 ἑλώδης *adj.* (*marshy, swampy*) = fī l-baṭāʾiḥi : ὁκόσα μὲν οὖν (*sc.* τῶν ὑδάτων) ἐστι στάσιμα καὶ ἑλώδεα καὶ λιμναῖα *Hippocr. Aer. 34.20* = inna l-miyāha l-kadirata l-rākidata fī l-sibāḫi wa-l-baṭāʾiḥi *versio B 47.13.*

بطائحيّ baṭāʾiḥiyyun *adj.*

1. *transl. derivatives of* ἕλος (*marsh*)

1.1 ἑλώδης (*marshy, swampy*) : ταῦτα δὲ χρὴ ἐνθυμεῖσθαι (*sc.* τὸν ἰατρόν) ... τῶν ὑδάτων πέρι ὡς ἔχουσι πότερον ἑλώδεσι χρέονται *Hippocr. Aer. 24.15** = yanbaġī an yunʿima (*sc.* al-ṭabību) l-naẓara fī ǧūdati l-miyāhi wa-radāʾatihā a-baṭāʾiḥiyyatun hiya *versio B 7.13, sim. versio A 7.5;* εἰσὶ γὰρ φύσιες, αἱ μὲν ὄρεσιν ἐοικυῖαι ... αἱ δὲ λειμακωδεστέροισί τε καὶ ἑλώδεσιν *Hippocr. Aer. 58.5* = inna mina l-nāsi man yušbihu ǧibālan ... wa-minhum man yušbihu arḍan baṭāʾiḥiyyatan zahruhā kaṯīrun *125.9; 60.2 = 131.1.*

1.2 ἕλειος (*of the marsh*) : ὁκόσαι δὲ (*sc.* τῶν πόλεων) ὕδασί τε ἑλείοισι χρέονται καὶ λιμνώδεσι *Hippocr. Aer. 50.12* = kullu madīnatin yašrabu ahluhā māʾan sibāḫiyyan aw baṭāʾiḥiyyan (baṭāʾiḥiyyan *codd. AC* : biṭāḥiyyan *cod. B, versio A*) *versio B 103.15*; *cf. versio A 103.7.*

بطخ

بطّيخ biṭṭīḫun

1. *transl.* πέπων (*a kind of melon*) *and its compounds*

1.1 πέπων (*a kind of melon*) : πέπονες <δὲ> (δὲ *Arab., add. Pack*) πρὸς μὲν φιλίας ... εἰσὶν ἀγαθοί, πέπον γὰρ τὸ προσφιλέστατον οἱ ποιηταὶ καλοῦσι *Artem. Onirocr. 74.6-8** = fa-ammā l-biṭṭīḫu fa-innahū ǧayyidun li-man arāda an yuḥibba āḫara ... li-anna l-šuʿarāʾa yusammūna l-maḥabbata bi-l-luġati l-yūnāniyyati bi-smi l-biṭṭīḫi *136.10-12* ⟼ ἡ δὲ τοῦ πέπονος σὰρξ καὶ αὐτὴ πεπτική, οὐρητικὴ ἐσθιομένη *Diosc. Mat. med. I, 206. 17* = al-biṭṭīḫu laḥmuhū munḍiǧun iḏā ukila adarra l-bawla *Ibn al-Bayṭār Ǧāmiʿ I, 98.28* = *vetus transl. Ullmann Unters., 183* ⟼ περὶ μηλοπεπόνων. οἱ μηλοπέπονες ἧττον μὲν τῶν πεπόνων εἰσὶν ὑγροί *Galen Alim. fac. VI, 566.5* = naḏkuru fīhi l-malbūna wa-hwa ṣinfun mina l-biṭṭīḫi ṭuwālun. al-malbūnu aqallu ruṭūbatan mina l-biṭṭīḫi *WGAÜ, 513.3* ⟼ σίκυος ἐδώδιμος ὁ μὲν ἤδη πέπων λεπτομερεστέρας ἐστὶν οὐσίας *Galen Simpl. medic. XII, 121.14* = ammā l-naḍīǧu wa-hwa l-biṭṭīḫu fa-ǧawharuhū laṭīfun *Ibn al-Bayṭār Ǧāmiʿ I, 98.21.*

1.2 μηλοπέπων (*melon*) : τοὺς δὲ μηλοπέπονας ποιήσεις ῥόδα πνεῖν, ἐὰν τὸ σπέρμα αὐτῶν μετὰ ξηρῶν ῥόδων ἀποθέμενος, καὶ φυράσας φυτεύσῃς *Cass. Bass. Geopon. XII, 20.2* = wa-iḏā unqiʿa bizru l-biṭṭīḫi fī wardin yābisin madqūqin mablūlin bi-l-māʾi ṯalāṯata ayyāmin ṯumma zuriʿa kānat rāʾiḥatu l-biṭṭīḫi l-nāšiʾi minhu miṯla rāʾiḥati l-wardi *WGAÜ Suppl. I, 686.16-17* ⟼ ὥσπερ ἔνιοι τῶν σικύων τε καὶ μηλοπεπόνων *Galen Simpl. medic. XI, 671.6* = bi-manzilati kaṯīrin mina l-ḫiyāri wa-l-biṭṭīḫi *WGAÜ Suppl. II, 280.14.*

2. *interpr.;* τὰ σικυήλατα (*[things grown in] cucumber-beds, kinds of cucumber*) = anwāʿun mina l-biṭṭīḫi wa-l-qiṯṯāʾi wa-l-qarʿi (*kinds of melon, cucumber, and gourd*) : ἐὰν δὲ ἀειζώου βοτάνης τῷ χυλῷ διαβρέξῃς τῶν σικυηλάτων τὰ σπέρματα, ἀβλαβῆ ταῦτα φυλάξεις *Cass. Bass. Geopon. XII,* 20.4 = wa-iḏā nuqiʿat buzūru hāḏihi l-anwāʿi l-ṯalāṯati mina l-biṭṭīḫi wa-l-qiṯṯāʾi wa-l-qarʿi fī māʾi ʿurūqi l-sūsi ṯumma zuriʿat salimat hāḏihi l-anwāʿu mina l-dūdi wa-l-āfāti *WGAÜ Suppl. II, 280.11.*

بطش

بَطْش I. **baṭšun** *maṣdar*

1. *transl.* ἰσχύς (*strength*) *and its derivatives*

1.1 ἰσχύς (*strength*) : ἰσχὺς δ’ ἐστὶ μὲν δύναμις τοῦ κινεῖν ἕτερον ὡς βούλεται *Arist. Rhet. I 5, 1361b15* = fa-ammā l-baṭšu fa-innahū quwwatun yuḥarriku bihā l-marʾu ġayrahū kayfa šāʾa *26.11.*

1.2 ἰσχυρός *adj.* (*strong*) = ḏū baṭšin : ὥστε ὁ ἰσχυρὸς ἢ πᾶσιν ἢ τούτων τισίν ἐστιν ἰσχυρός *Arist. Rhet. I 5, 1361b17* = fa-huwa (*sc.* al-marʾu) ḏū baṭšin lā maḥālata bi-kullin aw bi-l-nāsi *26.13.*

2. *interpr.*; δύναμις ἀγωνιστική (*the power to fight, athletic prowess*) : ἔτι τὰς τοῦ σώματος ἀρετάς, οἷον ὑγίειαν κάλλος ἰσχὺν μέγεθος δύναμιν ἀγωνιστικήν *Arist. Rhet. I 5, 1360b22* = ṯumma faḍāʾilu l-ǧasadi ayḍan miṯla l-ṣiḥḥati wa-l-ǧamāli wa-l-ǧaldi wa-l-ǧazālati wa-l-baṭši *23.9*; ἀγαθὴ δὲ (*sc.* νεότης) κατ’ ἀρετὴν σώματος, οἷον μέγεθος κάλλος ἰσχὺν δύναμιν ἀγωνιστικήν *I 5, 1361a3* = wa-ṣalāḥuhum (*sc.* al-fityāni) fī faḍāʾili l-ǧasadi ka-l-ǧazālati wa-l-ǧamāli wa-l-šiddati wa-l-baṭši *24.7.*

3. *sem.*; *def.*; ἀθλητής (*one who struggles and combats; athlete*) = ṣāḥibu l-ṣirāʿi wa-l-baṭši bi-l-aʿmāli l-šadīdati : οἷον ἐπὶ τῶν ἀθλητῶν συμβαίνει διὰ τὴν πολυφαγίαν *Arist. Gener. anim. IV 3, 768b29* = wa-hāḏā l-ʿaraḍu šabīhun bi-l-ʿaraḍi llaḏī yaʿriḍu li-aṣḥābi l-ṣirāʿi wa-l-baṭši bi-l-aʿmāli l-šadīdati li-ḥāli kaṯrati l-akli *147.24.*

باطش I. **bāṭišun** *act. part.*

1. ὁ ἀγωνιζόμενος *act. part.* (*to enter a contest and compete for a prize*) = *in hend.* al-muǧāhidu wa-l-bāṭišu : ὥσπερ δ’ Ὀλυμπίασιν οὐχ οἱ κάλλιστοι καὶ ἰσχυρότατοι στεφανοῦνται ἀλλ’ οἱ ἀγωνιζόμενοι *Arist. Eth. Nic. I 8, 1099a5* = ka-mā anna l-ǧawāʾiza laysa yanāluhā fī l-maydāni l-maharatu wa-l-ǧiyādu mina l-munāḍilīna lākini l-muǧāhidūna minhum wa-l-bāṭišūna (lākini l-muǧāhidūna minhum wa-l-bāṭišūna *cod.*; ... wa-l-mubāṭišūna *prop. Ullmann NE I, 66* : lākinna l-muǧāhidīna minhum wa-l-bāṭišīna *Akasoy / Fidora*) *141.2**.

مباطشة III. mubāṭašatun *maṣdar*

1. πρᾶξις (*action, performance*) : φύσις δὲ ἐν μὲν ἔργοις τοῦ ἔργου τῇ πρήξει, ὅ βούλεται τεκμαρτέον *Galen. In De off. med. 876. 14* = wa-mağrā l-ṭabʿi yanbağī an yutaʿarrafa mā yurīduhū wa-yaqtaḍīhi fī l-aʿmāli min (min *nos* : fī *ed.*) mubāṭašati l-ʿamali *52. 16**.

2. *sem.; def.;* ἆθλος (*athletic contest*) = mubāṭašatu aṣḥābi l-riyāḍati : ἢ κατὰ παλαίστραν ἢ ἐν ἄθλοις *Galen Loc. aff. VIII, 287.12* = fī mawḍiʿi l-ṣirāʿi aw fī mubāṭašati aṣḥābi l-riyāḍati *WGAÜ Suppl. I, 69.13.*

مباطش III. mubāṭišun *act. part.*

1. ὁ ἀγωνιζόμενος *act. part.* (*?*) : *see above,* bāṭišun 1.

بطق

بوطقة būṭaqatun → *s. r.* **b-w-ṭ-q.**

بطل

[1] **بَطَلَ I. baṭala,** *impf.* **yabṭulu,** *maṣdar* **buṭlānun** (*basic meaning: to be or become null, come to an end, be undone*)

1. *transl.* ἀναιρέομαι *pass.* (*to be abolished*) *and its compounds*

1.1 ἀναιρέομαι *pass.* (*to be abolished*) **(a)** *abs.* : ὥστε ἀκύρων γιγνομένων (*sc.* τῶν συνθηκῶν) ἀναιρεῖται ἡ πρὸς ἀλλήλους χρεία τῶν ἀνθρώπων *Arist. Rhet. I 15, 1376b13* = fa-in lam taṯbut tilka l-ašyāʾu wa-taṣiḥḥa baṭalat muʿāmalatu l-nāsi fī-mā baynahum *77.16* **(b)** *in hend.* irtafaʿa wa-baṭala : ἀναιρεθέντος γὰρ τοῦ ζώου ἀναιρεῖται καὶ ὁ ἄνθρωπος *Nicom. Arithm. 9.19* = wa-ḏālika anna l-insāna yartafiʿu wa-yabṭulu bi-rtifāʿi l-ḥayawāni *16.21.*

1.2 συναναιρέομαι *pass.* (*to be abolished together with s.th.*) = *in hend.*; irtafaʿa wa-baṭala bi-buṭlāni *c. gen.* : ἀλλʼ οὐ συναναιρεῖται (*sc.* ἡ ἀριθμητική) ὑπʼ αὐτῆς (*sc.* τῆς γεωμετρίας) *Nicom. Arithm. 10.21* = wa-lā yartafiʿu huwa (*sc.* ʿilmu l-ʿadadi) wa-yabṭulu bi-buṭlāni ʿilmi l-handasati *17.20.*

1.3 *sem. metathesis; act. / pass. transformation;* συναναιρέω *c. acc.* (*to abolish s.th. together with itself*) = *in hend.;* irtafaʿa wa-baṭala bi-rtifāʿi *c. gen.* (*to be abolished and annuled together with s.th.*) : ὅσῳ συναναιρεῖ μὲν (*sc.* ἡ ἀριθμητική) ἑαυτῇ τὰ λοιπά *Nicom. Arithm. 9.16* = wa-ḏālika anna l-ṣanāʾiʿa l-uḫara tartafiʿu wa-tabṭulu bi-rtifāʿi hāḏihi l-ṣināʿati *16.20;* συναναιρεῖ ἄρα ἡ ἀριθμητικὴ τὴν γεωμετρίαν *10.20* = inna ʿilma l-ʿadadi yartafiʿu wa-yabṭulu bi-rtifāʿihī wa-buṭlānihī ʿilmu l-handasati *17.19.*

2. *transl.* λύομαι *pass.* (*to be annulled, come to an end*) *and its derivatives*

2.1 λύομαι *pass.* (*to be annulled, come to an end*) : λύονται δὲ αἱ κινήσεις αἱ δημιουργοῦσαι εἰς τὰς ἐγγύς *Arist. Gener. anim. IV 3, 768a15* = wa-l-quwā llatī taḫluqu tabṭulu wa-tantaqilu ilā l-quwā l-aqrabi (*sic ed. pro* al-qurbā) *146.5*⊗ ⟼ λεχθέντος δὲ τοῦ αἰτίου ἐλύθη ἡ διαβολή *Arist. Rhet. II 23, 1400a28* = fa-lammā ḏukirati l-ʿillatu baṭalati l-tuhmatu *158.21* ⟼ οὕτω γὰρ ἂν λύοιτο τὸ τὴν νοῦσον παρέχον τῷ σώματι *Hippocr. Nat. hom. 200.16* = fa-innaka iḏā faʿalta ḏālika baṭalati l-ʿillatu l-muwallidatu li-l-maraḍi *23.13* ⟼ ἔπειτα φησὶ (*sc.* Εὐριπίδης) τὴν ἀνομίαν λυθῆναι νόμων εἰσαγωγῇ *Ps.-Plut. Placita 298a18* = wa-ḏakara (*sc.* Awrībīḏis) anna baʿda ḏālika baṭala l-fuǧūru bi-waḍʿi l-nawāmīsi *13.1.*

2.2 *sem. metathesis; act. / pass. transformation;* λύσιν ποιέω (*bringing to a resolution*) = baṭala (*come to an end*) : ἐχθροὺς δὲ προσαγορεύειν καὶ καταφιλεῖν δοκεῖν τῆς ἔχθρας λύσιν ποιεῖ *Artem. Onirocr. 101. 22* = fa-ammā in raʾā ka-annahū yuṣāfiḥu aw yuʿāniqu ʿaduwwan fa-inna ḏālika yadullu ʿalā anna ʿadāwatahū tabṭulu *188.1.*

3. *transl.* ἀπόλλυμαι *med.* (*to be undone, destroyed*) *and its compounds*

3.1 ἀπόλλυμαι (*to be undone, destroyed*) **(a)** *abs.* : ἔτι ὅταν ἐξ ἀέρος ὕδωρ γένηται, ἀπόλωλεν ὁ τόπος *Arist. Phys. IV 2, 210a10* = wa-ayḍan matā ḥadaṯa ʿani l-hawāʾi māʾun fa-qad baṭala l-makānu *289.1* ⟼ πρός τε τὸ προειδέναι κατὰ τὰ μεγάλα τραύματα ... τὴν ἀπολλυμένην ἐνέργειαν *Galen Anat. admin. II, 229.1* = fī l-taqaddumi bi-maʿrifati l-fiʿli llaḏī yabṭulu fī l-ǧirāḥāti l-ʿaẓīmati *16.20 Garofalo; 229.2* = *16.22* ⟼ τὸ δ' αὖ δόξῃ μετ' αἰσθήσεως ἀλόγου (ἀλόγου *om. Arab.*) δοξαστόν, γινόμενόν τε καὶ ἀπολλύμενον *Nicom. Arithm. 4.4** (= *Plato, Tim. 28A2-3*) = wa-ammā l-ṯānī minhumā fa-innahū yuẓannu annahū yakūnu wa-yabṭulu (*sic leg. pro* wa-yubṭalu *ed.*) bi-l-raʾyi maʿa l-ḥissi *12.23** **(b)** *in hend.* ḏahaba wa-baṭala : νεύρων μικρῶν κατὰ τὸ μετάφρενον βροχισθέντων ἀπόλλυσθαι τὴν φωνήν *Galen Anat. admin. II, 669.10* = yakūnu ʿinda mā rubiṭa (*sic leg. pro* rṭb *ap. Garofalo p. 504.5*) fī l-ẓahri aʿṣābun ṣiġārun ḏahaba l-ṣawtu wa-baṭala *WGAÜ Suppl. I, 150.17.*

3.2 ἐξαπόλλυμαι (*to be done away with*) : ἐὰν δὲ τὴν κ μεσότητα ἐμβάλλω εἰς τοὺς προκειμένους ἀρτίους ὅρους, ... ἐξαπόλλυνται δὲ τὰ τῆς ἀριθμητικῆς (*sc.* ἰδιώματα) *Nicom. Arithm. 138.7* = fa-ammā in naḥnu ǧaʿalnā l-ḥadda l-awsaṭa l-dāḫila fī-mā bayna l-ḥaddayni l-āḫarayni llaḏayni ḏakarnāhumā llaḏānī humā ʿadadāni zawǧāni ʿadada l-ʿišrīna fa-... tabṭulu ḫawāṣṣu l-tawassuṭi l-ʿadadiyyi *106.13.*

4. ἀπογίγνομαι (*to be or pass away*) : συμβεβηκὸς δέ ἐστιν ὃ γίνεται καὶ ἀπογίνεται χωρὶς τῆς τοῦ ὑποκειμένου φθορᾶς *Porph. Isag. 12.24* = wa-l-ʿaraḍu huwa mā yakūnu wa-yabṭulu min ġayri fasādi l-mawḍūʿi lahū *1086.5 / fol. 154a.*

5. ἀφανίζομαι *pass.* (*to be done away with, dissapear*) : ἀλλ᾽ εἰ ἕν τί γε ἐκλείποι, πάντα ἂν ἀφανισθείη *Hippocr. Nat. hom. 186.2* = lākin in nafida minhu šayʾun wāḥidun baṭala l-kullu *12.15.*

6. συγχέομαι (*to be obliterated*) : τέλος δ᾽ οὕτω συγχέονται (*sc.* αἱ κινήσεις) ὥστε μηθενὶ ἐοικέναι τῶν οἰκείων καὶ συγγενῶν *Arist. Gener. anim. IV 3, 768b10* = wa-fī aḫaratin tabṭulu tilka l-ḥarakatu tamāman wa-yaʿriḍu min ḏālika an lā yakūna l-mawlūdu šabīhan bi-aḥadin min ahlihī wa-ansibāʾihī *147.5.*

7. κατάληψις (*stopping [of sensation], catalepsy*) : καταφορὰ καὶ παράνοια, κατάληψις τῶν αἰσθητηρίων μετ᾽ ἀφωνίας *Paulus Aeg. III, 71.1* = ġašyun wa-ḏahābu l-ʿaqli wa-tabṭulu l-ḥawāssu wa-yanqaṭiʿu l-ṣawtu *versio A WGAÜ Suppl. I, 528.17.*

8. *sem. concentr.;* ἐκποδὼν γίνεται (*to be put out of the way, disappear*) : ἐὰν δὲ τὸν ις ἀντιλάβω μέσον ὅρον, πάλιν τὰ μὲν τῶν προτέρων δυοῖν μεσοτήτων ἰδιώματα ἐκποδὼν γίνεται *Nicom. Arithm. 138.18* = wa-ammā in naḥnu ǧaʿalnā l-ḥadda l-awsaṭa ʿadada l-sittata ʿašara badala l-ḥaddayni l-awsaṭayni llaḏayni qaddamnā ḏikrahumā fa-inna ḫawāṣṣa l-tawassuṭayni l-āḫarayni tabṭulu *106.21.*

9. *sem.; etym.; transl.* ὄλεθρος < ὄλλυμαι *med.* (*to perish, come to an end*) *in* ἀνώλεθρος (*indestructible*) = lā yabṭulu : τούτων δὲ οὕτως ἐχόντων ὁμολογητέον ἓν μὲν εἶναι τὸ κατὰ ταὐτὰ εἶδος ἔχον, ἀγέννητον καὶ ἀνώλεθρον *Plato Tim. 52A2* = fa-iḏā kāna hāḏā ha-kaḏā fa-yanbaġī an yusallama anna l-nawʿa llaḏī fī l-malāʾikati wāḥidun wa-annahū ġayru mukawwanin lā yabṭulu *Galen Comp. Tim. 14.4.*

10. *sem.; etym.; morph.; transl. the alpha privative in* ἀκινητίζω (*to be unmoving*) = baṭalat ḥarakatuhū : ἀκινητίζει τε φοβούμενα (*sc.* τὰ ἄναιμα) *Galen An. virt. 53.7* (= *Arist. Part. anim. II 4, 650b31*) = iḏā faziʿat (*sc.* al-ḥayawānu l-ʿadīmu l-dami) fa-baʿḍuhā tabṭulu (*sic leg. pro* yabṭulu *ed.*) ḥarakatuhū *25.11*⊗.

11. *sem. amplif.;* ξηραίνομαι *pass.* (*to dry up* [*and perish, of plants*]) = *in hend.* ǧaffa wa-baṭala : ἀμοιροῦντα δὲ (*sc.* τὰ φυτὰ ὑγροῦ) ξηραίνεται *Ps.-Plut. Placita 276a19* = in ʿudimati l-ruṭūbatu ǧaffa (*sc.* al-nabātu) wa-baṭala (wa-baṭala *nos* : wa-buṭṭila *ed.*) *3.20**.

بطلان I. **buṭlānun** *maṣdar*

1. *transl.* παραλύω (*to paralyze*) *and its derivatives*

1.1 παραλύω (*to paralyze*) : ὅ τι ἂν οἱ βραχίονες πάθωσι πένθος σημαίνουσιν ὅ τι δ’ ἂν οἱ πήχεις (ὅ τι δ’ ἂν οἱ πήχεις *non vert. Ar.*) παραλύουσι τῶν ἐν χερσὶ πραγμάτων *Artem. Onirocr. 48.2* = inna l-ḏirāʿa iḏā alimat fa-hiya tadullu ʿalā ḥuznin wa-buṭlāni l-ašyāʾi llatī tuʿmalu bi-l-yadi *90.15.*

1.2 *sem.; def.;* παραλυτικός (*paralytic*) = fāliǧun ʿāriḍun bi-buṭlāni ḥissi baʿḍi l-aʿḍāʾi wa-ḥarakatihā (*hemiplegia, consisting of partial loss of sensation and of movement*) : ἁρμόζει δὲ (*sc.* ὁ ὀπὸς) ... παραλυτικοῖς *Diosc. Mat. med. II, 91.12* = wāfaqat (*sc.* damʿatu l-nabāti) ... al-fāliǧa l-ʿāriḍa bi-buṭlāni <ḥissi> (*add. Dubler/Terés II, p. 275.10*) baʿḍi l-aʿḍāʾi wa-ḥarakatihā *Ibn al-Bayṭār Ǧāmiʿ IV, 208.18.*

2. ἀπώλεια (*perdition, loss*) : εἰς τὴν ὑπὸ τῶν ἰατρῶν γεγενημένην θεραπείαν εἰθισμένοις ἀναφέρειν τὴν ἀπώλειαν αὐτῆς (*sc.* ἐνεργείας) *Galen Anat. admin. II, 229.5* = min šaʾnihim an yaǧʿalū l-sababa fī buṭlāni l-fiʿli allaḏī yabṭulu ʿilāǧa l-ṭabībi *18.1 Garofalo.*

3. τὸ μὴ εἶναι (*non-existence*) : ἔνιοι τῶν φιλοσόφων ... καθόλου φασὶ μὴ εἶναι θεούς *Ps.-Plut. Placita 297a16* = inna baʿḍa l-awwalīna ... qālū bi-l-ǧumlati bi-buṭlāni l-ilāhi *12.18;* ταῦτ’ (*sc.* τὰ βιβλία) ἔστι τὰ περὶ τοῦ μὴ εἶναι θεούς *298a7* = yaʿnī bi-ḏālika kutubahū fī buṭlāni l-ālihati *12.22.*

4. στερίσκω (*to deprive*) = *in hend.* (*?*) <faqdun> aw buṭlānun : αὐξῆσαν δὲ (*sc.* τὸ αἰδοῖον) καὶ ἐπαύξει, ἀφαιρεθὲν δὲ στερίσκει *Artem. Onirocr. 52.9* = wa-iḏā ʿaẓuma (*sc.* al-iḥlīlu) dalla ʿalā tazayyudi l-šayʾi llaḏī yadullu ʿalayhi <wa-iḏā uḫiḏa dalla ʿalā faqdihī> (*add. nos; cf.* ἀφαίρεσις *234.26* = aḫḏun *433.16, and* στερίσκω *52.11* = faqdun *98.14*) aw buṭlānihī *98.12**.

5. ὑπερτίθεμαι *med.* (*to defer; to omit, abandon*) : ὁ δὲ μηδὲν ἀποκρινόμενος μάντις πᾶσαν ἐγχείρησιν καὶ πᾶσαν ὁρμὴν ὑπερτίθεται *Artem. Onirocr. 212.11* = fa-ammā iḏā raʾā l-insānu ka-anna l-ʿarrāfa <lā> (<lā> *add. Endress, p. 344*) yuǧībuhū bi-šayʾin fa-inna l-ruʾyā tadullu ʿalā buṭlāni kulli mā faʿala wa-kulli irādatin li-šayʾin *385.3**.

6. κατάληψις (*stopping* [*of sensation*], *catalepsy*) : καταφορὰ καὶ παράνοια, κατάληψις τῶν αἰσθητηρίων μετ' ἀφωνίας *Paulus Aeg. III, 71.1* = subātun wa-ḫtilāṭun wa-buṭlānu l-ḥawāssi wa-buṭlānu l-ṣawti *versio B WGAÜ Suppl. I, 528.18*.

7. *transl.* φθείρω (*to destroy*) *in act. and med.*

7.1 φθείρω *act.* (*to ruin, destroy*) : εἰ ἀφαιρεθεῖσα (*sc.* ἡ κίνησις) φθείροι ἂν τὸν οὐρανόν *Theophr. Princ. 6a14* = hal iḏā zālat (*sc.* al-ḥarakatu) kāna bi-zawālihā buṭlānu l-samāʾi *184.8 (cf. app. crit. ad loc. et Gutas, p. 185 note 74)*.

7.2 φθείρομαι *med.* (*to be annihilated, perish*) : ἅμα τῷ πεπαῦσθαι (*sc.* τῆς περιφορᾶς) φθείροιτ' ἂν (*sc.* ὁ οὐρανός) *Theophr. Princ. 6a8* = maʿa sukūnihā (*sc.* al-ḥarakati) yakūnu buṭlānu l-samāʾi *184.5*.

8. διίστημι (*to set apart, dissolve*) = *in hend.* buṭlānun wa-mufāraqatun : διὸ καὶ γάμους καὶ κοινωνίας διίστησι (*sc.* ἔρρωσο καὶ ὑγίαινε λέγειν) *Artem. Onirocr. 99.12* = wa-li-ḏālika tadullu hāḏihi l-ruʾyā fīman yurīdu an yuʿrisa ʿalā buṭlāni ʿursihī wa-ʿalā mufāraqati l-šurakāʾi *183.7*.

9. *sem.; etym.; morph.; transl. the alpha privative, followed by the gen. of the negated word*

9.1 ἀνορεξία (*lack of desire*) = buṭlānu l-bāhi : οἱ θέρμοι ... στομάχου ἄσην πραΞνουσι καὶ ἀνορεξίαν ἰῶνται *Diosc. Mat. med. I, 184.16* = al-turmusu ... yusakkinu ġaṯayāna l-maʿidati wa-karbahā wa-yanfaʿu min buṭlāni l-bāhi *versio B WGAÜ Suppl. I, 129.13*.

9.2 ἀφωνία (*voicelessness*) = buṭlānu l-ṣawti : *v. supra,* buṭlānun 6.

9.3 ἀπραγέω (*to do nothing, be unemployed*) = *in hend.* buṭlānu l-ʿamali wa-ʿuṭlatun : οἷα δ' ἂν γράμματά τις μὴ δύνηται γράφειν ἢ ἀναγινώσκειν, ἀπραγήσει *Artem. Onirocr. 60.27* = wa-ammā l-kitābu llaḏī lā yumkinu l-insānu an yaqraʾahū <a>w (*add. Fahd*) an yaktubahū fa-innahū yadullu ʿalā buṭlāni l-aʿmāli wa-ʿuṭlatin *112.10.*

9.4 ἀναισθησία (*lack of sensation*) = *in hend.* ʿusru l-ḥissi wa-buṭlānuhū : τὸ δὲ μὴ ἔχειν ῥῖνα ἀναισθησίαν πᾶσι σημαίνει *Artem. Onirocr. 35.25* = fa-in ʿadimū (*sc.* al-nāsu) l-anfa fī l-manāmi fa-inna ḏālika yadullu ʿalā ʿusri l-ḥissi wa-buṭlānihī *67.5.*

باطل **bāṭilun** *act. part. → at the end of the verbal stems*

[2]بَطَلَ **I. baṭala,** *impf.* **yabṭulu,** *maṣdar* **biṭālatun** *but also* **buṭlānun** (*basic meaning: to be idle, inactive*)

1. *transl.* ἀργέω (*to be idle, unemployed*) *and its derivatives*

1.1 ἀργέω (*to be idle, unemployed*) : πονήσαντες γὰρ μᾶλλον δύνανται ὀχεύειν ἢ ἀργοῦντες *Arist. Hist. anim. VI 20, 574b29* = aʿnī annahā iḏā taʿibat (*post* taʿibat <fī l-ʿamali> *add. Badawī*) kānat aqwā ʿalā l-sifādi minhā iḏā baṭalat *297.10* ↔ ἐκθηλύνεται γὰρ ἅπαν ἀργοῦν (ἀργοῦν *Arab. ut vid.* : ἀρωγὸν *P* : ἀργούντων *ed.*) σῶμα καὶ ἄῤῥωστον γίνεται *Galen In De off. med. 880.1** = wa-ḏālika anna kulla ǧismin yabṭulu fa-hwa ḍaʿīfun wa-yaṣīru ḫāmila l-quwwati *56.7.*

1.2 ἀργός εἶναι *c. gen.* (*to be void of s.th.*) : ὁ μὲν γὰρ χειμὼν ἀργὸς ἔργων *Hippocr. Humor. 16:8* = wa-ḏālika anna l-šitāʾa tabṭulu l-aʿmālu fīhi *29.6.*

2. *transl.* σχολάζω (*to have leisure*) *and its derivatives*

2.1 σχολάζω (*to be unoccupied, have leisure*) : δοκεῖ τε ἡ εὐδαιμονία ἐν τῇ σχολῇ εἶναι· ἀσχολούμεθα γὰρ ἵνα σχολάζωμεν *Arist. Eth. Nic. X 7, 1177b5* = wa-yuẓannu (*sic leg. pro* wa-naẓunnu *ed.*) anna l-saʿādata fī l-biṭālati min aǧli annā naštaġilu li-nabṭula (*sic leg. Ullmann pro* li-nubaṭṭila *ed.*) *559.11*.*

2.2 σχολὴν ἔχειν (*to have leisure*) : τί ἂν εἴη ἄλλο ἢ τὸ μὴ σχολὴν ἔχειν (ἔχειν *Arab. ut vid., add. Hercher* : *om. codd.*) ἀλλ' ἀπὸ τῆς τέχνης πορίζειν *Artem. Onirocr. 91.20** = fa-laysa ḏālika illā ṭalabuhu l-maʿāša min ṣināʿatin yuʿāliǧuhā wa-lā yabṭulu (*sic leg. pro* yubaṭṭilu *ed.*) *168.16*.*

3. ἀπρακτέω (*to be inactive*) : δοκεῖ γὰρ ἐνδέχεσθαι καὶ καθεύδειν ἔχοντα τὴν ἀρετὴν ἢ ἀπρακτεῖν διὰ βίου *Arist. Eth. Nic. I 5, 1095b33* = wa-ḏālika annā naʿlamu annahū qad yumkinu an yanāma l-insānu wa-maʿahu l-faḍīlatu wa-yumkinu an yabṭula dahrahū kullahū *123.8.*

بطالة **I. biṭālatun** *maṣdar* (*also vocalized* baṭālatun *or* buṭālatun, *cf. Lane s.v.* baṭala)

1. *transl.* ἀργία (*idleness, unemployment*) and *its derivatives*

1.1 ἀργία (*idleness, unemployment*) : ἀργία γάρ ἐστιν ὁ ὕπνος τῆς ψυχῆς *Arist. Eth. Nic. I 13, 1102b7* = li-anna l-nawma innamā huwa biṭālatun mina l-nafsi *151.7;* διὰ δειλίαν καὶ ἀργίαν *IX 4, 1166b10* = li-l-ǧubni aw li-l-biṭālati *499.2* ⟼ οἷον "χωρὶς γὰρ ἄλλης ἧς ἔχουσιν ἀργίας, φθόνον ... ἀλφάνουσι δυσμενῆ" *Arist. Rhet. II 21, 1394a33* (= *Euripides, Medea* 297) = ka-qawli l-qāʾili inna fī ġayri l-biṭālati ayḍan mutakalliman li-l-ḥussādi *137.13* ⟼ ὅτι χρῆσις κρατύνει, ἀργίη δὲ τήκει *Galen In De off. med. 879.9* / *Hippocr. Off. med. 42. 19* = inna l-istiʿmāla yuṣaḥḥiḥu (*sic leg. in Gal.*) wa-l-biṭālatu tuḏawwibu *54. 26** / *16.11.*

1.2 *sem. concentr.;* ἀργία καὶ σχολή (*unemployment and leisure*) : χειροτέχναις δὲ ἀργίαν καὶ σχολήν (*sc.* τὰ λευκὰ ἱμάτια σημαίνει) *Artem. Onirocr. 102.17* = fa-ammā man kāna ṣāniʿan bi-yadihī wa-raʾā ka-annahū lābisu ṯiyābin bīḍin fa-inna ḏālika yadullu fīhi ʿalā biṭālatihī *189.11.*

1.3 ἀργός (*idle*) : πότερον οὖν τέκτονος μὲν καὶ σκυτέως ἔστιν ἔργα τινὰ καὶ πράξεις, ἀνθρώπου δ' οὐδέν ἐστιν ἀλλ' ἀργὸν πέφυκεν; *Arist. Eth. Nic. I 7, 1097b30* = a-fa-turā li-l-naǧǧāri wa-l-iskāfi afʿālan wa-aʿmālan wa-l-insānu maṭbūʿun ʿalā l-biṭālati *133.15.*

1.4 ἀργότερον *adv.* (*in a more idle way*) = *in hend.* ḏū l-ʿuṭlati wa-l-biṭālati : καὶ τοῖς ἀργότερον βιοῦσι πλεονάζουσα (*sc.* φαίνεται ἡ πιμελή) *Galen Anat. admin. II, 566.7* = wa-yakṯuru (*sc.* al-šaḥmu) fī abdāni ḏawī l-ʿuṭlati wa-l-biṭālati *378.4 Garofalo.*

1.5 *sem. amplif.; added as objective complement to* baṭṭāl *transl.* περίεργος (*superfluous*) : ἄνθρωπος τἄλλα περίεργος ἱκανῶς *Galen Simpl. medic. XI, 793.14* = kāna raǧulan baṭṭālan ġāyata l-biṭālati *versio B WGAÜ, 184.25* (*cf. infra,* baṭṭālun 1.2b).

2. *transl.* σχολή (*leisure*) *and its derivatives*

2.1 σχολή (*leisure*) : δοκεῖ τε ἡ εὐδαιμονία ἐν τῇ σχολῇ εἶναι *Arist. Eth. Nic. X 7, 1177b4* = wa-yuẓannu (*sic leg. pro* wa-naẓunnu *ed.*) anna l-saʿādata fī l-biṭālati *559.11** ⟼ τοῖς μὲν γὰρ (*sc.* ἐπιδίφριον τὴν ἐργασίαν ἔχουσι) σχολὴν σημαίνει τὸ ὄναρ *Artem. Onirocr. 128.22* = wa-ḏālika anna l-ruʾyā tadullu fī hāʾulāʾi ʿalā biṭālati l-rukkābi *233.12; cf. supra* biṭālatun 1.2.

2.2 τὸ σχολαστικόν (*leisureliness*) : αὕτη δὲ (*sc.* ἡ ἡδονὴ) συναύξει τὴν ἐνέργειαν καὶ τὸ αὔταρκες δὴ καὶ σχολαστικὸν καὶ ἄτρυτον *Arist. Eth. Nic. X 7, 1177b22* = wa-hāḏihi l-laḏḏatu bi-numūwihā yanmī l-fiʿlu wa-l-kifāyatu wa-l-biṭālatu wa-l-rāḥatu *561.6.*

3. *transl.* ἀπραξία (*inaction*) *and its derivatives*

3.1 ἀπραξία (*inaction, unemployment*) : ἐν μνήμασι δὲ ... καθεύδειν τοῖς μὲν νοσοῦσι θάνατον προαγορεύει, τοῖς δὲ ἐρρωμένοις ἀπραξίαν *Artem. Onirocr. 99.6* = fa-ammā in raʾā l-insānu ka-annahū nāʾimun fī maqbaratin ... fa-inna ḏālika yadullu fī l-marḍā ʿalā l-mawti wa-fī l-aṣiḥḥāʾi ʿalā biṭālatin *182.17;* τοῖς δὲ ἄλλοις μεγάλην ἀπραξίαν προαγορεύει (*sc.* τὸ νοσεῖν) *212.23* = wa-ammā fī sāʾiri l-nāsi fa-innahū (*sc.* al-maraḍa) yadullu ʿalā biṭālatin kabīratin *386.6;* τῶν γραμμάτων ... τὰ μὲν φωνήεντα φόβους καὶ ἀπραξίας (ἀπραξίας *Arab.* : ταραχὰς *LV, Pack*) σημαίνει, τὰ δὲ ἡμίφωνα ἀπραξίας μὲν οὐχί φόβους δὲ ἐπάγει *218.12*-13* = al-aḥrufu ... inna ḏawāti l-ṣawti tadullu ʿalā ḫawfin wa-biṭālatin wa-llatī fīhā niṣfu ṣawtin fa-innahā tadullu ʿalā biṭālatin ġayra annahū lā yatbaʿuhā ḫawfun *398.4-5; 166.14 = 298.7; etc.*

3.2 ἄπρακτος (*ineffective, unprofitable*) : αὐτὸ μὲν τὸ καθεύδειν δοκεῖν ἄπρακτον, καὶ τὸ μέλλειν ὑπνοῦν καὶ αὐτὸ ἄπρακτον καὶ πονηρὸν πᾶσι *Artem. Onirocr. 98.18-19* = iḏā raʾā l-insānu fī manāmihī ka-annahū nāʾimun aw ka-annahū yurīdu an yanāma fa-inna ḏālika yadullu ʿalā biṭālatin wa-hwa radīʾun li-ǧamīʿi l-nāsi *182.4;* αἱ δὲ κατάντεις (*sc.* ὁδοὶ) πᾶσίν εἰσιν ἄπρακτοι *150.23* = fa-in kānati l-ṭuruqu munqaṭiʿatan fīhā māniʿun fa-innahā tadullu ʿalā biṭālatin li-ǧamīʿi l-nāsi *272.4;* πρὸς δὲ τὰς πράξεις ἄπρακτοι (*sc.* οἱ πέπονες) *74.9* = fa-ammā man arāda an yaʿmala l-aʿmāla <fa-hwa> (*add. Fahd; sc.* al-biṭṭīḫu) radīʾun lahū wa-yadullu ʿalā biṭālatin *136.13; etc.*

4. ἀνεργασία (*unemployment*) : κίτρια (κίτρια *codd., Arab.* : κινάρα *Hercher* : †κίτρια† *Pack, sed v. Schmitt 39, adnot. 7*) δὲ διὰ τὸ ἀκανθῶδες καὶ ὀξὺ ὀδύνας σημαίνει καὶ (καὶ *codd., Arab.* : <ἔτι> καὶ *Pack*) ἀνεργασίας διὰ τὸ δύσπεπτον (διὰ τὸ δύσπεπτον *codd., Arab.* : *secl. Pack*) ἔστι γὰρ ἄτροφα *Artem. Onirocr. 73.15** = <fa-ammā> (*add. nos*) al-utruǧǧu bi-sababi šawkihī wa-ḥarāfatihī (ḥarāfatihī *cod., cf. Strohmaier 274* : ḥurāqatihī *Fahd*) wa-ḥumūḍatihī fa-innahū yadullu ʿalā waǧaʿin wa-biṭālatin li-annahū baṭīʾu l-ihtiḍāmi radīʾu l-maṭʿami *135.8**; ὄρη δὲ καὶ νάπαι ... δυσθυμίας καὶ φόβους καὶ ταραχὰς καὶ ἀνεργασίας σημαίνουσι *150.12* = fa-ammā l-ǧibālu wa-l-rawābī ... fa-innahā tadullu ʿalā ġammin šadīdin wa-fazaʿin wa-ḍṭirābin wa-biṭālatin *271.7.*

5. ἔκλυτος (*relaxed, loosened*) : καὶ γὰρ τὸ ἔκλυτον πέπον καλεῖται *Artem. Onirocr. 74.9* = li-anna l-biṭālata ayḍan tusammā bi-hāḏā l-ismi (*sc.* ismi l-biṭṭīḫi) *136.14.*

6. *in hend.;* ἀπαλαττόμενος *med.* (*one who is free, released [from being occupied with s.o. or s.th.]*) = ʿinda l-mufāraqati wa-ʿinda l-biṭālati : οὔτε γὰρ προσιόντες ἀλλήλοις ... ταῦτα (*sc.* ἔρρωσο καὶ ὑγίαινε) λέγουσιν οἱ ἄνθρωποι, ἀλλὰ ἀπαλλαττόμενοι ἀλλήλων καὶ πρὸς ὕπνον τρεπόμενοι *Artem. Onirocr. 99.11* = wa-ḏālika anna l-nāsa lā yuwaddiʿu baʿḍuhum baʿḍan illā ʿinda l-mufāraqati wa-ʿinda l-biṭālati wa-iḏā arādū l-nawma *183.5.*

7. *periphr.;* ἀφορία (*non-productivity*) = *in hend.* šiddatun wa-biṭālatun : ἀκρίδες δὲ καὶ πάρνοπες καὶ οἱ λεγόμενοι μάστακες γεωργοῖς μὲν ἀφορίαν ἢ φθορὰν τῶν καρπῶν προαγορεύουσι *Artem. Onirocr. 139.17* = fa-ammā l-ǧarādu wa-l-farāšu wa-l-ṭayru llaḏī yusammā masṭaqis wa-hwa ⁎ ΞΞ(*lac. ind. cod.*) fa-innahā tadullu fī l-akarati ʿalā šiddatin wa-biṭālatin wa-halāki l-ġallati *251.3**.

بطلان I. **buṭlānun** *maṣdar*

1. *in hend.;* ἀργότατος (*most lazy*) = kaṯīru l-kasali wa-l-buṭlāni : ὁ δ' ἀστερίας ὁ ἐπικαλούμενος ὄκνος μυθολογεῖται μὲν γενέσθαι ἐκ δούλων τὸ ἀρχαῖον, ἔστι δὲ κατὰ τὴν ἐπωνυμίαν τούτων ἀργότατος *Arist. Hist. anim. IX 18, 617a7* = fa-ammā llaḏī yusammā asṭāriyās wa-tafsīruhū l-baḥrī (*sic cod.* [?] : al-naǧmī *coni. Badawī*) fa-innahū yuqālu fī l-amṯāli inna ḫilqatahū min ḫilqati ʿabīdin wa-fiʿluhū šabīhun bi-smihī li-annahū kaṯīru l-kasali wa-l-buṭlāni *405.7.*

بطّال **baṭṭālun**

1. *transl.* ἀργός (*idle, unemployed*) and *its compounds*

1.1 ἀργός (*idle, unemployed*) **(a)** *abs.* : τούς τε κηφῆνας ἀργοὺς ἅτ' οὐδὲν ἔχοντας ὅπλον πρὸς τὸ διαμάχεσθαι *Arist. Gener. anim. III 10, 760b11* = fa-ammā llatī tusammā qīfīnās fa-innahā tabqā baṭṭālatan li-annahū laysa lahā ʿuḍwun muwāfiqun li-l-qitāli *126.7* ⊣ ἀπὸ συλλαβῆς δέ "τί ἂν ἔπαθες δεινόν, εἰ ἄνδρ' εἶδες ἀργόν;" *Arist. Rhet. III 9, 1410a35* = wa-ammā l-maqāṭiʿu fa-kamā qīla ayyu šarrin nālaka in kunta raǧulan baṭṭālan *198.13* (*either Ar. understood* εἶ *or* ἦσθα *for* εἶδες – *cf. Lyons, p. 382 — or the Arabic text should be corrected to read,* in kunta <raʾayta>) ↔ ἀργοῖς δὲ καὶ ἀπόροις πράξεις σημαίνει (*sc.* τὸ ὄναρ) καὶ ἐργασίας· οὔτε γὰρ ἀργὸς ὁ στρατιώτης οὔτε ἐνδεής ἐστι *Artem. Onirocr. 154.11-12* = wa-tadullu (*sc.* al-ruʾyā) fī man kāna baṭṭālan lā yaʿmalu šayʾan ʿalā ʿamalin yaʿmalūnahū wa-ḏālika anna l-ğundiyya laysa bi-baṭṭālin wa-lā bi-muḥtāğin *279.10, 12*; ὁ δὲ ἀσσιδάριος ἀργὴν καὶ μωρὰν εἶναι τὴν γυναῖκα σημαίνει *155.17* = asīdāriyūs, fa-inna l-ruʾyā tadullu ʿalā annahū yatazawwağu mraʾtan baṭṭālatan lā ʿaqla lahā *281.13* **(b)** *in hend.* baṭṭālun lā yaʿmalu šayʾan : αἱ δὲ φαναὶ καὶ λαμπραί (*sc.* μέλιτται), ὥσπερ γυναῖκες ἀργαί *Arist. Hist. anim. IX 40, 627a15* = fa-ammā l-naḥlu l-ṣāfī l-naqiyyu fa-hwa šabīhun bi-l-nisāʾi l-baṭṭālāti llātī lā yaʿmalna šayʾan *439.9.*

1.2 περίεργος (*overdoer, superfluous*) **(a)** *abs.* : καθάπερ καὶ Ξενοκράτης ὁ Ἀφροδισιεὺς ἐποίησεν, ἄνθρωπος τἄλλα περίεργος ἱκανῶς καὶ γοητείας οὐκ ἀπηλλαγμένος *Galen Simpl. medic. XI, 793.14* = kamā faʿala Kasānūqrāṭīs al-Afrūdīsiyyu fa-innahū kāna rağulan baṭṭālan ġāyata l-biṭālati wa-yaḏhabu maḏhaban mā huwa bi-baʿīdin ʿan maḏhabi l-saḥarati *versio B WGAÜ, 184.25 (cf. infra,* bāṭilun 4.2) **(b)** *in hend.* baṭṭālun aw mutaʿaṭṭilun : εἴ τις περίεργος ἀφαιρεθῇ *Arist. Rhet. I 4, 1359b27* = in kāna fīhā insānun baṭṭālun aw mutaʿaṭṭilun nuḥḥiya *20.6.*

2. *transl.* ἀπραγέω (*to do nothing*) *and its derivatives*

2.1 ἀπραγέω (*to do nothing, be idle*) : ἢ γὰρ ἀναλαμβάνοντες ἢ ἀπραγοῦντες εἰς θερμὰ πορεύονται *Artem. Onirocr. 70.12* = li-anna llaḏīna yaġtasilūna fī l-ḥammāmāti hum immā marḍā wa-immā baṭṭālūna *129.12.*

2.2 ἄπρακτος (*doing nothing*) : ἄπρακτοι γὰρ οἱ ἀποθανόντες *Artem. Onirocr. 182.5* = wa-ḏālika anna l-mawtā hum baṭṭālūna *329.12;* ὑπτίους γὰρ τοὺς ἀπράκτους λέγομεν *194.6* = wa-ḏālika anna man kāna baṭṭālan yuqālu innahū mustalqin ʿalā qafāhu *351.10;* ἄπρακτοι γὰρ οἱ νοσοῦντες *212.23* = wa-ḏālika anna l-marḍā baṭṭālūna *386.6; etc.*

[3] بَطُلَ **I. baṭula,** *impf.* **yabṭulu,** *maṣdar* **baṭālatun** (*basic meaning*: *to be brave*)

بَطالة **I. baṭālatun** *maṣdar*

1. τολμάω (*to be bold, dare*) : τὸ πολλὰ τολμᾶν πόλλʼ ἁμαρτάνειν ποιεῖ *Men. Mon. I 300b* = laysa fī l-baṭālati l-kaṯīrati šayʾun mina l-ḫayri *Ullmann Bem., 87.*

بطل baṭalun, *pl.* **abṭālun**

1. γενναῖος (*valiant, brave*) : εἴπομεν ὦ γενναῖε, μὴ ῥητορικῶς ἡμῶν κατάτρεχε χωρὶς ἀποδείξεως *Galen. Nat. fac. II, 61.11* = fa-naqūlu ayyuhā l-baṭalu lā taṭʿun ʿalaynā ʿalā ṭarīqi aṣḥābi l-rīṭūrīqā min ġayri burhānin *WGAÜ Suppl. I, 239.*

2. *paraphr.;* μονομάχος (*gladiator*) = *in hend.* baṭalun mubārizun (*brave combatant; v. supra* mubārizun 1, *II 197.27*) : ἐπί τε στρατιωτῶν ἐν πολέμοις τετρωμένων, καὶ τουτωνὶ τῶν καλουμένων μονομάχων *Galen Anat. admin. II, 345.8* = fī qawmin mina l-muqātilati aṣābathum ǧirāḥātun fī l-ḥarbi wa-qawmin mina l-abṭāli l-mubārizīna (*sic leg. pro* mubādizīna *ed.*) *136.20* Garofalo.*

بطّل II. baṭṭala

1. *sem. concentr.;* ποιεῖν τινὰ ἀνενεργές (*to make s.th. ineffective, frustrate*) : ποιεῖ δὲ τὸ σπέρμα αὐτῆς ἀνενεργῆ τὰ θανάσιμα προπινόμενον *Diosc. Mat. med. I, 186.7* = ṯamaratuhū tubaṭṭilu (*vel* tubṭilu) quwwata l-adwiyati l-qattālati šurban qablahā *versio B WGAÜ Suppl. I, 123.22.*

تبطيل II. tabṭīlun *maṣdar*

1. λύσις (*dissolution*) : εἰ δὲ ὑπὸ τῆς ἑαυτοῦ γυναικὸς ἢ ἐρωμένης δόξειέ τις ἀρρητοποιεῖσθαι, ἔχθρα ἢ λύσις τοῦ γάμου ἢ τῆς φιλίας ἔσται *Artem. Onirocr. 95.15* = in raʾā l-insānu ka-anna mraʾatahū aw ṣadīqatahū tafʿalu bihī mā lā yaǧūzu ḏikruhū fa-inna ḏālika yadullu ʿalā muʿādātihī wa-nṣirāfi maḥabbatihī ʿanhā wa-tabṭīli ʿursi l-marʾati (al-marʾati *nos* : al-mamālīki *cod., ed.*) *175.5*.*

أبطل IV. abṭala *c. acc.* (*and vulgarly* **II. baṭṭala** *c. acc.*)

1. *transl. compounds of* αἱρέω (*to take*)

1.1 ἀναιρέω (*to annul, abolish, eliminate s.th.*) : τὸ δὲ φάναι ... ἀναιρεῖν ἐστι τῶν δεδομένων τι *Arist. Cael. I 12, 283a6* = fa-ammā man qāla ... fa-qad yubṭilu baʿḍa l-muqaddamāti llatī waḍaʿnā wa-l-maqāyīs [*sic leg. cum mss.*] *versio B 217.12 Badawī* ⟼ ἔτι τὸ ἐπίστασθαι ἀναιροῦσιν οἱ οὕτως λέγοντες *Arist. Metaph. α 2, 994b20* = wa-ayḍan fa-inna man qāla bi-hāḏā l-qawli abṭala l-ʿilma *36.2* / wa-ayḍan inna l-qāʾilīna bi-miṯli hāḏā l-qawli yubṭilūna l-ʿilma *36v1* ⟼ ὅλως δ᾽ ἀναιρεῖ ὁ οὕτως λέγων τὰ φύσει τε καὶ φύσιν *Arist. Phys. II 8, 199b14* = wa-bi-l-ǧumlati inna man qāla bi-hāḏā l-qawli fa-innamā yubṭilu mā yakūnu bi-l-ṭabīʿati wa-l-ṭabīʿata *154.16*; γένεσιν οὖν ἀναιρεῖ καὶ φθορὰν οὗτος ὁ λόγος *VIII 3, 254a10* = fa-hāḏā l-qawlu l-āna yubṭilu l-kawna wa-l-fasāda *828.3* ⊢ ὅσοι δὲ τῶν λόγων ψεῦδος συλλογίζονται, λυτέον ἀναιροῦντα παρ' ὃ γίνεται τὸ ψεῦδος· οὐ γὰρ ὁ ὁτιοῦν ἀνελὼν λέλυκεν, οὐδ' εἰ ψεῦδός ἐστι τὸ ἀναιρούμενον *Arist. Top. VIII 10, 160b24-25* = wa-mā kāna min al-aqāwīli muntiğan li-l-kiḏbi fa-qad yanbaġī an nanquḍahū bi-ibṭāli mā ʿanhu yantiğu l-kiḏbu wa-ḏālika annahū laysa bi-ibṭālika ayya šayʾin ittafaqa takūnu qad naqaḍta mā yağibu naqḍuhū wa-lā in kāna mā (mā *nos* : mimmā *ed.*) tubṭiluhū kiḏban *751.8-10* / fol. 322b; 160b32, 34 = 752.1, 3 / fol. 322b; VIII 12, 162b19 = 760.9 / fol. 325a; etc.* ⊢ καὶ ἡ μεγάλη συζυγία ... τὴν φωνὴν ἀναιρεῖν πέφυκεν *Galen Nerv. diss. II, 842.16* = wa-zawğu l-aʿṣābi l-ʿaẓīmu ... qad yubṭilu l-ṣawta *106.14* ⊢ ἁμαρτάνει (*sc.* Ἀναξίμανδρος) ... τὸ ... ποιοῦν αἴτιον ἀναιρῶν *Ps.-Plut. Placita 278a4* = wa-qad aḫṭaʾa (*sc.* Anaqsimandurus) ... min qibali annahū ... abṭala l-ʿillata l-fāʿilata *4.4;* Ξενοφάνης καὶ Ἐπίκουρος ἀναιροῦσι τὴν μαντικήν *415a17* = fa-ammā Kasānūfānis wa-Ibīqūrus fa-innahumā yubaṭṭilāni (*vel* yubṭilāni) l-ʿirāfata l-battata *63.7; 320a6, 12 = 21.9, 13; etc.* ⊢ οἱ γὰρ ἁπάντων ζητοῦντες λόγον ἀναιροῦσιν λόγον, ἅμα δὲ καὶ τὸ εἰδέναι *Theophr. Princ. 9b21* = fa-inna llaḏīna ṭalabū l-ḥuğğata fī l-ʿulūmi <kullihā> qad yubṭilūna l-ḥuğğata wa-yubṭilūna maʿa ḏālika l-maʿrifata *208.4-5.*

1.2 ἐξαιρέω (*to remove, make away with s.th.*) : οἱ τὸ ἄπειρον ποιοῦντες ... ἐξαιροῦντες τὴν τοῦ ἀγαθοῦ φύσιν *Arist. Metaph. α 2, 994 b12* = allaḏīna yağʿalūna l-ašyāʾa ġayra mutanāhiyatin yubṭilūna ṭabīʿata l-ğūdi *31.2.*

1.3 περιαιρέω (*to take off, remove s.th.*) : πρὸς τὸ τὴν δριμύτητα περιαιρεῖν *Diosc. Mat. med. I, 114.18* = li-yubṭila ḥiddatahū *vetus transl. Ullmann Unters., 183.*

2. *transl.compounds and derivatives of* λύω (*to loose*)

2.1 *sem. metathesis; active / passive transformation*; παραλύω *c. acc.* (*to disable, paralyse s.th.*) = ubṭila *c.* bi- : αἱ γὰρ ... τομαὶ παραλύουσι τὴν ἐνέργειαν *Galen Anat. admin. II, 229.14* = fa-inna l-qaṭʿa ... tubṭalu bihī afʿālu l-ʿaḍali *18.7 Garofalo.*

2.2 *in hend.;* λυτικός *c. gen.* (*alleviating s.th.*) = aḏhaba wa-abṭala *c. acc.* : νάρκη γὰρ μετρίη ὀδύνης λυτική *Galen Loc. aff. VIII, 71.17* (= *Hippocr. Aphor. V 25)* : wa-l-ḫadaru l-yasīru yuḏhibu l-wağaʿa wa-yubṭiluhū *WGAÜ Suppl. I, 647.17.*

3. ἀπόλλυμι (*to undo, destroy*) **(a)** *abs.* : ἀλλ' ὁ μὲν ἣν ἔχει διάθεσιν, ταύτην ἀπόλλυσι *Them. In De an. 55.32* = lākinna ḏāka yubṭilu l-ḥāla llatī huwa ʿalayhā *81. 5* **(b)** *sem. metathesis; med. / active transformation* : ἤτοι παραλυθέντων τῶν ἄλλων, ἢ καὶ παντάπασιν ἀπολομένων *Galen Anat. admin. II, 394.1* = ḥadaṯa bi-ǧamīʿi l-aʿṣābi l-uḫari immā stirḫāʾun wa-immā āfatun tubṭiluhā (tubṭiluhā *nos* : tubṭiluhū *ed.*) ǧumlatan *186.20* Garofalo.*

4. *medic.; transl. compounds and expressions containing derivatives of the word* ἐνεργέω (*to be active, effective* [*of medicament*]) *used negatively*

4.1 ἀντενεργέω (*to be efficacious against*) : δύναμιν δὲ ἔχει ... ἀντενεργεῖν θανασίμοις *Diosc. Mat. med. I, 109.8* = abṭala quwwata l-adwiyati l-qātilati *vetus transl. Ullmann Unters., 183.*

4.2 *sem. concentr.;* ποιεῖν τινὰ ἀνενεργές (*to make s.th. ineffective, frustrate*) : ποιεῖ δὲ τὸ σπέρμα αὐτῆς ἀνενεργῆ τὰ θανάσιμα προπινόμενον *Diosc. Mat. med. I, 186.7* = wa-iḏā tuquddima fī šurbin bizruhū abṭala l-adwiyata l-qattālata *versio A* = ṯamaratuhū tubṭilu (*vel* tubaṭṭilu) quwwata l-adwiyati l-qattālati šurban qablahā *versio B WGAÜ Suppl. I, 123.22.*

5. ἀποστρέφω (*to prevent, hinder*) : συνουσίαν ἀποστρέφει *Diosc. Mat. med. I, 207.14* = yubṭilu šahwata l-ǧimāʿi *vetus transl. Ullmann Unters., 183.*

6. εἴργω (*to hinder, prevent*) : ἐπεὶ γὰρ ὁ νόμος τὰ φανερὰ τῶν ἀδικημάτων εἴργειν ἠδύνατο *Ps.-Plut. Placita 298a20* = min aǧli anna l-nāmūsa innamā kāna yaqdiru ʿalā an yubṭila mā kāna mina l-ǧawri ẓāhiran *13.2.*

7. περιγράφω (*to cancel, annul*) : καὶ ἐὰν μὲν ἕπηται αὐτοῖς πόνος ἢ αἷμα ἢ σαρκία, τέλεον περιγράφουσι καὶ ἀναιροῦσι τὰ προκείμενα *Artem. Onirocr. 39.2* = fa-in kāna maʿa ḏālika waǧaʿun aw ḫurūǧu damin aw laḥmin fa-inna ḏālika yubṭilu wa-yufsidu l-amra llaḏī yurādu *73.6.*

8. *in hend.;* καταβάλλω (*to put down, refute*) = naqaḍa wa-abṭala : τἄλλα πάντα τὰ καταβάλλοντα τὸν λόγον αὐτῶν *Galen An. virt. 75.2* = ǧamīʿu l-ašyāʾi l-uḫari llatī tanquḍu (tanquḍu *nos* : tunqiṣu *ed.*) kalāmahum hāḏā wa-tubṭiluhū *40.6-7*.*

9. ἀμαυρόω (*to obscure, eclipse s.th.*) : πεφυκότος τοῦ ἰσχυροτέρου πυρὸς τὸ ἀσθενέστερον ἀμαυροῦν *Ps.-Plut. Placita 358 a12* = wa-ḏālika anna l-nāra l-aqwā tubṭilu (tubṭilu *nos* : yubṭilu *ed.*) l-nāra l-aḍʿafa *36.3**.

10. *sem. metathesis; neg. / affirm. transformation* οὐδὲν ἀληθὲς εἰπεῖν (*it is not true to say*) = *in hend.* abṭala wa-kaḏaba fī qawlihī (*he rejected and lied as he spoke*) : οὐδέν γ' ἀληθὲς εἰπεῖν νῦν ὅτι ἔστι πέρυσιν, οὐδὲ πέρυσιν ὅτι νῦν ἔστιν *Arist. Cael. I 12, 283b6* = wa-ḏālika anna man qāla inna l-āna huwa ʿāma l-awwali wa-inna ʿāma l-awwali huwa l-āna abṭala wa-kaḏaba fī qawlihī hāḏā [*sic leg. cum mss.*] *221.2 Badawī.*

11. *periphr.;* διαφέρει (*'it makes a difference,' sc., with regard to invalidating an argument*) τάχα γὰρ ἐνσταίη τις ἂν ὡς οὐκ ἀνάγκη τὸ λεχθέν· ... ἀλλ' οὐδὲν διαφέρει πρὸς τὸν λόγον *Arist. Cael. I 11, 281a23* = fa-laʿalla aḥadan yuḫālifu qawlanā fa-yaqūlu inna ḥaddana llaḏī ḥaddadnā bihī l-quwwata laysa bi-muḍṭarrin wa-lā ṣawābin ... fa-naqūlu inna hāḏā laysa mimmā yubṭilu qawlanā *versio B 206.11 Badawī.*

إبطال **IV. ibṭālun** *maṣdar*

1. ἀναιρεῖν (*annulling, eliminating*) **(a)** *abs.* : οὐ γὰρ χαλεπὸν ἀνελεῖν τὰς ἀτόμους γραμμάς *Arist. Phys. III 6, 206a17* = fa-innahū laysa yaṣʿubu ibṭālu l-ḫuṭūṭi llatī lā tanqasimu *250.15* ⟼ *Arist. Top. VIII 10, 160b24-25* = *751.8-10 / fol. 322b* (*see above,* abṭala 1.1) **(b)** *sem.; expr.* = saʿā fī ibṭāli *c. gen.* : τὸ δὲ φάναι ... ἀναιρεῖν ἐστι τῶν δεδομένων τι *Arist. Cael. I 12, 283a6* = fa-ammā man qāla innahū ... fa-innahū yasʿā fī ibṭāli baʿḍi l-muqaddamāti llatī taqaddamnā fa-waḍaʿnāhā wa-l-maqāyīsi ayḍan *versio A 96a4.*

2. κρατεῖν *c. gen.* (*overpowering, suppressing*) : κατάδηλος γίγνεται ὅτι ἄτονός τε καὶ ἐξίτηλός ἐστιν ἡ ἰσχὺς, ὡς μηδὲ κρατῆσαι τῆς τοῦ φαρμάκου δυνάμεως *Galen Ther. Pis. 270.2* = ʿulima annahū (*sc.* al-maʿǧūna) ... qad ʿatuqa ǧiddan wa-ḏālika annahū lam yaqwa ʿalā ibṭāli quwwati l-dawāʾi l-mushili *123a14.*

3. *sem. metathesis; neg. / affirm. transformation* τὸ μὴ εἶναι (*non-being, inexistence*) = al-ibṭālu : εἰ δή ἐστιν ἔνια δυνατὰ καὶ εἶναι και μή, ἀνάγκη χρόνον τινὰ ὡρίσθαι τὸν πλεῖστον καὶ τοῦ εἶναι καὶ τοῦ μή *Arist. Cael. I 11, 281a30* = in kāna li-šayʾin mina l-ašyāʾi quwwatu an yakūna wa-lā yakūna, fa-lā budda min zamānin yafṣila bayna kawnihī wa-bayna ibṭālihī *versio B 207.1 Badawī.*

مبطل IV. mubṭilun *act. part.*

1. *transl. compounds of* αἱρέω (*to take*)

1.1 ἀναιρέω (*to annul, abolish, eliminate*) : τὸ δὲ ἄλλο τι ζητεῖν αἴτιον ... ἀνελεῖν ἐστι τὴν βουλήν *Alex. An. mant. [Lib. arb.] 173.35* = wa-ṭalabunā li-sababin āḫara ... mubṭilun li-l-rawiyyati *199.9*.

1.2 ἀφαιροῦμαι *med., c. dupl. acc.* (*to deprive s.o. of s.th.*) : οὐκ ἀφαιρεῖται δ' ὁ λόγος οὐδὲ τοὺς μαθηματικοὺς τὴν θεωρίαν *Arist. Phys. III 7, 207b27* = wa-laysa hāḏā l-qawlu mubṭilan li-ʿilmi aṣḥābi l-taʿālīmi *265.8*.

2. μάταιος (*futile*) : μάταιος δὲ φαίνεται μᾶλλον ἢ κακός *Arist. Eth. Nic. IV 7, 1127b11* = an yakūna mubṭilan awlā <minhu> bi-an yakūna radīʾan *167.5 Badawī (Akasoy / Fidora om.)*.

3. *periphr.;* διαφέρει (*'it makes a difference,' sc. with regard to invalidating an argument*) (τάχα γὰρ ἐνσταίη τις ἂν ὡς οὐκ ἀνάγκη τὸ λεχθέν·) ... ἀλλ' οὐδὲν διαφέρει πρὸς τὸν λόγον *Arist. Cael. I 11, 281a23* = wa-naḥnu naqūlu bi-anna hāḏā ġayru mubṭilin li-qawlinā *versio A 103b9*; *see above,* abṭala 11.

باطل bāṭilun, *pl.* **abāṭīlu,** *and, in advervial use,* **bāṭilan** *or* **bi-l-bāṭili**

(N.B. bāṭilun, *though morphologically active participle of* I. baṭala, *has no verbal force and is used as adjective and adverb only)*

1. *transl.* μάταιος (*vain*) *and its derivatives and compounds*

1.1 μάταιος (*vain*) **(a)** *abs.* : ὥστε μάταιον ἔσται τὸ εἶδος *Arist. Eth. Nic. I 6, 1096b20* = fa-yaṣīru l-nawʿu li-ḏālika bātilan *127.15* ⟼ μάτην φαμὲν βαδίσαι καὶ ἡ βάδισις ματαία *Arist. Phys. II 6, 197b25* = qulnā innahū mašā bāṭilan wa-inna mašyahū bāṭilun *130.18* ⟼ ἐὰν δὲ ἀγνοῇ τὴν περαινομένην (*sc.* γυναῖκα) μjαταίοις ἐπιχειρήσει πράγμασιν *Artem. Onirocr. 97.11* = fa-ammā in kānat lā taʿrifu l-marʾata llatī tuǧāmiʿuhā fa-inna ḏālika yadullu ʿalā annahā tafʿalu fiʿlan bāṭilan *178.14;* καὶ πάλιν αὖ ἐφάνη τις μικρὰ προσδοκία ἀγαθῶν ἢ κακῶν ψευδὴς οὖσα καὶ ματαία *234.4* = fa-inna l-insāna qad yatawaqqaʿu mirāran kaṯīratan ḫayran yasīran aw šarran yasīran fa-yakūnu mā tawaqqaʿahū min ḏālika kiḏban bāṭilan *432.13* ⟼ ἔτι δ' ἐν αὐτοῖς τοῖς ζῴοις τὰ μὲν ὥσπερ μάταια *Theophr. Princ. 10b8* = wa-qad yakūnu fī l-ḥayawāni ayḍan ašyāʾu ka-annahā bāṭilatun *214.5* **(b)** bi-l-bāṭili : οὐδὲν δέομαι τό γε νῦν μεμνῆσθαι τῆς ματαίας φλυαρίας αὐτῶν *Galen Diff. febr. VII, 281.3* = fa-lastu aḥtāǧu fī hāḏā l-mawḍiʿi an aḏkura ġabāwatahum wa-haḏayānahum bi-l-bāṭili *WGAÜ Suppl. I, 663.16*.

1.2 ματαίως *adv.* (*in vain*) **(a)** *abs.* : ἔτι δὲ τοῖς πάθεσιν ἀκολουθητικὸς ὢν (*sc.* ὁ νέος) ματαίως ἀκούσεται καὶ ἀνωφελῶς *Arist. Eth. Nic. I 4, 1095a5* = wa-li-annahū (*sc.* al-ḥadaṯa) ayḍan tābiʿun li-mā tadʿūhu nafsuhū ilayhi mina l-šahawāti ṣāra stimāʿuhū li-kalāminā bāṭilan lā manfaʿata fīhi *117.12* **(b)** *in hend.* bāṭilun lā manfaʿata fīhi : κρεμασθήσεται οὖν μετὰ τὰ ἅμματα περιττὰ πρὸς τῷ ματαίως ἐξηρτῆσθαι *Galen In De off. med. 752.15* = kāna l-fāḍilu minhu baʿda l-ʿaqdi muʿallaqan fa-yağtamiʿu ʿalā l-marīḍi amrāni aḥaduhumā an yabqā minhu muʿallaqan fa-yakūnu bāṭilan lā manfaʿata lahū fīhi *24.15.*

1.3 μάτην *adv.* (*in vain*) **(a)** *abs.* : εἰ δὲ μὴ οὕτως ἔχοι τὸ Γ πρὸς τὸ Δ ὥστε ποιεῖν συλλογισμόν, μάτην ἔσται εἰλημμένα *Arist. An. pr. I 25, 42a23* = fa-in lam takun nisbatu Ḥ ilā D nisbatan yakūnu minhā qiyāsun fa-inna aḫḏahumā (aḫḏahumā *nos* : aḫḏahā *ed. Ğabr* : aḥadahumā *ed. Badawī*) yakūnu bāṭilan *210.19* / fol. 92b* ⟝ εἰ δὲ καὶ ἦν ἡ κύκλῳ τῇ κύκλῳ (*sc.* κινήσει) ἐναντία, μάτην ἂν ἦν ἡ ἑτέρα *Arist. Cael. I 4, 271a 23* = wa-aqūlu ayḍan inna l-ḥarakata l-mustadīrata law kānat muḍāddatan li-l-ḥarakati l-mustadīrati la-kānat iḥdāhumā bāṭilan *versio B*; ὥστ' εἰ ἀμφότερα (*sc.* σώματα) ἦν, μάτην ἂν θάτερον ἦν σῶμα μὴ κινούμενον τὴν αὑτοῦ κίνησιν· μάτην γὰρ ὑπόδημα τοῦτο λέγομεν, οὗ μή ἐστιν ὑπόδεσις, ὁ δὲ θεός καὶ ἡ φύσις οὐδὲν μάτην ποιοῦσιν *271a31, 32, 33* = wa-law kāna ḏālika ka-ḏālika la-kāna ğirmun min ağrāmi l-dāʾirati bāṭilan ḥayṯu lam takun ḥarakatuhū bi-ḏātihī, ka-qawlinā inna l-ḫuffa bāṭilun iḏā lam yakun lahū lābisun, fa-ammā l-ṭabīʿatu fa-lā tafʿalu šayʾan ʿabaṯan wa-lā bāṭilani l-batatta *versio B*; wa-law kāna ḏālika ka-ḏālika la-kānat iḥdā l-ḥarakatayni bāṭilatan ḥayṯu lam takun mawğūdatan, fa-innā naqūlu inna wuğūda l-ḫuffi yakūnu bāṭilan iḏā lam yakun lahū lābisun, wa-l-ṭabīʿatu lā tafʿalu fiʿlan bāṭilan *versio C 147.4, 5, 6 Badawī* ⟝ τὸ γὰρ ἄρρεν μάτην ἂν ἦν, ἡ δὲ φύσις οὐδὲν ποιεῖ μάτην *Arist. Gener. anim. II 5, 741b4-5* = wa-law kāna ḏālika la-kānat ḫilqatu l-ḏakari bāṭilan wa-l-ṭibāʿu lā yafʿalu šayʾan bāṭilan *76.10* ⟝ διόπερ οὐδὲ πλατεῖς ἔχουσιν ὀδόντας (*sc.* οἱ ἰχθύες) ... μάτην ἂν οὖν εἶχον *Arist. Part. anim. III 14, 675a8* = wa-li-ḏālika laysa li-l-samaki asnānun ʿarīḍatun ... wa-law kānat li-l-samaki asnānun ʿarīḍatun la-kānat bāṭilan *95.19; II 13, 658a9 = 50.6; III 1, 661b24 = 59.6; etc.* ⟝ σημεῖον δὲ τὸ μάτην, ὅτι λέγεται ὅταν μὴ γένηται τὸ ἕνεκα ἄλλου ἐκείνου ἕνεκα *Arist. Phys. II 6, 197b22* = wa-l-dalīlu ʿalā mā qulnāhu annahū yuqālu fī l-šayʾi innahū bāṭilun matā kāna l-šayʾu llaḏī yakūnu min ağli ġayrihī lā yakūnu min ağli ḏālika l-ġayri *130.15;*

οὕτω δὴ τὸ αὐτόματον καὶ κατὰ τὸ ὄνομα ὅταν αὐτὸ μάτην γένηται *197b30* = fa-ka-ḏālika ayḍan yaǧrī l-amru fī awṭūmāṭun ay fī tilqāʾi l-nafsi fa-innahū yakūnu ʿalā ḥasabi smihī mā yakūnu (*sic leg. pro* innamā yakūnu *ed.*) iḏā kāna awṭūmāṭin ay iḏā kāna l-šayʾu bi-nafsihī bāṭilan *131.8**; οὔτε γὰρ πάντες (πάντες *E Arab.* : *om. codd. cett., Ross*) μάτην οἷόν τε αὐτὸ εἶναι *III 4, 203b5** = fa-laysa bāṭilan ẓannū kulluhum annahū mawǧūdun *212.4; II 6, 197b25 = 130.18* (*cf. supra*, bāṭilun 1.1); *etc.* ⟼ ἢ γὰρ ἐκκρούσει τὸ πάθος ἢ μάτην εἰρημένον ἔσται τὸ ἐνθύμημα *Arist. Rhet. III 17, 1418a13* = fa-innaka immā an tarfaʿa l-alama wa-immā an taǧʿala l-tafkīra maqūlan bāṭilan *217.10* ⟼ ὡς οὐκ ἂν ἠρωτημένα μάτην *Arist. Soph. el. I 15, 174a37* = ka-annahum (ka-annahum *nos* : ka-annahū *ed.*) laysa yasʾalūna bāṭilan *versio Ibn ʿAdī 919.7** *(fol. 353b)* / anna masʾalatahum lam takun bāṭilatan *versio Ibn Zurʿa 921.1 (fol. 353b)* / annahum lam yasʾalū bāṭilan *versio vetusta 922.9 (fol. 354a)* ⟼ σαλαμάνδρα ... μάτην πιστευθὲν μὴ καίεσθαι *Diosc. Mat. med. I, 140.*16 = salāmandarā ... bāṭilun mā qīla fīhi annahū iḏā udḫila l-nāra lam yaḥtariq *Ibn al-Bayṭār Ǧāmiʿ III, 3.20 = WGAÜ, 597* ⟼ εἰ μή τε μακρολογίας ἔμελλον ἀποίσεσθαι δόξαν ἀναλίσκειν τε τὸν χρόνον μάτην *Galen An. virt. 57.10* = law lā annanī ufnī l-zamāna bāṭilan wa-an yuẓanna bī annī muṭīlu l-kalāmi *28.9* ⟼ ἔς τʼ ἂν δὲ μὴ δύνανται δεῖξαι ταῦτα μάτην παραδείγματα γράφουσι *Galen In De off. med. 908.14* = fa-mā dāmū lā yaqdirūna an yubayyinū hāḏā fa-iṯbātuhum fī kutubihimi l-miṯālāti llatī tamaṯṯalū bihā innamā kāna bāṭilan *80.26* ⟼ εἰ γάρ ἐστιν ἐν ὅλοις μὲν τοῖς φυτοῖς ἡ κινητικὴ δύναμις, οὐ κινεῖ δὲ ..., οὐκοῦν μάτην ἔσται ἐν ὅλοις τοῖς εἴδεσι τῶν φυτῶν· ὅπερ ἐστὶν ἄτοπον, τὸ λέγειν μάτην τι γίνεσθαι ὑπὸ τῆς φύσεως *Philop. In De an. 576.34-35* ≈ wa-ḏālika annahū law kānat li-l-nabāti quwwatun yataḥarraku bihā l-ḥarakata l-makāniyyata wa-lam yataḥarrak kānat hāḏihi l-quwwatu fīhi bāṭilan wa-l-ṭabīʿatu lā tafʿalu šayʾan bāṭilan *339.8* ⟼ εἰ μὲν γὰρ ἄλλως ἐνεργῶν νοεῖ (*sc.* ὁ νοῦς), τί μάτην αὐτῷ προσάπτουσι τὴν περιφοράν; *Them. In De an. 22.9* = li-annahū in kāna (*sc.* al-ʿaqlu) bi-fiʿlin āḫara yaʿqilu fa-limā yaqrinūna bihī l-dawarāna bāṭilan *5.9;* διόπερ οὐδὲ γεύσει προσχρῆται (*sc.* τὰ φυτά), ὅτι μάτην ἂν ἐχρῆτο *124.12* = wa-min qibali hāḏā lam yuġḏa (*sc.* al-nabātu) bi-l-maḏāqi fa-innahū law ǧuʿila fīhi la-kāna stiʿmāluhū lahū bāṭilan *230.10* ⟼ πάνθʼ ἕνεκά του καὶ μηδὲν μάτην *Theophr. Princ. 10a22* = anna l-ašyāʾa kullahā innamā takūnu min aǧli šayʾin wa-annahū laysa šayʾun bāṭilun *212.5* **(b)** *in hend.* ʿabaṯan wa-bāṭilan : ὁ δὲ θεός καὶ ἡ φύσις οὐδὲν μάτην ποιοῦσιν *I 4, 271a33* = fa-ammā l-ṭabīʿatu fa-lā tafʿalu šayʾan ʿabaṯan wa-lā bāṭilani l-batatta *versio B.*

1.4 ματαιότερος *comp. expressing a weaker positive sense* (*rather pointless*) = *in hend.* ʿanāʾun bāṭilun : ἁπάσας μὲν οὖν ἐξετάζειν τὰς δόξας ματαιότερον ἴσως ἐστίν *Arist. Eth. Nic. I 4, 1095a29* = wa-ḫalīqun an yakūna l-baḥṯu ʿan ǧamīʿi hāḏihi l-ārāʾi fīhi ʿanāʾan bāṭilan (*sic leg., v. Ullmann NE II, 125*) *119.11**.

1.5 *sem.; etym.;* ματαιοπονία (*labor in vain*) **(a)** taʿabun bāṭilun : περσικὰ δὲ καὶ βερικόκκια καὶ κεράσια ... σημαίνει παρὰ δὲ τὸν καιρὸν ματαιοπονίας *Artem. Onirocr. 79.20* = al-ḫawḫu wa-l-mišmišu wa-l-iǧǧāṣu ... fī ġayri waqtihā ... tadullu ʿalā taʿabin bāṭilin *146.15;* ἀσπάλαξ ... σημαίνει ... ματαιοπονίαν διὰ τὸν μάταιον τοῦ ζῴου πόνον *232.12* = al-ḫuldu fī l-ruʾyā yadullu ... ʿalā taʿabin bāṭilin wa-ḏālika anna taʿaba hāḏā l-ḥayawāni bāṭilun *429.4* **(b)** *in hend.* taʿabun wa-ʿanāʾun bāṭilun : τοῖς δὲ λοιποῖς ματαιοπονίας σύμβολα καθίστανται (*sc.* πύξοι) *Artem. Onirocr. 145.8* = fa-ammā fī sāʾiri l-nāsi fa-innahā (*sc.* šaǧara l-buksū) tadullu ʿalā taʿabin wa-ʿanāʾin bāṭilin *260.15* **(c)** *in hend.* aʿmālun bāṭilatun wa-taʿabun : ὅσοι δὲ τῶν ἰχθύων εἰσὶ σελάχιοι, οἱ μὲν μακροὶ πάντες ματαιοπονίαν σημαίνουσι *Artem. Onirocr. 131.14* = fa-ammā l-samaku llaḏī laysa lahū qišrun fa-inna kulla mā kāna minhu ṭawīlan fa-innahū yadullu ʿalā aʿmālin bāṭilatin wa-taʿabin *237.9.*

2. *transl.* ψεῦδος (*falsehood*) *and its derivatives and compounds*

2.1 ψευδής (*false*) : τὸ δὲ λέγειν ... ἔοικε τὸ μὲν ψευδεῖ τὸ δ' ἀληθεῖ *Arist. Eth. Nic. III 7, 1113b15* = fa-ammā l-qawlu ... fa-yušbihu an yakūna baʿḍuhū bāṭilan wa-baʿḍuhū ḥaqqan *207.5* ⟝ ἡ μὲν οὖν (*sc.* δόξα) ὅτι οὐκ ἀγαθὸν τὸ ἀγαθὸν τοῦ καθ' αὑτὸ ὑπάρχοντος ψευδής, ἡ δὲ τοῦ ὅτι κακὸν τοῦ κατὰ συμβεβηκός *Arist. Int. 14, 23b19* = wa-kāna l-ʿaqdu fī ḫayrin mā annahū laysa bi-ḫayrin ʿaqdan bāṭilan li-amrin ḏātiyyin wa-l-ʿaqdu fīhi annahū šarrun ʿaqdan bāṭilan li-amrin ʿaraḍiyyin *32.14 / fol. 190b20;* ψευδὴς γὰρ αὕτη (ψευδὴς γὰρ αὕτη *Σα, Arab.* : ἀληθὴς *post* ψευδὴς *add. in ras. n* : οὐκ ἀληθὴς *post* ψευδὴς *add. Δ* : γὰρ αὕτη *om. Λ* : ψευδὴς ... αὕτη *secl. Minio-Paluello*) *24a1** = wa-ḏālika anna hāḏā bāṭilun *33.16 / fol. 191a17; 23a38 = 31.14 / fol. 190b3; etc.* ⟝ καὶ γὰρ ψευδῆ λαμβάνουσι καὶ ἀσυλλόγιστοί εἰσιν (*sc.* Μέλισσος καὶ Παρμενίδης) *Arist. Phys. I 2, 185a9* = wa-ḏālika annahumā (*sc.* Mālisus wa-Barminīdis) yaqtaḍiyāni (*sic leg. pro* yaqtaḍibāni *ed.*) ašyāʾa bāṭilatan wa-mā huwa ġayru lāzimin li-l-qiyāsi *8.4*;* εἴπερ οὖν ἔστιν δόξα ψευδής *VIII 3, 254a27* = fa-in kāna hāhunā ẓannun bāṭilun *829.10* ↦ ἀνάγκη τὸ αὐτὸ ἀπειράκις νοεῖν, ψευδὴς ἄρα ἡ τοιαύτη ὑπόθεσις *Philop. In De an. 128.10* = fa-l-šay'u l-wāḥidu taʿlamuhu <l-nafsu> mirāran kaṯīratan wa-hāḏā bāṭilun *199.13* ↦ τότε τις σοφὸς ἀνὴρ ἐπέστησεν, ὡς δεῖ ψευδεῖ λόγῳ τυφλῶσαι τὴν ἀλήθειαν *Ps.-Plut. Placita 298a23* = qaṣada rağulun ḥakīmun li-iṣlāḥi ḏālika bi-an ʿamiya (*sc.* al-nāsu) ʿani l-ḥaqqi bi-bāṭilin waḍaʿahū *13.4;* οἱ Στωικοὶ τὰς μὲν αἰσθήσεις ἀληθεῖς, τῶν δὲ φαντασιῶν τὰς μὲν ἀληθεῖς, τὰς δὲ ψευδεῖς. Ἐπίκουρος ... τῶν ... δοξῶν τὰς μὲν ἀληθεῖς, τὰς δὲ ψευδεῖς *396a5, 8* = ammā aṣḥābu l-riwāqi fa-yarawna anna l-ḥawāssa ḥaqqun wa-anna l-taḫayyulāti minhā ḥaqqun wa-minhā bāṭilun wa-ammā Abīqūrus fa-yarā anna ... mina l-ārā'i mā huwa ḥaqqun wa-minhā mā huwa bāṭilun *53.20, 22.*

2.2 ψεῦδος (*falsehood*) **(a)** *abs.* : οἷον τὸ ἄνθρωπος ἢ λευκόν ... οὔτε γὰρ ψεῦδος οὔτε ἀληθές πω *Arist. Int. 1, 16a15* = mithālu ḏālika qawlunā insānun aw bayāḍun ... fa-innahū laysa huwa baʿdu ḥaqqan wa-lā bāṭilan *100.4 / fol. 179a13;* τοῦτο δὲ ψεῦδος *13, 22b36* = wa-hāḏā ayḍan bāṭilun *128.5 / fol. 189b12; 14, 23b4 = 130.18 / fol. 190b8; etc.* ↦ οὐ γὰρ οἷόν τε πρὸς τὸ φανὲν ψεῦδος μὴ ἀνανεῦσαι *Them. In De an. 88.40* = fa-innahū laysa yumkinunā allā nağḥada mā ẓahara lanā annahū bāṭilun *155.7;* ἐν οἷς οὔπω τὸ ἀληθὲς ἢ τὸ ψεῦδός ἐστι *109.7* = allatī lā yakūnu fīhā baʿdu lā l-ḥaqqu wa-lā l-bāṭilu *198.12;* ἔστι μέντοι καθάπερ τῇ αἰσθήσει τὸ ἡδὺ καὶ τὸ λυπηρόν, οὕτως αὖ πάλιν τῷ θεωρητικῷ τὸ ἀληθὲς καὶ τὸ ψεῦδος, τὸ ἀληθὲς μὲν ἀντὶ τοῦ ἀγαθοῦ, τὸ ψεῦδος δὲ ἀντὶ τοῦ κακοῦ *114.5-6* = wa-kamā li-l-ḥissi l-laḏīḏu wa-l-mu'ḏī ka-ḏālika ayḍan li-l-naẓariyyi l-ḥaqqu wa-l-bāṭilu fa-l-ḥaqqu makāna l-ḫayri wa-l-bāṭilu makāna l-šarri *208.6-7; 109.8 = 198.14; 112.11-13 = 204.19-205.1; etc.* **(b)** *in hend.* kiḏbun bāṭilun : τοῦτο δ' ὅτι ψεῦδος, φανερόν *Arist. Cael. III 8, 307a18* = fa-hāḏā kiḏbun wa-bāṭilun *353.7 Badawī.*

2.3 ψευδῶς *adv.* (*falsely*) = *in hend.* kāḏibun wa-bāṭilun : ἀφροσύνης δέ ἐστι ... τὸ ψευδῶς δοξάζειν περὶ τῶν εἰς τὸν βίον ἀγαθῶν καὶ καλῶν *Ps.-Arist. Virt. 6, 1250b45* = wa-ammā afʿālu l-ğahli fa-... an ... yataqallaba (*sc.* al-insānu) fī l-ahwā'i l-kāḏibati wa-l-ārā'i l-bāṭilati *versio Q 42.23.*

2.4 ψεύδομαι (*to be untrue, false*) : οὐδὲ λύειν ἅπαντα προσήκει, ἀλλ' ἢ ὅσα ἐκ τῶν ἀρχῶν τις ἐπιδεικνὺς ψεύδεται *Arist. Phys. I 2, 185a15* = fa-innahū laysa yanbaġī an nanquḍa (*sic leg. pro* tunqaḍa *ed.*) kullahā bal innamā yanbaġī an naqṣida bi-l-naqḍi minhā li-mā kāna bayānuhū mabniyyan ʿalā l-mabādi'i illā annahū bāṭilun *8.12*.*

2.5 *sem.; etym.;* ψευδογραφέω (*to draw a fallacious figure*) = rasama šaklan bāṭilan : οὔτε γὰρ ἐξ ἀληθῶν καὶ πρώτων συλλογίζεται ὁ ψευδογραφῶν *Arist. Top. I 1, 101a10* = li-anna llaḏī yarsumu šaklan bāṭilan laysa yaʿmalu qiyāsan min muqaddimātin ṣādiqatin awwaliyyatin *491.4 / fol. 422a.*

3. *transl.* κενός (*futile*) *and its compounds*

3.1 κενός (*futile, useless*) : τὸ γάρ, διότι (ἐπεί *post* διότι *secl. Bruns, om. Ar.*) ἀφεστῶτες αἰσθανόμεθα τοῦ ὁρωμένου, ἐκεῖ καὶ τὴν ἀντίληψιν ἡγεῖσθαι γίνεσθαι, κενόν *Alex. An. mant.* [*Vis.*] *145.23** = wa-ḏālika anna raʾya man yarā anna idrāka l-mubṣari innamā yakūnu huwa fī l-buʿdi minnā fī l-mawāḍiʿi llatī nuḥissuhū <fīhā> bāṭilun *157.119* ⟼ οὗτος μὲν οὖν ὁ λόγος καθόλου λίαν καὶ κενός· οἱ γὰρ μὴ ἐκ τῶν οἰκείων ἀρχῶν λόγοι κενοί *Arist. Gener. anim. II 8, 748a8-9* = fa-hāḏā l-qawlu ʿāmmun ǧiddan wa-huwa bāṭilun li-anna l-kalāma llaḏī <lā> yakūnu min awāʾilihi l-ahliyyati bāṭilun *93.5;* τὸ δὲ κενὸν δοκεῖ μὲν εἶναί τι, ἔστι δ’ οὐθέν *748a11* = fa-ammā l-bāṭilu fa-huwa yuẓannu annahū šayʾun wa-laysa huwa ka-ḏālika *93.8* ⟼ διὰ τοῦτο ἔφη νῦν ὁ Ἱπποκράτης, μὴ εἰς τὸ ἐνεὸν κείσεται, τουτέστιν εἰς τὸ κενόν, ὅπερ δηλονότι καὶ ἄχρηστόν ἐστι καὶ μάταιον. ἔδοξε δέ τινι τῶν ἐξηγουμένων τὸ βιβλίον κενεὸν ἡγεῖσθαι τὸ κενὸν χωρίον *Galen In De off. med. 751.9-11* = fa-bi-hāḏā l-sababi qāla Abuqrāṭ kay-mā lā yakūna mawḍūʿan bāṭilan fa-inna mā huwa bāṭilun fa-l-amru fīhi maʿlūmun annahū lā manfaʿata fīhi wa-lā maʿnā lahū wa-qad ẓanna raǧulun mimman fassara hāḏā l-kitāba anna qawla Abuqrāṭ hāhunā bāṭilun innamā yurīdu bihi l-mawḍiʿa l-ḫālī *22.21* ⟼ μηδὲν γὰρ ἐλλείπων (*sc.* εἰς εὐδαιμονίαν ὁ θεὸς) κεναῖς ἔμελλεν ἐπιχειρεῖν πράξεσι *Ps.-Plut. Placita 301a6* = wa-law kāna (*sc.* Allāhu) nāqiṣan fī l-saʿādati lam yakun maġbūṭan wa-kāna manqūṣan fāʿilan afʿālan bāṭilatan *14.9.*

3.2 διὰ κενῆς *adv.* (*to no purpose*) : τὴν δ’ οὐσίαν οἰόμενοι λέγειν αὐτῶν ἑτέρας μὲν οὐσίας εἶναί φαμεν, ὅπως δ’ ἐκεῖναι τούτων οὐσίαι, διὰ κενῆς λέγομεν *Arist. Metaph. A 9, 992a28* = fa-iḏā qaṣadnā li-l-kalāmi fī l-ǧawhari qulnā inna ǧawāhira uḫara ḥattā annā in qulnā inna tilka ǧawāhiru hāḏihī kāna qawlan bāṭilan *146.11.*

3.3 διάκενος (*empty, idle*) : φανταστικὸν δέ ἐστι διάκενος ἑλκυσμός ... φάντασμα δέ ἐστιν, ἐφ’ ὃ ἑλκόμεθα κατὰ τὸν φανταστικὸν διάκενον ἑλκυσμόν *Ps.-Plut. Placita 402a10, 18* = wa-ammā l-muḫayyilu fa-innahu nǧiḏābun ilā l-nafsi yaǧrī maǧrā l-abāṭīli ... wa-ammā l-ḫayālu fa-huwa l-šayʾu llaḏī nanǧaḏibu ilayhi bi-l-taḫayyuli l-bāṭili *55.21, 25.*

4. *transl. derivatives and compounds of* *ἔργω (*to do work*)

4.1 ἀργός (*idle*) : ἐγὼ μὲν οὖν, ἐπειδὴ οὔτε φθονεῖσθαι δεῖ οὔτ' ἀργὸν εἶναι, οὔ φημι χρῆναι παιδεύεσθαι *Arist. Rhet. II 21, 1394b30* = ammā anā fa-innī li-kay-lā uḥsada aw uddaʿā bāṭilan azʿumu annahū lā yanbaġī lī an ataʾaddaba *139.4.*

4.2 περίεργος (*overdoer, superfluous*) **(a)** *abs.* : καθάπερ καὶ Ξενοκράτης ὁ Ἀφροδισιεὺς ἐποίησεν, ἄνθρωπος τἄλλα περίεργος ἱκανῶς καὶ γοητείας οὐκ ἀπηλλαγμένος *Galen Simpl. medic. XI, 793.15* = šibha mā faʿala Kasanūqrāṭīs al-Afrudīsiyūs fa-inna hāḏā l-insānu kaṯīru l-abāṭīli ġayru ʿadīmi l-siḥri *versio A WGAÜ, 184.24* (*cf.* baṭṭālun 1.2a) **(b)** *sem. amplif.* nawʿun bāṭilun / nawʿu l-bāṭili : τὸ δ' οὕτω γίγνεσθαι (*sc.* τὸ συλλαβεῖν) περίεργον, ἡ δὲ φύσις οὐδὲν ποιεῖ περίεργον *Arist. Gener. anim. II 4, 739b19-20* = wa-kaynūnatu l-ḥamli miṯla hāḏihi l-ḥāli min anwāʿi l-bāṭili wa-laysa yafʿalu l-ṭibāʿu šayʾan mina l-ašyāʾi bi-nawʿin bāṭilin *71.10-11.*

5. ἠλίθιος (*vain*) : σπουδάζειν δὲ καὶ πονεῖν παιδιᾶς χάριν ἠλίθιον φαίνεται καὶ λίαν παιδικόν *Arist. Eth. Nic. X 6, 1176b32* = wa-l-ḥirṣu wa-l-taʿabu min aǧli l-laʿbi bāṭilun [wa-] (*secl. nos*) ẓāhirun wa-lāʾiqun bi-l-ṣibyāni ǧiddan *555.16**.

6. ἄλογος (*absurd*) : καὶ ἐν ἑκάστῳ ἄρα μορίῳ πολλαὶ ψυχαί, ὅπερ ἄλογον *Philop. In De an. 149.8* ≈ waǧaba an takūna fīnā anfusun kaṯīratun wa-huwa bāṭilun *211.4.*

7. εἰς ἄχρηστον *adv.* (*to no purpose*) : διὰ τὴν εἰς ἄχρηστον ἀπόκρισιν τοῦ σπέρματος *Artem. Onirocr. 96.5* = li-anna l-maniyya yulqā fī miṯli hāḏā l-fiʿli bāṭilan *176.7.*

8. τυχόντως *adv.* (*to no purpose and by chance*) = *in hendiatrion* ʿalā waǧhi l-bāṭili wa-ka-mā ǧāʾa wa-bi-l-baḫti : τὸ γὰρ μὴ τυχόντως ἀλλ' ἕνεκά τινος ἐν τοῖς τῆς φύσεως ἔργοις ἐστὶ καὶ μάλιστα *Arist. Part. anim. I 5, 645a24* = li-annahū lam yuṭbaʿ šayʾun minhā ʿalā waǧhi l-bāṭili wa-lā ka-mā ǧāʾa wa-lā bi-l-baḫti bal kullu mā (*sic leg. pro* kullamā *ed.*) yakūnu min aʿmāli l-ṭibāʿi innamā yakūnu li-šayʾin *20.22**.

9. *transl.* ἐνεός (*useless*) *in adverbial use*

9.1 ἐνεόν (*in vain*) = bi-l-bāṭili : τὸ δὲ ἅμμα μήτε ἐν τρίβῳ μήτε ἐν ἔργῳ μήτε ἐκεῖσε, ὅκου ἐνεὸν, ὡς μὴ ἔσται (ἔσται *P Arab.* : ἔσω *ed.*) ἐνεὸν κείσεται *Galen In De off. med. 749.3** (= *Hippocr. De off. med. II, 35.5-7 Kühlewein*) = wa-ammā l-ʿaqdu fa-lā yakūnu fī mawḍiʿi l-muḥākkati wa-lā fī mawḍiʿi l-ʿamali wa-lā fī mawḍiʿi l-ʿaṭali kay-mā lā yakūna mawḍūʿan bi-l-bāṭili *20.8.*

9.2 εἰς τὸ ἐνεόν (*in vain*) = bāṭilan : διὰ τοῦτο ἔφη νῦν ὁ Ἱπποκράτης, μὴ εἰς τὸ ἐνεὸν κείσεται *Galen In De off. med. 751.8-9* = fa-bi-hāḏā l-sababi qāla Abuqrāṭ kay-mā lā yakūna mawḍūʿan bāṭilan *22.20.*

10. εἰκῇ (*at random, in vain*) **(a)** *abs.* bāṭilan : οὐδὲν γὰρ τῶν καλῶν εἰκῇ καὶ ὡς ἔτυχε γίνεται *Ps.-Plut. Placita 293a4* = laysa šayʾun mina l-ḫayrāti yakūnu bāṭilan wa-lā bi-l-ittifāqi *10.12* ⟼ ἀλλ' ὥσπερ σάρξ, εἰκῇ κεχυμένων (κεχυμένων α Λ : κεχυμένη *ut intell. Arab.*) ὁ κάλλιστος ... κόσμος (= *Heraclitus, frag. 124 Diels/Kranz*) *Theophr. Princ. 7a14* = lākin aǧallu l-umūri bi-manzilati laḥmin manṯūrin bāṭilan *192.1* ⟼ *v. also WGAÜ Suppl. II, 623 ult.-624.1* **(b)** *in hend.* bāṭilan wa-ʿabaṯan : ἀλλ' ἵνα ἐπιδείξῃ μηδὲν εἰκῇ γεγονὸς ὑπὸ τῆς φύσεως *Galen Anat. admin. II, 286.6* = bal li-yadulla bihī ʿalā annahū laysa fī l-ḫilqati šayʾun ǧuʿila bāṭilan wa-ʿabaṯan *78.10 Garofalo.*

11. *sem. metathesis; neg. / affirm. transformation* : οὐκ ... ἀληθής (*not true*) = bāṭilun : ἐπεὶ δ' οὐκ ἔστιν ἀληθὴς ὁ λόγος οὗτος, ὡς δείξομεν *Galen Ther. Pis. 250.15* = fa-qad ʿulima l-āna anna aqāwīla-hum hāḏihī bāṭilun ʿalā mā bayyannā *116b17.*

12. *sem.; def.;* ἀλαζονεία (*boastfulness and false swagger*) = *in hend.* maḥabbatu l-kibri wa-l-takabburu bi-l-bāṭili : καὶ τὴν ἀλαζονείαν καὶ τὴν ἐπιθυμίαν καὶ τὴν ἀκρασίαν *Ceb. Tab. 17.11* = wa-maḥabbatu l-kibri wa-l-takabburu bi-l-bāṭili wa-l-šahawātu wa-l-laḏḏātu l-mūbiqatu wa-l-sarafu *246.5.*

13. *paraphr.;* ἀνήκοος (*sc.* εἶναι, *c. gen.*) (*to be ignorant, not to have heard of s.th.*) = ištabaha (*c.* ʿalayhi) wa-ẓanna ẓannan bāṭilan (*to be in doubt about and hold a false opinion*) : ἵνα δὲ μὴ ἀνήκοοι ὦμεν κολούρων καὶ δικολούρων *Nicom. Arithm. 104.1* = wa-li-allā yaštabiha ʿalaynā l-amru wa-naẓunna ẓannan bāṭilan [innā] (*secl. nos*) iḏā qulnā qūlūrun ... wa-dīqūlūrūn *81.12*.*

14. *paraphr.;* ἄδικος (*unjust*) = *in hend.* bāṭilun ḫāʾibun (*futile and unsuccessful*) : δεῦτε οὗ ... ὁ πλάσας Ζᾶνα (Ζεὺς *ut intell. Arab.*) γέρων ἀλαζὼν ἄδικα βιβλία ψήχει *Ps.-Plut. Placita 298a6* (= *Callimachos, frag. 86*) = fa-tanẓurū ilā šayḫin ʿatīqin ḫalaqahū Zāwus yaktubu kutuban bāṭilatan ḫāʾibatan *12.21.*

15. *paraphr.;* παραιώρησις (*leaving a component in a state of suspense, 'in the air'; cf. Th. Heath, Mathematics I Aristotle, Oxford 1949,*

176) = nuqiḍa ... bāṭilun lā yustaʿmalu : οὐδ' ἐν τοῖς διαλυομένοις ἡ τῶν τριγώνων παραιώρησις εὔλογος *Arist. Cael. III 7, 306a21* = an yaqūlū inna fī l-usṭuqussāti muṯallaṯātun qad nuqiḍat, wa-laysa ḏālika mina l-wāǧibi wa-lā mimmā yanbaġī, fa-innahū qad yaʿriḍu an yakūna fī nuqlati l-usṭuqussāti baʿḍihā ilā baʿḍin muṯallaṯātun bāṭilatun lā tustaʿmalu *347.15 Badawī.*

بواطيل **bawāṭīlu** (*irregular plural word made from a singular form* bāṭūlun *or* buṭālun, *none of which exists; cf. Wright I, 229)*

1. *paraphr.; used in the transl. of* γόης (*sorcerer, trickster*) *implied in* γοητείαι (*kinds of jugglery and deception*) = sāḥirun ǧāhilun ṣāḥibu maḫārīqa wa-bawāṭīla : περὶ δὲ τοῦ πύου καὶ ὅσα τοιαῦτα παρίημι λέγειν τοῖς τὰ τοιαῦτα δεινοῖς ἅμα γοητείαις τισίν *Galen Simpl. medic. XII, 290.12* = wa-ammā l-qayḥu fa-lastu aḏkuruhū li-annahū qaḏirun ǧiddan wa-ammā llaḏīna ḏakarūhu fa-saḥaratun ǧuhhālun aṣḥābu maḫārīqa wa-bawāṭīla *WGAÜ, 185.4.*

2. παράσημος, *of men* (*eccentric, inane*) = muḥibbun li-l-fuḍūli wa-l-bawāṭīli : ὡς περίεργός τε καὶ παράσημος καταγνωσθήσεται *Galen Simpl. medic. XII, 193.17* = ḏammahū ʿalā ḏālika wa-ʿaḏalahū ǧamīʿu l-aṭibbāʾi wa-anzalūhu manzilata insānin fāriġin muḥibbin li-l-fuḍūli wa-l-bawāṭīli *WGAÜ, 499.7.*

بطم

بطم **buṭmun** *coll.*

1. *transl. the botanical and medical meanings of* τέρμινθος

1.1 τέρμινθος *bot.* (*terebinth, Pistacia Terebinthus*) : καρπὸς δὲ βοτρυδίοις ἐοικώς, πυκνός, κατὰ μέγεθος τερμίνθου *Diosc. Mat. med. I, 101.11* = wa-ṯimāruhū tušbihu l-ʿanāqīda multazzatun wa-huwa kaṯīrun ʿaẓīmun ka-l-buṭmi *versio C WGAÜ Suppl. II, 447.18* = ... wa-hiya fī l-ʿiẓami miṯlu l-ḍirwi wa-huwa l-buṭmu *vetus transl. Ullmann Unters., 183* ⟼ τερμίνθου καὶ ὁ φλοιὸς καὶ τὰ φύλλα καὶ ὁ καρπὸς ἔχουσί τι στυπτικόν *Galen. Simpl. medic. XII, 137.15* = ḏikru šaǧarati l-buṭmi liḥāʾu hāḏihi l-šaǧarati wa-ṯamaruhā wa-waraquhā fī ǧamīʿihā šayʾun qābiḍun *WGAÜ, 671.5* ⟼ δριμύ τε τερμίνθου δάκρυ

Λιβυστιάδος *Galen Ther. Pis. Androm. 140* = wa-ṣamġu l-buṭmi al-ḥirrīfu llaḏī yuǧlabu min Lībuwī *120a12.*

1.2 *sem.; def.;* τέρμινθος *medic.* (*a swelling like the fruit of the terebinth-tree*) = al-baṯru l-maʿrūfu bi-l-buṭmi : οἱ αἱμορροΐδας ἔχοντες οὔτε πλευρίτιδι ... οὔτε τερμίνθοισιν ἁλίσκονται *Hippocr. Humor. 20:3* = wa-llaḏīna tanfatiḥu fīhim afwāhu l-ʿurūqi llatī fī l-siflati lā tuṣībuhum ḏātu l-ǧanbi ... wa-lā l-buṯūru l-maʿrūfatu bi-l-buṭmi *33.9.*

2. τερεβίνθινος *bot.* (*of the terebinth*) = al-buṭm *in gen. construction* : βῆχάς τε ἰᾶται (*sc.* κάλαμος ἀρωματικὸς) ὑποθυμιώμενος καθ' ἑαυτὸν καὶ σὺν ῥητίνῃ τερεβινθίνῃ *Diosc. Mat. med. I, 23.21* = wa-yubriʾu (*sc.* qaṣabu l-ḏarīrati) mina l-suʿāli tuduḫḫina bihī waḥdahū aw maʿa ṣamġi l-buṭmi *Ibn al-Bayṭār Ǧāmiʿ IV, 22.32;* τὸ τερεβίνθινον (*sc.* ἔλαιον) *I, 41.12* = duhnu l-ḍirwi wa-huwa l-buṭmu *vetus transl. Ullmann Unters., 183*; ἡ τερεβινθίνη (*sc.* ῥητίνη) ἀφεψομένη ἄχρις ὅτου ἂν ἄοσμος γένηται *I, 54.9* = wa-ammā ṣamġu l-buṭmi fa-innahū yuṭbaḫu ḥattā taḏhabu rāʾiḥatuhū *versio A Dubler/Téres I, 57.11;* κοιλίαν τε κούφως μαλάττει (*sc.* ὁ στύραξ) καταπινόμενος ὀλίγος μετὰ ῥητίνης τερεβινθίνης *I, 60.11* = wa-iḏā btuliʿa minhu (*sc.* al-asṭuraki) šayʾun yasīrun maʿa ṣamġi l-buṭmi layyana l-baṭna talayyunan ḫafīfan *versio A Dubler/Téres I, 63.7* ⟼ ῥητίνης τερεβινθίνης στατῆρας τέσσαρας *Theomn. Hippiatr. I, 178.22* = wa-min ʿilki l-buṭmi arbaʿatu asātīra *100.5; I, 42.3 = 64.13; I, 178.3 = 98.1.*

بطن

بَطَنٌ I. baṭanun *maṣdar of* baṭina

1. διάρροια (*diarrhea*) : τοῦ γὰρ θέρεος δυσεντερίαι τε πολλαὶ ἐμπίπτουσι καὶ διάρροιαι καὶ πυρετοὶ τεταρταῖοι πολυχρόνιοι *Hippocr. Aer. 36.9* = wa-yaʿriḍu lahum fī l-qayẓi ḫtilāfu l-aġrāsi wa-l-baṭanu wa-ḥummā ribʿin ṭawīlatun muzminatun *versio A 53.1.*

2. δυσεντερία (*dysentery*) : τοῖσι δὲ ἀνδράσι (*sc.* ἐπιπίπτειν) δυσεντερίας καὶ διαρροίας καὶ ἠπιάλους *Hippocr. Aer. 28.12* = inna sukkāna hāḏihi l-madīnati mina l-riǧāli man yaʿriḍu lahumu l-baṭanu (al-baṭanu *nos, prop. Ullmann WGAÜ, 197.4* : al-bġr *ed., cod. ut vid.* : al-zaḥīr *prop.*

Mattock & Lyons) wa-ḫtilāfu l-dami wa-l-saqamu llaḏī yudʿā ibiyālūs (*sic leg. pro* ʾībālūs *ed.*) *versio A 19.3**.

مبطون **I. mabṭūnun** *pass. part. of* baṭina

1. κοιλιακός ([*suffering*] *of the bowels*) : ἡ ῥίζα ... ποιεῖ πρὸς ... κοιλιακούς *Diosc. Mat. med. II, 20.7* = aṣluhā yanfaʿu l-mabṭūnīna *vetus transl. Ullmann Unters., 184.8*.

استبطن **X. istabṭana** *c. acc.*

1. *transl. compounds of* κεῖμαι (*to lie*)

1.1 ὑπόκειμαι (*to lie under*) : προσκείμενον (προσκείμενον *Arab., Garofalo* : ὡς κείμενον *P*) οὖν (οὖν *ed.* : νῦν *ut intell. Arab.*) ἐᾷν χρὴ κατὰ τὰ ὑποκείμενα σώματα τὸ δέρμα κατὰ τοῦτο τὸ χωρίον *Galen Anat. admin. II, 292.13** = fa-yanbaġī laka l-āna an tadaʿa l-ǧilda lāziman fī hāḏā l-mawḍiʿi li-mā yastabṭinuhū *84.20 Garofalo*.

1.2 ἔγκειμαι (*to lie in or near s.th.*) : ἢν ὑστέρῃ ἐν τῷ ἰσχίῳ ἐγκειμένη διαπυήσῃ, ἀνάγκη ἔμμοτον γενέσθαι *Hippocr. Aphor. V.47* = matā taqayyaḥa l-raḥimu ḥayṯu yastabṭinu l-warika waǧaba ḍarūratan an yuḥtāǧa ilā l-futuli *48. 4*.

2. περιτίθημι (*to place around s.th.*) : φυλακτέον δὲ τοὺς τῶν ποιμνίων φύλακας κύνας, ὠμὴν βύρσαν τοῖς τραχήλοις αὐτῶν περιθέντας *Cass. Bass. Geopon. XIX, 1.2* = wa-yanbaġī an tuttaḫaḏa li-kilābi l-māšiyati wiqāyatun min ǧulūdi l-baqari l-madbūġati tastabṭinu aʿnāqahā *WGAÜ Suppl. I, 233.25*.

3. *in hend.;* ὑποζώννυμι (*to undergird s.th.*) = ġašiya wa-stabṭana : ὀνομάζεται ... οὕτω τοῦθ' ὑπεζωκώς, ἐπειδὴ τὰς πλευρὰς ὅλας ἔσωθεν ὑπέζωκεν ... τὰς μὲν πλευρὰς ὑπέζωκεν *Galen Anat. admin. II, 591.9, 13* = ka-ḏālika yusammā hāḏā l-ġišāʾu l-mustabṭinu li-l-aḍlāʿi mustabṭinan min qibali annahū yaġšā l-aḍlāʿa kullahā min dāḫilin wa-yastabṭinuhā ... wa-huwa mustabṭinun li-l-aḍlāʿi kullihā yaġšāhā (*sic leg.*) min dāḫilin *408.5, 8* Garofalo*.

مستبطن **X. mustabṭinun** *act. part.*

1. ὑπεζωκώς (*undergirding*) *act. part. perf. of* ὑποζώννυμι (*to undergird s.th.*) : ὀνομάζεται ... οὕτω τοῦθ' ὑπεζωκὼς ... ἀκριβὴς δὲ καὶ οὗτος ὁ ὑπεζωκὼς ὀνομαζόμενος ... ἀλλ' ὁ ὑπεζωκὼς οὗτος ἐπιτείνεται *Galen Anat. admin. II, 591.8, 17, 592.4* = ka-ḏālika yusammā hāḏā l-ġišāʾu l-mustabṭinu li-l-aḍlāʿi mustabṭinan ... wa-l-ġišāʾu l-mustabṭinu li-l-aḍlāʿi ayḍan ḥaqīqiyyun ḫāliṣun ... wa-hāḏā l-ġišāʾu l-mustabṭinu li-l-aḍlāʿi yamtaddu *408.5, 10, 15 Garofalo;* ὁ τὰς πλευρὰς ὑπεζωκὼς ὑμήν *II, 664.5* = al-ġišāʾu l-mustabṭinu li-l-aḍlāʿi *496.20 Garofalo*; *etc.*

مستبطن **X. mustabṭanun** *pass. part.*

1. ὑποκείμενος (*underlying*) *act. part. of* ὑπόκειμαι (*to lie under*) = mustabṭanun : μήπως κατὰ τοῦτο τὸ χωρίον ἀποσπάσῃς ἅμα τῷ δέρματι τὸν ὑποκείμενον αὐτῷ τένοντα *Galen Anat. admin. II, 292.10* = kay-lā taqlaʿa maʿa l-ǧildi fī hāḏā l-mawḍiʿi l-watara l-mustabṭana lahū *WGAÜ Suppl. II, 547.14.*

بَطْنٌ **baṭnun,** *pl.* **buṭūnun**

1. *transl.* κοιλία (*cavity of the gastro-intestinal tract; a cavity or ventricle of the body*) *and its derivatives and compounds*

1.1 κοιλία (*belly; stomach; intestine*) : τόπος (*sc.* τοῖς κατὰ φύσιν περιττώμασι) ... τῆς τροφῆς τῆς ξηρᾶς ἡ κάτω κοιλία ... καὶ τῆς χρησίμης ἡ ἄνω κοιλία *Arist. Gener. anim. I 18, 725b1-2* = faḍlat al-ṭaʿāmi l-yābisi makānuhu <l-baṭnu> l-asfalu ... wa-makānu l-ṭaʿāmi llaḏī yuḥtāǧu ilayhi l-baṭnu l-aʿlā *32.21-33.2* ⟝ τὴν δὲ κοιλίαν σαρκώδη καὶ στιφρὰν οἱ πλεῖστοι (*sc.* ὄρνιθες) ἔχουσι *Arist. Hist. anim. II 17, 508b32* = fa-ammā buṭūnu <akṯari> (*nos*) aṣnāfi l-ṭāʾiri fa-ḫilqatuhā min laḥmin wa-hiya ṣulbatun *93.1*; 509a6, 8 = 93.9, 10; IV 4, 529a1 = 169.4; etc.* ⟝ ὁ γὰρ σπλὴν ἀντισπᾷ ἐκ τῆς κοιλίας τὰς ἰκμάδας τὰς περιττευούσας *Arist. Part. anim. III 7, 670b4* = fa-ammā l-ṭiḥālu fa-huwa yaǧḏibu mina l-baṭni faḍla l-ruṭūbati *83.14;* ὥσπερ ἀπὸ τῆς ἄνω κοιλίας δέχεται στενώτερον ἔντερον, οὕτως ἐκ τοῦ κώλου καὶ τῆς εὐρυχωρίας ἐν τῇ κάτω κοιλίᾳ πάλιν εἰς στενώτερον ἔρχεται (*sc.* τὸ περίττωμα) *III 14, 675b18-19* = yuqbalu l-ṭaʿāmu ilā miʿāʾin aḍyaqa aʿnī annahū yaqbaluhū mina l-baṭni l-aʿlā wa-ka-ḏālika ayḍan mina l-ʿuḍwi llaḏī yusammā qūlūn wa-min saʿati l-mawḍiʿi yaṣīru fī l-baṭni l-asfali wa-minhu yaṣīru ilā miʿāʾin aḍyaqa *97.16-17; etc.* ⟝ ὅσοι <δὲ> τῶν ἰχθύων ἐκταράσσουσι τὴν κοιλίαν ἡμῶν καὶ ἀποκρίνουσι τὰ σκύβαλα *Artem. Onirocr. 130.9* = inna l-samaka llaḏī yuḫriǧu l-zibla wa-l-fuḍūla wa-yushilu l-baṭna *235.14* ⟝ κοιλίαν δὲ ὑπάγει μετρίως (*sc.* ἡ ἀκαλήφη) *Galen Simpl. medic. XI, 818.6* = wa-qad tushilu (*sc.* al-anǧuratu) l-baṭna *versio A* = wa-huwa yuṭliqu l-baṭna iṭlāqan muʿtadilan *versio B WGAÜ, 351.21-22; etc.* ⟝ τάς τε κοιλίας αὐτῶν πυκνὰ ἐκταράσσεσθαι *Hippocr. Aer. 28.4* = wa-buṭūnuhum kaṯīratu l-iḫtilāfi dāʾimatan *versio A 15.8, sim. versio B 15.17;* ὅκου ἂν κοιλίαι ὑγραὶ ἔωσι *28.16* = man kāna baṭnuhū ladnan layyinan *versio A 19.8; 26.21* = *versio A 13.9/versio B 13.17; etc.* ⟼ ἀποκρίσιες κατὰ φύσιν, κοιλίης, οὔρων, ἱδρῶτος *Hippocr. Alim. 142.7* = inna l-maḫraǧa (al-maḫraǧa *nos* : al-mrḫḏ *cod., ed.*) al-ṭabīʿiyya huwa l-baṭnu wa-l-bawlu wa-l-ʿaraqu *5.8*; 142.10* = *5.10; etc.* ⟼ οἷσιν ἡ κοιλίη ὑγροτέρη τοῦ καιροῦ ἐν τῇσι νούσοισιν *Hippocr. Diaet. acut. 66.21* = man kāna baṭnuhū fī maraḍihī layyinan bi-akṯara mimmā yanbaġī *43.2* ⟼ καὶ ἤ τε κοιλίη φυσᾶται *Hippocr. Genit. 60.2* = wa-yunfaḫu l-baṭnu *56.13* ⟼ εἰσὶ δὲ καὶ ἀπὸ τῆς κοιλίης φλέβες *Hippocr. Nat. hom. 196.6* = wa-fī l-badani ayḍan ʿurūqun ... manšaʾuhā mina l-baṭni *20.10;* ὅσοι δὲ μὴ ἀνεμέουσι τὰ σιτία, ἢ καὶ κοιλίας ἔχουσιν ὑγράς *214.12* = man lam yaḥtaǧ ilā l-qayʾi aw kāna baṭnuhū layyinan *32.12; 214.8* = *32.8; etc.* ⟼ ἐσθιέτω ... καυλὸν σιλφίου καὶ ὅτι φῦσαν ἐμποιέει ἐν τῇ κοιλίῃ *Hippocr. Superf. 84.10* = wa-l-taʾkul ... al-maḥrūṯa (al-maḥrūṯa *cod., cf. Ullmann p. 266* : al-maḥrūt *ed.*) wa-kulla mā yanfuḫu l-baṭna *12.3*; 76.3* = *4.5* ⟼ ἡ κοιλία καὶ πολλὰ χωρεῖ κὠλίγα *Men. Mon. I.226* = inna l-baṭna yašbaʿu qalīlan wa-kaṯīran *WGAÜ Suppl. I, 566.20.*

1.2 κοιλία (*ventricle*) : ἐν ἑκάστῃ γὰρ ἔχει (*sc.* ἡ καρδία) αἷμα τῶν κοιλιῶν, λεπτότατον δ' ἐστὶ τὸ ἐν τῇ μέσῃ *Arist. Hist. anim. I 17, 496b10* = li-annahū (*sc.* al-dama) yakūnu fī ǧamīʿi buṭūnihī (*sc.* al-qalbi) wa-l-damu llaḏī fī l-baṭni l-awsaṭi laṭīfun daqīqun ṣāfin ǧiddan *48.8* ⟼ αὗται μὲν αἱ ἐμπρόσθιαι κοιλίαι αἱ κατὰ τὸν ἐγκέφαλον εἰς τὸ πρόσω φερόμεναι στενοῦνται *Galen Nerv. diss. II, 832.1* = wa-ḏālika anna l-baṭnayni llaḏayni fī muqaddami l-dimāġi yaḍīqāni fī mamarrihimā ilā quddāmin *98.12; cf. also M. Simon, Sieben Bücher Anatomie, Vol. 1 (Glossary), p. 334.*

1.3 κοιλιακός (*of the bowels*) **(a)** *abs.;* baṭnun *c. gen.* : πρὸς δυσεντερίαν καὶ κοιλιακὴν διάθεσιν καὶ ἄσην στομάχου *Diosc. Mat. med. I, 189.9* = li-qurūḥi l-amʿāʾi wa-li-nṭilāqi l-baṭni wa-li-ġaṯayāni l-maʿidati *versio B WGAÜ Suppl. I, 567.12* = nafaʿa min waǧaʿi l-amʿāʾi wa-l-baṭni *vetus transl. Ullmann Unters., 184.3* **(b)** *sem. amplif.;* κοιλιακός ([*suffering*] *of the bowels*) = **(b1)** inḥilālu l-baṭni : ἁρμόζουσι δὲ καὶ δυσεντερικοῖς καὶ κοιλιακοῖς *Diosc. Mat. med. I, 100.21* = wa-yanfaʿu ayḍan li-aṣḥābi qurūḥi l-miʿāʾi wa-li-nḥilāli l-baṭni *versio C WGAÜ Suppl. I, 567.7* **(b2)** istirḫāʾu l-baṭni : διὸ καὶ κοιλιακοὺς ... ὠφελεῖ *Galen Simpl. medic. XI, 819.3* = wa-yanfaʿu li-ḏālika ... mini stirḫāʾi l-baṭni *versio A WGAÜ, 352.22* **(b3)** istiṭlāqu l-baṭni : διὸ καὶ κοιλιακοὺς ... ὠφελεῖ *Galen Simpl. medic. XI, 819.3* = wa-li-ḏālika ṣāra yanfaʿu mini stiṭlāqi l-baṭni *versio B WGAÜ, 352.23.*

1.4 *sem.; etym.; transl. the word* κοιλία (*belly, etc.*) *in compounds containing it*:

1.4.1 εὐκοίλιος (*easing the bowels, diarrhetic*) **(a)** ashala l-baṭna : κράμβη ἥμερος εὐκοίλιος ἀκρόζεστος ἐσθιομένη *Diosc. Mat. med. I, 193.1* = al-kurunbu l-bustāniyyu in suliqa salqatan ḫafīfatan wa-ukila ashala l-baṭna *WGAÜ, 272.22*; *I, 178.1, 195.10* = *vetus transl. Ullmann, Unters., 183.19* ⟼ ὄσπριον (*sic leg.*) φυσῶδες, τρόφιμον, εὐκοίλιον, οὐρητικὸν *Galen. Simpl. medic. XI, 876.13** = hāḏā ṣinfun mina l-qaṭāniyyi kaṯīru l-ġiḏāʾi nāfiḫun mushilun li-l-baṭni yuġzaru minhu l-bawlu *versio A WGAÜ, 272.19* **(b)** aṭlaqa l-baṭna : *Diosc. Mat. med. I, 191.3* = *vetus transl. Ullmann Unters., 183.22* **(c)** layyana l-baṭna : βλίτον λαχανεύεται καὶ τοῦτο· ἔστι δὲ εὐκοίλιον *Diosc. Mat. med. I, 191.3* = al-baqlatu l-yamāniyatu hāḏihi l-baqlatu ayḍan tuʾkalu wa-hiya mulayyinatun li-l-baṭni *versio A* = *Ibn al-Bayṭār, Ǧāmiʿ I, 104.2* = baqlatun yamāniyatun ... wa-hiya tulayyinu l-baṭna *versio B WGAÜ Suppl. I, 416.3; I, 191.6* = *WGAÜ Suppl. I, 416.5* ⟼ ὄσπριον (*sic leg.*) φυσῶδες, τρόφιμον, εὐκοίλιον, οὐρητικὸν *Galen. Simpl. medic. XI, 876.13** = hāḏā ǧinsun mina l-ḥubūbi yanfuḫu wa-yaġḏū wa-yulayyinu l-baṭna wa-yudirru l-bawla *versio B WGAÜ, 272.20* **(d)** anzala l-baṭna : *Diosc. Mat. med. I, 191.6* = *vetus transl. Ullmann Unters., 183.21.*

1.4.2 δυσκοίλιος (*bad for the bowels, constipating*) = šadīdun ʿalā l-baṭni : *Diosc. Mat. med. I, 98.16* = *vetus transl. Ullmann, Unters., 184.3.*

1.4.3 μονοκοίλιος (*with a single stomach*) = lahū baṭnun wāḥidun *vel sim.* : ὥσπερ καὶ τοῖς ἄλλοις τοῖς μονοκοιλίοις *Arist. Hist. anim. I 16, 495b31* = kamā yakūnu fī sāʾiri l-ḥayawāni llaḏī laysa lahū illā baṭnun wāḥidun *46.1* ⟼ ἔχουσι δὲ τὴν καλουμένην πυετίαν ... τῶν ... μονοκοιλίων δασύπους *Arist. Part. anim. III 15, 676a7* = fa-ammā l-ḥayawānu llaḏī lahū baṭnun wāḥidun fa-laysa tūǧadu fī baṭnihī maswatun mā ḫalā l-ḥayawāna llaḏī yusammā l-azabba l-riǧlayni *98.17; 676a12f.* = *98.21; IV 3, 677b17* = *103.19.*

1.4.4 πολυκοίλιος (*with many stomachs*) = lahū buṭūnun kaṯīratun : ἔχουσι δὲ τὴν καλουμένην πυετίαν τὰ μὲν πολυκοίλια πάντα *Arist. Part. anim. III 15, 676a6* = wa-fī buṭūni l-ḥayawāni ayḍan maswatun wa-ḫāṣṣatan ǧamīʿi l-ḥayawāni llaḏī lahū buṭūnun kaṯīratun *98.16f.; IV 3, 677b17* = *103.19.*

1.4.5 μεγαλοκοίλιος (*with large ventricles*) = ʿaẓīmu l-buṭūni : διὸ τῶν μεγαλοκοιλίων οὐδὲν οὐδὲ τῶν μεγαλοφλέβων πῖόν ἐστι *Arist.*

Part. anim. III 4, 667a28 = wa-li-ḏālika annahū lā yakūnu samīnan šayʾun mina l-ḥayawāni l-ʿaẓīmi l-buṭūni wa-lā l-ḥayawāni l-ʿaẓīmi l-ʿurūqi *75.2.*

1.4.6 μικροκοίλιος (*with small ventricles*) = ṣaġīru l-buṭūni : ἀλλὰ πάντα ἢ τὰ πλεῖστα τῶν τοιούτων (*sc.* πίονα κατὰ σάρκα ζῴων) ἀδηλόφλεβα καὶ μικροκοίλια φαίνεται *Arist. Part. anim. III 4, 667a30* = bal ǧamīʿu l-ḥayawāni l-ṣaġīri l-buṭūni wa-l-ṣaġīri l-ʿurūqi yakūnu samīna l-laḥmi *75.3.*

! 1.5 *sem. amplif.* (*mistaken*); *added to supply the presumed reference to* κοιλία (*stomach*) *of the word read as* ἑτέρου (*the other*) *for* ἐντέρου (*intestine*) : ἡ δὲ τῆς κυνὸς (*sc.* κοιλία) μικρὰ τὸ μέγεθος καὶ οὐ πολὺ τοῦ ἑτέρου (ἑτέρου *SΣ, Arab.* : ἐντέρου *codd. cet., ed.*) ὑπερβάλλουσα *Arist. Part. anim. III 14, 675a30** = fa-ammā baṭnu l-kalbi fa-ṣaġīrun wa-laysa huwa awsaʿa mina l-baṭni kaṯīran *96.15.*

2. *transl.* γαστήρ (*belly, stomach*; *womb*) *and in compounds*

2.1 γαστήρ (*belly, stomach*) : ἔνια αὐτῶν ἔσω πρὸς τῷ τέλει τῆς γαστρὸς (*sc.* ἔχει τοὺς ὄρχεις) *Arist. Gener. anim. I 3, 716 b27* = minhu mā yakūnu unṯayāhu dāḫilan (*sic leg. pro* dāḫil *ed.*) fī āḫiri l-baṭni *6.5** ⟼ ἰδίως γὰρ ἡ γαστὴρ καὶ τὰ ἔντερα δανειστῇ ἔοικε *Artem. Onirocr. 73.18* = li-anna l-baṭna wa-l-amʿāʾa ḫāṣṣatan tušabbahu bi-l-muqriḍīna *135.11;* λύει δὲ τὴν γαστέρα λαμβανόμενα (λαμβανόμενα *om. V et fort. Arab.*) πάντα τὰ ὀστρακόδερμα *130.12** = wa-innamā yushilu l-baṭna mina l-samaki kullu mā kāna minhā ṣulba l-qišrati *235.16* ⟼ ὡς ἕκαστον ἔδεσμα καταπίνεται μὲν πρῶτον εἰς τὴν γαστέρα *Galen An. virt. 66.19* = anna ǧamīʿa l-ṭaʿāmi iḏā btuliʿa nazala awwalan ilā l-baṭni *34.15* ⟼ καὶ μὴν οὐκ ἐνδέχεται φιλόπονον εἶναί τινα ... αἰδοίοις καὶ γαστρὶ δουλεύοντα *Galen Med. phil. 6.8* = wa-laysa yumkinu an yakūna aḥadun muʾṯiran li-l-naṣabi ʿalā l-ḫafḍi iḏā kāna ... ʿabdan li-farǧihī wa-baṭnihī *93* ⟼ ἐμπνευματώσεις τε τὰς κατὰ γαστέρα καθίστησιν *Galen Simpl. medic. XI, 833.17* = wa-yuṭliqu arwāḥa l-baṭni wa-qarqaratahū *versio A* = wa-yuḏhibu l-nafḫa l-ḥādiṯa fī l-baṭni *versio B WGAÜ, 175.14-15;* εἰς δυσεντερίας καὶ ῥεύματα γαστρὸς καὶ ἀτονίας ... ἐπιτήδεια φάρμακα *XI, 848.19* = fī l-adwiyati wa-l-aḫlāṭi l-nāfiʿati mini ḫtilāfi l-aġrāsi wa-stiṭlāqi l-baṭni wa-ḍuʿfi l-maʿidati *versio A* = wa-yanfaʿu ... min qurūḥi l-amʿāʾi wa-li-stiṭlāqi l-baṭni wa-li-ḍuʿfi l-maʿidati wa-l-amʿāʾi *versio B WGAÜ, 175.16-18; etc.* ⟼ τοῖσι δὲ πίνουσι ... τὰς γαστέρας σκληράς τε καὶ λεπτὰς καὶ θερμάς (*sc.* εἶναι) *Hippocr. Aer. 36.1* = inna llaḏīna yašrabūna min hāḏihi l-miyāhi takūnu buṭūnuhum ǧāsiyatan naḥīfatan ḥārratan *versio A 49.7, sim. versio B 49.17* ⟼ ὥσπερ τοῖσι δένδρεσιν ἡ γῆ οὕτω τοῖσι ζώοισιν ἡ γαστήρ· ... ὥσπερ γῆ κοπρευομένη χειμῶνος θερμαίνει, οὕτως ἡ γαστὴρ θερμὴ γίνεται *Hippocr. Humor. XI.2-4* = bi-manzilati mā l-arḍu li-l-nabāti ka-ḏālika l-baṭnu li-l-ḥayawāni ... ka-mā anna l-arḍa iḏā surqinat (iḏā surqinat *nos* : iḏā ʾsrqt *cod., ed.*) fī l-šitāʾi tusaḫḫinu ka-ḏālika l-baṭnu takūnu fī hāḏihi l-waqti ḥārratan *23.5-8*; XI.11 = 23.14* ⟼ ἔπειτα ὑπὲρ τῆς γαστρὸς ἐς τὸ αἰδοῖον τελευτῶσιν (*sc.* αἱ τέταρται φλέβες) *Hippocr. Nat. hom. 196.4* = ṯumma yamtaddu (*sc.* al-zawǧu l-rābiʿu) ʿalā l-baṭni min ḫāriǧin ilā an yantahiya ilā l-farǧi *20.7* ⟼ νάρκη ἐμπίπτει ἐν τῇ γαστρί *Hippocr. Superf. 84.26* = fa-innahā taǧidu ṯiqalan wa-ḫadaran fī baṭnihā *13.7* ⟼ στόμα γὰρ καὶ γαστὴρ καὶ φλέβες ... ὄργανα τῆς τροφῆς *Them. In De an. 42. 7* = fa-inna l-fama wa-l-baṭna wa-l-ʿurūqa ... hiya ālātun li-l-ġiḏāʾi *50.7; cf. also WGAÜ Suppl. I, 237.*

2.2 γαστήρ (*womb*) : οἱ Στωικοὶ μέρος εἶναι αὐτὸ (*sc.* τὸ ἔμβρυον) τῆς γαστρός *Ps.-Plut. Placita 425a19* = wa-ammā l-riwāqiyyūna fa-yarawna annahū (*sc.* al-ǧanīnu) ǧuzʾun mina l-baṭni *69.15*; τὰ ζῷα ἐν γαστρὶ ὄντα *433a6* = al-ḥayawānātu iḏā kānat fī l-baṭni *73.20; 425a6 = 69.9; 427a4 = 70.12; etc.*

2.3 *sem.; etym.; transl. the word* γαστήρ (*belly, stomach*) *in compounds containing it*:

2.3.1 γαστροκνημία (*calf of the leg*) = baṭnu l-sāqi : καὶ ταύτης (*sc.* τῆς κνήμης) τὸ μὲν πρόσθιον ἀντικνήμιον, τὸ δ' ὀπίσθιον γαστροκνημία *Arist. Hist. anim. I 15, 494a7* = wa-muqaddamu l-sāqi yuqālu lahū anfu l-sāqi wa-muʾaḫḫaruhū yuqālu <lahū> baṭnu l-sāqi *39.17* ⟼ διόπερ τὰ ἰσχία σαρκώδη ἐποίησε καὶ μηροὺς καὶ γαστροκνημίας *Arist. Part. anim. IV 10, 689b15* = wa-li-ḏālika ṣayyara l-warikayni kaṯīrayi l-laḥmi wa-mā yalī l-faḫiḏayni wa-buṭūna l-sāqayni *137.7* ⟼ κατὰ τὸν τῆς γαστροκνημίας καλούμενον τόπον *Galen Anat. admin. II, 316.6* = fī mawḍiʿi baṭni l-sāqi *WGAÜ Suppl. I, 237.22* ⟼ καὶ κνήμης ἡ (*sc.* περιβολή) ὑπὲρ γαστροκνημίης *Galen In De off. med. 763.11* = yaqaʿu (*sc.* laffu l-ḫiraqi) ... mina l-sāqi fī l-mawḍiʿi llaḏī fawqa baṭni l-sāqi *34.28.*

2.3.2 γαστρορραφία (*sewing up of a belly-wound*) = ḫiyāṭatu l-baṭni : ὥστε καὶ τὴν καλουμένην γαστροραφίαν ... μετὰ τῆς ἀπονευρώσεως, ἣν λέγω *Galen Anat. admin. II, 551.9* = ḥattā anna ḫiyāṭata l-baṭni ... maʿa hāḏā l-watari llaḏī ḏakartuhū *358.15 Garofalo.*

2.3.3 ἐπιγάστριον (*the epigastrium*) = marāqqu l-baṭni : ἅτε (ἅτε *ed., Arab.* : οὔτε *Garofalo*) μέρος εἶναί τινος ἄλλου νομισθῆναι δυνάμενος, ὥσπερ ὁ παρὰ τῷ στέρνῳ (*sc.* μῦς) τοῦ κατ' ἐπιγάστριον *Galen Anat. admin. II, 497.11** = kamā yuẓannu bi-l-ʿaḍalati llatī taʾtī l-qassa annahā ǧuzʾun mina [l-ʿaḍalati llatī hiya] (*seclusimus*) l-ʿaḍalati llatī ʿalā marāqqi l-baṭni *292.19* Garofalo; II, 656.16 = 488.7-8* ⟛ ὥστε καὶ τοῦ ἐπιγαστρίου καταχριομένου κοιλίαν ὑπάγει *Galen Simpl. medic. XII, 50.19* = idā ṭuliya ʿalā marāqqi l-baṭni aṭlaqa l-baṭna *WGAÜ, 254.2* ⟛ ἡ δὲ ἀρχαιοτέρη τροφὴ διὰ τοῦ ἐπιγαστρίου, ᾗ ὀμφαλός *Hippocr. Alim. 144.14* = ammā l-ġidāʾu l-awwalu l-nuzūli fa-l-kāʾinu mina l-surrati wa-marāqqi l-baṭni *13.2.*

2.3.4 τὸ ὑπογάστριον (*the lower belly from the navel downwards*) = asfalu l-baṭni : τὰ δὲ πλευρὰ κάτω καθήκει συνάπτοντα πρὸς τὸ ὑπογάστριον *Arist. Hist. anim. II 11, 503a17* = fa-ammā aḍlāʿuhū fa-ṭawīlatun tantahī ilā qurbi asfali baṭnihī *71.13;* ἐὰν ... βλέπωσιν αἱ ὑστέραι ... πρὸς τὸ ὑπογάστριον *X 2, 634b40* = wa-idā ... kānat (*sc.* al-raḥimu) muttaǧihatan ... nāḥiyata asfali l-baṭni *489.21* ⟛ ἢν ... ὀδύνη ἐμπίπτῃ ἐς τὸ ὑπογάστριον ... τὰ περὶ τὴν κύστιν πονεῖ *Hippocr. Aphor. IV.80* = man ... aṣābahū waǧaʿun fī asfali baṭnihī ... fa-inna mā yalī maṯānatahū waǧiʿun *40.4.*

2.3.5 γαστρίμαργος (*greedy of belly, i.e., gluttonous*) = ṣāḥibu baṭnin : διὸ λέγονται οὗτοι γαστρίμαργοι, ὡς παρὰ τὸ δέον πληροῦντες αὐτήν *Arist. Eth. Nic. III 11, 1118b19* = wa-li-ḏālika yuqālu (*sic leg. pro* yql *ed.*) li-hāʾulāʾi aṣḥābu buṭūnin li-annahum yamlaʾūna buṭūnahum akṯara mimmā yaḥtāǧūna ilayhi *229.7.*

2.4 *sem.; def.;* προγαστρότερος, *moderating comp. of* προγάστωρ (*potbellied*) = baṭnuhū kabīrun : τὰ τοιαῦτα εἴδεα προγαστρότερα εἶναι καὶ σπληνώδεα *Hippocr. Aer. 80.4* = kānat ṣuwaru hāʾulāʾi l-nāsi muḫtalifatan wa-buṭūnuhum takūnu kibāran wa-aṭḥilatuhum miṯla ḏālika *157.7.*

3. νηδύς (*belly, stomach*) : ὁκόσων δὲ μαλακαὶ αἱ νηδύες καὶ ὑγραί εἰσι καὶ φλεγματώδεες *Hippocr. Aer. 38.22* = wa-man kāna mina l-nāsi baṭnuhū layyinan ladnan balġamiyyan *versio A 65.9, sim. versio B 65.18;* οὐ γὰρ οἷόν τε νηδὺν ἀναξηραίνεσθαι ἐν τοιαύτῃ χώρῃ *68.18* = wa-ḏālika anna buṭūnahum lā yumkinu an taǧiffa wa-taybasa fī miṯli hāḏihi l-bilādi *141.10.*

4. στόμαχος (*stomach*) : πνευματωτικὸς στομάχου καὶ ἐντέρων *Diosc. Mat. med. I, 181.6* = yuhayyiǧu l-riyāḥa fī l-baṭni wa-l-amʿāʾi *vetus transl. Ullmann Unters., 184.5.*

5. ὑποχόνδριον (*part of the body below the cartilage, abdomen*) : κατὰ τοῦ στόματος τῆς γαστρὸς ἢ τῶν ὑποχονδρίων ὅλων ἐπιτιθέμενος *Galen Simpl. medic. XI, 630.17* = matā wuḍiʿa ʿalā fami l-maʿidati aw ʿalā ǧamīʿi l-baṭni *WGAÜ Suppl. II, 560.7.*

6. αἱ λαγόνες (*in context*: [*the cavity between*] *the flanks, hence, belly*) : ὥσπερ οἴκῳ κτήματα, οὕτω τὰ σπλάγχνα ταῖς λαγόσιν ἔγκειται *Artem. Onirocr. 50.14* = wa-qiyāsu l-aḥšāʾi fī l-baṭni ka-qiyāsi matāʿi l-manzili fī l-manzili *95.5.*

7. ἔδαφος (*the text proper* [*as opposed to what is written in the margins*]) : εἶθ' εὑρόντα τὸν βιβλιογράφον ἐνίας μὲν (*sc.* λέξεις) αὐτῶν ἐν τοῖς μετώποις γεγραμμένας ... πάσας ἔγραψε τῷ ἐδάφει τοῦ συγγράμματος *Galen In De off. med. 864.4* = fa-iḏā waǧada l-nāsiḫu li-l-kitābi baʿda ḏālika baʿḍa l-kalāmi muṯbatan fī l-ẓahri nasaḫahā kullahū fī baṭni l-kitābi *40.10.*

8. τὸ κάτω (*what is beneath*) : ὅτι τὸ κάτω τῆς γῆς τοῦ μὲν χειμῶνος θερμόν ἐστι *Hippocr. Nat. puer. 71.15* = li-anna baṭna l-arḍi ḥārrun fī l-šitāʾi *72.11;* τοῦ θέρεος τὸ κάτω τῆς γῆς ψυχρόν ἐστι *75.7* = yakūnu l-māʾu llaḏī fī baṭni l-arḍi fī l-ṣayfi bāridan *74.16.*

9. *sem.; def.;* ἕρψις (*creeping*) = *in hend.* sayrun ʿalā l-baṭni wa-dabbun (*moving on the ground and creeping*) : ἡ τῶν ζῴων πορεία ... διαφέρει γὰρ πτῆσις καὶ νεῦσις καὶ βάδισις καὶ ἕρψις *Arist. Part. anim. I 1, 639b3* = fa-inna fī aṣnāfi masīri l-ḥayawāni ḫtilāfan aʿnī anna minhu mā yaṭīru wa-minhu mā yaʿūmu wa-minhu mā yamšī wa-minhu mā yasīru ʿalā baṭnihī wa-yadibbu *6.6.*

10. *sem.; expr.; used in expressions translating Greek words pertaining to the anatomy of the abdomen*

10.1 ὑποχόνδριον (*part of the body below the cartilage, abdomen*) : marāqqu l-baṭni : *Diosc. Mat. med. I, 90.11* = *vetus transl. Ullmann Unters., 184.6* ⟼ ἀκίνητοι μὲν αἱ ὠμοπλάται εἰσὶ, τὸ δ' ὑποχόνδριον ἔμπαλιν *Galen Anat. admin. II, 679.10* = fa-l-katifāni yakūnāni ġayra mutaḥarrikayni wa-ammā marāqqu l-baṭni fa-tataḥarraku bi-ḫilāfi mā kāna yataḥarraku (*sc.* al-ḥiǧābu) *WGAÜ Suppl. II, 560.3* ⟼ τὸ χαμαίμηλον ... καὶ διὰ τοῦτο καὶ ὑποχονδρίοις εὐμενὲς εἴπερ τι ἄλλο *Galen Simpl. medic. XI, 563.4* = wa-li-ḏālika ṣāra (*sc.* al-bābūnaǧu) min ašaddi l-ašyāʾi taskīnan wa-alyanihā fī mudāwāti l-aḥšāʾi llatī min warāʾi marāqqi l-baṭni *WGAÜ Suppl. II, 560.6.*

10.2 ἦτρον (*the lower part of the abdomen*) = marāqqu l-baṭni : τέμνουσι δὲ τὸ ἦτρον *Arist. Hist. anim. IX 50, 632a24* = ṯumma yuqṭaʿu l-ǧildu llaḏī fī marāqqi l-baṭni *455.3* ⟼ πνεῦμα πυκνότερον ... κοπῶδες ὑποχονδρίων καὶ ἤτρου *Hippocr. Diaet. acut. 42.14* = al-tanaffusu ... azyadu tawāturan ... yutʿibu mā dūna l-šarāsīfi wa-marāqqa l-baṭni *9.1-2*.

10.3 ἐπίπλοον (*fold of the peritoneum*) = al-ṯarbu llaḏī ʿalā l-baṭni : ἔτι δ' ἄλλαι ἀπὸ τῆς μεγάλης φλεβὸς ἀποσχίζονται, ἡ μὲν ἐπὶ τὸ ἐπίπλοον *Arist. Hist. anim. III 4, 514b10* = wa-taftariqu ʿurūqun uḫaru mina l-ʿirqi l-ʿaẓīmi wa-yaʾḫuḏu l-ʿirqu l-wāḥidu minhā bi-l-ṯarbi llaḏī ʿalā l-baṭni *113.13*.

10.4 τὰ αἰδοῖα (*pudenda*) = muntahā l-baṭni : τὸ ἀπ' αὐχένος μέχρι αἰδοίων κύτος, ὃ καλεῖται θώραξ *Arist. Hist. anim. I 7, 491a29* = wa-ǧamīʿu mā bayna l-ʿunuqi ilā muntahā l-baṭni yuqālu lahū tannūrun *28.10*.

11. *sem.; expr.; used in expressions translating Greek words denoting abdominal diseases*

11.1 διάρροια (*diarrhea*) **(a)** iḫtilāfu l-baṭni : ὥσπερ οὖν ἐν ταῖς κοιλίαις διὰ τὴν ἀπεψίαν γίγνεται διάρροια *Arist. Gener. anim. I 20, 728a22* = wa-ka-miṯli mā yaʿriḍu ḫtilāfu l-baṭni li-ḥāli l-tuḫamati *40.19* ⟼ ἡ πυετία ... συμφέρει ... πρὸς τὰς διαρροίας *Arist. Hist. anim. III 21, 522b10* = wa-l-maswatu ... muwāfiqatun li-iḫtilāfi l-baṭni (li-iḫtilāfi l-baṭni *cod.* : li-iṭlāqi l-baṭni *scripsit Badawī*) *144.1**; ἁλίσκεται δὲ (*sc.* ὁ ἐλέφας) καὶ διαρροίᾳ *VIII 26, 605a27* = wa-yuṣībuhā (*sc.* al-fiyalata) ḫtilāfu l-baṭni *360.15* **(b)** iṭlāqu l-baṭni : ὥστε καὶ διάρροιαν ἰᾶται *Galen Simpl. medic. XI, 812.17* = ʿaqalat iṭlāqa l-baṭni *versio A WGAÜ, 196.16* **(c)** istiṭlāqu l-baṭni : τὸ δὲ σπέρμα αὐτῶν ἔχει τι σαφῶς καὶ στυπτικόν, ὡς καὶ δυσεντερίας καὶ διαρροίας ἰᾶσθαι *Galen Simpl. medic. XII, 56.16* = fa-ammā bizru l-ḥummāḍi fa-fīhi qabḍun bayyinun ḥattā innahū <yašfī> (*suppl. Ullmann*) qurūḥa l-amʿāʾi wa-stiṭlāqa l-baṭni *WGAÜ, 196.21*.

11.2 δυσεντερία (*dysentery*) = iḫtilāfu baṭnin min qurūḥi l-maṣārīni : ἕως δυσεντερίας γενομένης καὶ κινδυνεύσασα ὑπ' αὐτῆς ἔτεκε σάρκα ἣν καλοῦσι μύλην *Arist. Gener. anim. IV 7, 775b32* = fa-ʿaraḍa lahā ḫtilafu baṭnin min qurūḥi l-maṣārīni wa-laqiyat minhu šiddatan wa-kādat tahliku ḥattā waladat biḍʿata laḥmin yusammā mūlī *166.12*.

11.3 λειεντερία (*passing one's food undigested, dysentery*) = istirḫāʾu l-baṭni : καὶ λειεντερίαι καὶ ὕδρωπες τελευτῶσι τοῖσι νοσεύμασιν ἐπιγίγνονται *Hippocr. Aer. 50.16* = qad yatbaʿu ayḍan hāḏihi l-asqāma stirḫāʾu l-baṭni fa-yusammā liyanṭariyā wa-l-māʾu l-aṣfaru *versio A 105.7, sim. versio B 105.16.*

11.4 ἕλμινς (*intestinal worm*) **(a)** *abs.* ḥayyatu l-baṭni : ἕλμινθας ἀποκρίνειν διὰ τῆς ἕδρας ἢ διὰ τοῦ στόματος ... σημαίνει *Artem. Onirocr. 207.17* = fa-ammā ḥayyātu l-baṭni fa-inna l-insāna iḏā raʾā ka-annahū yulqīhā mina l-maqʿadati aw mina l-fami fa-inna ḏālika yadullu ʿalā... *375.1;* ἐνοικοῦσι μὲν γὰρ τῷ σώματι οἱ ἕλμινθες *207.22* = wa-ḏālika anna ḥayyāti l-baṭni takūnu (*fort.* taskunu *leg.*) fī l-badani *375. 6** **(b)** *in hend.* ḥayyatu l-baṭni wa-dūduhū : καὶ διὰ τοῦτο πρὸς τὰς πλατείας ἕλμινθας ἐπιτηδεία *Galen Simpl. medic. XI, 813.9* = yuḫriğu mā fī l-baṭni mina l-ḥayyāti wa-l-dūdi l-ʿarīḍi *versio A WGAÜ, 235.2* **(c)** mā fī l-baṭni min ḥabbi l-qarʿi : καὶ τῷ μὲν πικρῷ τὰς ἕλμινθας ἀναιρεῖ *Galen Simpl. medic. XI, 883.12* = fa-yaqtulu mā fī l-baṭni min ḥabbi l-qarʿi li-ḥāli marāratihī *versio A WGAÜ, 235.4.*

11.5 στρόφος (*twisting of the bowels, colic*) : *Diosc. Mat. med. I, 7.2, 114.9* = maġaṣu l-baṭni *vetus transl. Ullmann Unters., 184.6.*

11.6 βορβορυγμός (*intestinal rumbling*) = qarqaratun fī l-baṭni : *Paulus Aeg. III, 71.1* = *WGAÜ Suppl. I, 224.23.*

11. *sem.; expr.; used in expressions translating Greek words signifying birth*

11.1 *used in expressions transl.* τίκτω (*to give birth*) *and its derivatives*

11.1.1 τίκτω (*to give birth*) = waḍaʿat mā fī baṭnihā : ὁρέομεν ... ταῦτα τίκτει τῇ αὐτῇ ἡμέρῃ *Hippocr. Nat. puer. 83.12* = qad narāhā taḍaʿu mā fī baṭnihā mina l-awlādi fī yawmin wāḥidin *85.5.*

11.1.2 πρωτοτόκος (*having born her first-born*) = awwalu baṭnin waḍaʿat : ἱστοροῦσι δέ τινες τὸ τῆς πρωτοτόκου κυνὸς γάλα ψιλοῦν τρίχας καταχρισθέν *Diosc. Mat. med. I, 145.20* = wa-qad zaʿama qawmun anna labana l-kalbati fī awwali baṭnin taḍaʿu iḏā luṭṭiḫa ʿalā l-šaʿari ḥalaqahū *versio A WGAÜ Suppl. II, 218.17.*

11.2 πολύγονος (*producing many offspring at one birth*) = talidu awlādan kaṯīratan fī baṭnin wāḥidin : καὶ τὰ πολύγονα τῶν ζῴων πλείους ἔχει (*sc.* κόλπους) τῶν ὀλίγα κυεόντων *Hippocr. Nat. puer. 83.2* = wa-l-ḥayawānu llatī talidu awlādan kaṯīratan fī baṭnin wāḥidin ... fī arḥāmi-hinna aḥḍānun kaṯīratun akṯaru mina llatī lā talidu kaṯīran *84.15.*

11.3 *used in expr. transl.* κύω (*to be pregnant with child*)

11.3.1 *sem. amplif.;* κύουσα *act. part. fem.* (*pregnant woman*) = baṭnu l-ḥāmili : οἷον τὴν ἄνθρωπον ἣν λέγουσι τὰς κυούσας ἀνασχίζουσαν τὰ παιδία κατεσθίειν *Arist. Eth. Nic. VII 5, 1148b20* = miṯla l-insānata (al-insānata *Badawī, Ullmann in WGAÜ Suppl. I, 609* : al-insāniyyata *F, ed.*) llatī qīla innahā kānat tašuqqu buṭūna l-ḥawāmili wa-ta'kulu l-ağinnata *389.9**.

11.3.2 κυόμενος *pass. part.* (*embryo*) = fī baṭni ummihī : τὰ δὲ κυόμενα παιδία ἀσθενῆ γίνεται *Ps.-Arist. Probl. phys. I 9, 860a21* = wa-takūnu (*sc.* al-ruṭūbātu) qātilatan li-l-aṭfāli fī buṭūni ummahātihim *I 7, 16.12*.

12. *sem.; expr.;* πρηνής (*prone,* [*lying*] *on one's belly*) = ʿalā l-baṭni : ὥσπερ τὰ ὀπισθουρητικά, ὅταν τὸ μὲν ὕπτιον τὸ δὲ πρανὲς ἐπαλλάξῃ τὰ οὐραῖα *Arist. Gener. anim. I 14, 720b10* = miṯla mā yasfadu l-ḥayawānu llaḏī yabūlu ilā ḫalfu iḏā kāna aḥaduhumā ʿalā l-ẓahri wa-l-āḫaru ʿalā l-baṭni wa-baddala waḍʿa l-aḏnābi *18.5*.

13. *metaphorically;* ὀσφῦς (*loins*) : βαρύτητες ἐν τῇ ὀσφύϊ καὶ ἐν τοῖσι γούνασι, καὶ θέρμαι γίνονται *Hippocr. Nat. hom. 212.6* = wa-yaḥduṯu ... ṯiqalun fī l-baṭni wa-l-rukbatayni wa-ltihābun *30.13* (*for this apparently Christian metaphorical use of the word* [*"fruit of the loins"*] *v. WGAÜ, 479.1-2*).

14. *interpr.;* μήτηρ (*mother*) : ἐπεὶ γὰρ οὐκ ἐκτρέφονταί γε ἐν τῇ μητρὶ τὰ ᾠοτοκούμενα *Arist. Gener. anim. III 3, 753b33* = li-anna l-bayḍa llaḏī yubāḍu lā yuġaḏḏā fī l-baṭni *108.16*.

! 15. πάγκρεας (*pancreas*) : ἔτι δ' ἄλλαι ἀπὸ τῆς μεγάλης φλεβὸς ἀποσχίζονται, ἡ μὲν ἐπὶ τὸ ἐπίπλοον, ἡ δ' ἐπὶ τὸ καλούμενον πάγκρεας *Arist. Hist. anim. III 4, 514b11* = wa-taftariqu ʿurūqun uḫaru mina l-ʿirqi l-ʿaẓīmi wa-ya'ḫuḏu l-ʿirqu l-wāḥidu minhā bi-l-ṯarbi llaḏī ʿalā l-baṭni wa-l-āḫaru ilā l-baṭni (al-baṭni *cod.* : mā yusammā bi-l-bankriyās *corr. Badawī; cf. WGAÜ Suppl. I, 1*) *113.13**.

بطانة biṭānatun

1. οἱ οἰκεῖοι (*kinsmen, people of the private sphere*) = *in hend.* al-ḫawāṣṣu wa-ahlu l-biṭānati : ἀλλὰ καὶ τῶν οἰκείων *Galen Loc. aff. VIII, 8.7* = lākin min ḫawāṣṣihī wa-ahli biṭānatihī ayḍan *WGAÜ Suppl. I, 750.2*.

باطن bāṭinun

1. *transl.* ἐν (*in*) *and its derivatives*

1.1 ἐν *prep. c. dat.* (*in*) **(a)** min bāṭini *c. gen.* : κυπάρισσος ... καὶ πολύπους τοὺς ἐν τοῖς μυκτῆρσιν ἰᾶται *Diosc. Mat. med. I, 74.6* =

ǧawzu l-sarwi ... wa-abraʾa fūlūbus wa-huwa laḥmun yanbutu fī l-anfi min bāṭinihī *versio A WGAÜ Suppl. I, 706.17* **(b)** fī bāṭini *c. gen.* : τὸ δὲ κέντρον τὰ μὲν ἔχει ἐν αὑτοῖς, οἷον αἱ μέλιτται καὶ οἱ σφῆκες *Arist. Hist. anim. IV 7, 532a15* = wa-rubbamā kānat tilka l-ḥumatu fī bāṭinihā miṯla ḥumati l-dabri <wa-l-naḥli> (*add. Badawī*) *180.3* ↦ ἕλκη ... τὰ ἐν μυκτῆρσι *Diosc. Mat. med. I, 104. 12* = al-qurūḥ allatī fī bāṭini l-anfi *Ibn al-Bayṭār, Ǧāmiʿ II, 144.23.*

1.2 ἐντός *adv.* (*within, inside*) **(a)** *abs.* : ξηραίνεται δὲ πάντα ... ὑπὸ τῆς ἐντὸς θερμότητος ἢ τῆς ἔξω *Arist. Meteor. IV 5, 382b18* = wa-l-ašyāʾu l-raṭbatu taǧiffu ... min aǧli l-ḥarārati l-bāṭinati fī l-šayʾi aw mina l-ḥarārati l-ḫāriǧati l-muḥīṭati bihī *1153* ↦ οἱ μὲν κατὰ τὸ ἐντὸς καὶ κατὰ τὸ ἐκτός εἰσιν ἀγαθοί, ... οἱ δὲ κατὰ <μὲν> τὸ ἐντὸς ἀγαθοὶ κατὰ δὲ τὸ ἐκτὸς κακοί, οἱ δὲ κατὰ μὲν τὸ ἐντὸς κακοὶ κατὰ δὲ τὸ ἐκτὸς ἀγαθοί *Artem. Onirocr. 14.10-12*= fa-baʿḍuhā maḥmūdun fī l-ẓāhiri wa-l-bāṭini wa-baʿḍuhā maḥmūdun fī l-ẓāhiri maḏmūmun fī l-bāṭini wa-baʿḍuhā maḏmūmu l-ẓāhiri maḥmūdu (maḥmūdu *cod., Rosenthal, p. 141* : wa-maḥmūdu *ed.*) l-bāṭini *28.11-13*; 15.3 = 30.1; etc.* ↦ διαφοροῦν καὶ μαλάσσον πᾶσαν φλεγμονὴν ἐντός τε καὶ ἐκτός *Diosc. Mat. med. I, 177.6* = ḥallala l-awrāma l-ḥārrata wa-layyanahā ẓāhiratan kānat aw bāṭinatan *versio A* = yufiššu l-falġamūnī l-bāṭina wa-l-ẓāhira *versio B WGAÜ Suppl. I, 362.8* = yulayyinu l-awrāma l-ẓāhirata wa-l-bāṭinata *vetus transl. Ullmann Unters., 184.7* **(b)** fī bāṭini *c. gen.* : τὰ δ' ἔχει μὲν ὄρχεις, ἐντὸς δ' ἔχει τούτους πρὸς τῇ ὀσφύι *Arist. Gener. anim. I 3, 716b18* = wa-minhu mā lahū unṯayāni wa-humā fī bāṭini ǧasadihī qarībun mina l-ṣulbi *5.18* ↦ ὥστε καὶ τὰ ἐντὸς ἀποστήματα ῥήσσει *Galen Simpl. medic. XI, 886.18* = fa-yufaǧǧiru l-awrāma l-kāʾinata fī bāṭini l-badani *versio A WGAÜ, 246.20.*

1.3 *sem. amplif.;* τὰ ἐντόσθια (*inwards, entrails*) = al-aʿḍāʾ al-bāṭina : ὁ πνεύμων πάντων τῶν ἐντοσθίων λεπτότατον ἔχει τὸν ὑμένα *Theomn. Hippiatr. I, 46.11* = wa-huwa anna ṣifāqa l-riʾati araqqu ǧamīʿi ṣifāqāti l-aʿḍāʾi l-bāṭinati *60.9.*

1.4 ἔνδον *adv.* (*inside, within*) : ὑποτεταγμένους τῷ ψιλῷ καὶ ἀτρίχῳ τῆς ἄκρας χειρός, ὅπερ ἔνδον αὐτῆς ἐστιν *Galen Anat. admin. II, 234.6* = taḥta l-ǧuzʾi l-amlasi l-azʿari mina l-kaffi wa-huwa bāṭinuhā *22.20 Garofalo.*

1.5 ἔνδοθεν *adv.* (*from within, on the inside*) : εἰς καινὰ κεράμια βεβαμμένα ἔνδοθεν γύψῳ ἢ ἀμόργῃ ἔμβαλε *Cass. Bass. Geopon. IX 19.11* = fa-ǧʿalhu fī awʿiyatin min faḫḫārin madhūnati l-bāṭini (*variant reading:* min ḫazafin muǧaṣṣaṣin baṭinuhū) *WGAÜ Suppl. I, 354.10* ↦

κεφάλια περιφερῆ, ἔνδοθεν μὲν λευκὸν καὶ χρυσίζον ἀνθύλλιον ἔχοντα *Diosc. Mat. med. II, 146. 5* = ruʾūsun mustadīratun ṣiġārun fī bāṭini baʿḍihā zahrun abyaḍu wa-fī baʿḍihā zahrun miṯlu lawni l-ḏahabi *Ibn al-Bayṭār, Ǧāmiʿ I, 73.8.*

2. ὑπέρ *prep. c. acc.* (*over, on*) = fī bāṭini *c. gen.* : ὁ ὑπὲρ τὴν δεξιὰν ἀγκύλην τοῦ αὐτοῦ Διδύμου *Ptol. Syntaxis mathematica vol. I.2, p. 92.15* = al-kawkabu llaḏī fī bāṭini l-faḫiḏi l-yumnā ʿinda l-rukbati min hāḏā l-tawʾami *WGAÜ Suppl. I, 56.9.*

3. βάθος (*depth*) : ἕλκεται γὰρ οὖν (*sc.* ἡ θαψία) ἐκ βάθους *Galen Simpl. medic. XI, 885.5* = wa-hāḏā l-dawāʾu yaǧḏibu mina l-bāṭini l-fuḍūla *versio A WGAÜ, 157.*

4. *paraphr.; transl. compounds of* φαίνομαι (*to appear*) *that negate its basic meaning and denote little or no explicit view*

4.1 ὑπόφασις (*"under-" or slight appearance*) = al-bāṭinu *and* mā ẓahara min bāṭinin : σκοπεῖν δὲ χρὴ καὶ τὰς ὑποφάσιας τῶν ὀφθαλμῶν ἐν τοῖσιν ὕπνοισιν *Hippocr. Aphor. VI.52* = qad yanbaġī an yutafaqqada bāṭinu l-ʿaynayni fī waqti l-nawmi *58.14* = *Hippocr. Progn. II, 196.6* = qad yanbaġī an tatafaqqada mā yaẓharu min bāṭini l-ʿaynayni fī waqti l-nawmi *207.3.*

4.2 ἀφανῶς *adv.* (*not apparently at all, hiddenly*) = fī l-bāṭini : ἐπειδὴ οὐ ταὐτὰ φανερῶς ἐπαινοῦσι καὶ ἀφανῶς, ἀλλὰ φανερῶς μὲν τὰ δίκαια καὶ τὰ καλὰ ἐπαινοῦσι μάλιστα *Arist. Rhet. II 23, 1399a30* = min qibali <anna l-nāsa laysa> (*suppl. nos pro lac. ms* : <anna l-nāsa lā> *Sālim, Badawī*) madḥuhum fī l-ẓāhiri wa-l-bāṭini wāḥidan lākinnahum fī l-ẓāhiri yamdaḥūna ʿalā ḥasabi l-ʿadli wa-fī l-bāṭini ʿalā ḥasabi l-ǧamīli (*where the second* fī l-bāṭin *either interprets* μάλιστα *as meaning "in truth," "in their hearts," or transl. the following* ἰδίᾳ *in the Greek text, a misplaced variant of which as* ἡδέα, *however, is also transl. as* laḏīḏāt *in what follows in the Arabic* [*cf. Lyons, p. 352*]) *154.20*.*

5. *paraphr.;* κρυπτός (*hidden*) : ὠφελεῖ καρκινώματα κρυπτά *Diosc. Mat. med. I, 224.7* = nafaʿa mina l-saraṭāni l-bāṭini *WGAÜ, 370.*

6. *interpr.;* ῥάμφος (*beak*) = bāṭinu l-fami (*the interior of the mouth*) : οἱ θαλάττιοι ὄρνιθες ἐὰν ἑλκωθῶσι τὸ ῥάμφος *Cass. Bass. Geopon. XV, 1.24* = min amri ṭayri l-baḥri ... iḏā aṣāba bāṭina afwāhihā ǧurḥun *WGAÜ Suppl. II, 241.12.*

! 7. περιεκτικός (*containing*) = bāṭinun (*internal, contained*) : ὁ γὰρ τὰ περιεκτικὰ τῶν φροντίδων ἀπολέσας εἰκότως ἄλυπός ἐστιν *Artem. Onirocr. 50.24* = li-anna man ḏahabat ʿanhu ġumūmuhu l-bāṭinatu bi-l-wāǧibi mā ṣāra mustarīḥan mina l-hammi wa-l-aḏā *95.17* (*where* περιεκτικός *was apparenly misunderstood as* περιεχόμενος).

بطى

باطية bāṭiyatun, *pl.* **bawāṭin**

1. κύλιξ (*cup, wine-cup*) : κατασκευάζουσι δὲ ἔνιοι ... κύλικας *Diosc. Mat. med. I, 82.19* = yaʿmalūna bawāṭiya *vetus transl. Ullmann Unters., 184.*

بعث

بعث I. baʿaṯa

1. πέμπω *c. acc. et* εἰς (*to send s.o./s.th. to*) = baʿaṯa *c.* bi- *r. et* ilā : ὁ πατὴρ εἰς διδασκάλου πέμπων τὸν υἱόν *Artem. Onirocr. 89.26* = al-raǧulu ... yabʿaṯu bi-l-ṣabīyi ilā l-muʿallimi *165.8.*

2. ἄγω *c. acc.* (*to draw s.th. along*) = baʿaṯa *c. acc. r. et* ilā : ἀκτέα (*sc.* οἱ χυμοί), ᾗ ῥέπει τῶν συμφερόντων χωρίων, πλὴν ὧν οἱ πεπασμοὶ ἐκ τῶν χρόνων *Hippocr. Humor. 1.3* = yanbaġī an tubʿaṯa (*sc.* al-aḫlāṭu) ilā ḥayṯu tamīlu mina l-nawāḥī l-muwāfiqati illā mā kāna minhā lam yanḍaǧ *1.4.*

3. ἐφίημι *c. acc. pers.* (*to incite s.o.*) = baʿaṯa *c. acc. pers. et* ʿalā : ὅς τ' ἐφέηκε (*sc.* ὁ οἶνος) πολύφρονά περ μάλ' ἀεῖσαι *Galen An virt. 40.17* (= *Homer* ξ *464*) = innahā (*sc.* al-ḫamra) tabʿaṯu l-rakīna l-ʿāqila ʿalā an yataġannā *16.3.*

4. στέλλομαι *pass., c.* ἐπί (*to be sent, commissioned to do s.th.*) = buʿiṯa *c.* bi- *pers. et* fī : μάλιστα τοῖς ὄχλου προΐστασθαι βουλομένοις καὶ τοῖς ἐπὶ τὸ ἄρχειν στελλομένοις (καὶ ... στελλομένοις *V, Arab.* : *om. L, secl. Pack*) καὶ σοφισταῖς καὶ διδασκάλοις ἔργων (ἔργων *L, Arab.* : *om. V* :

*secl. Pack) Artem. Onirocr. 119.12** = wa-bi-ḫāṣṣatin li-man kāna yurīdu an yarʾusa qawman wa-yudabbirahum wa-li-man buʿiṯa bihī fī wilāyatin wa-li-man kāna fiʿluhū fiʿla l-sufisṭīna (*form?*) wa-l-muʿallimīna *218.2**.

5. διηθέω (*to strain through, filter*) = baʿaṯa *c. acc. r. et* ilā : Φιλόλαος ὁ Πυθαγόρειος ὑαλοειδῆ τὸν ἥλιον (τὸν ἥλιον *Stobaeus, Arab.* : *om. Ps.-Plut.*), ... διηθοῦντα δὲ πρὸς ἡμᾶς τό ... φῶς *Ps.-Plut. Placita 349a10** = wa-ammā Fīlūlāwus al-Fūṯāġūriyyu fa-innahū yarā anna ǧirma l-šamsi ka-l-zuǧāǧi ... wa-yabʿaṯu al-ḍawʾa ilaynā *33.7.*

انبعث **VII. inbaʿaṯa** *abs. or c.* min *or* ʿan *of the source or origin*

1. *transl.* πέμπω (*to send*) *and its compounds in sem. metathesis, act. / pass. transformation*

1.1 πέμπω (*to send*) : τὰ μὲν ἀπέριττα σώματα βραχύ τι τοῖς ἕλκουσι πέμπουσι, τὰ δὲ περιττωματικά τε καὶ πληθωρικὰ τοσούτῳ πλέον, ὅσῳπερ ἂν ἐξεστήκῃ τοῦ κατὰ φύσιν *Galen Diff. febr. VII, 387.3* = wa-matā kāna l-badanu kaṯīra l-fuḍūli mumtaliʾan kāna mā yanbaʿiṯu minhu ilā tilka l-aʿḍāʾi azyada bi-ḥasabi miqdāri ḫurūǧihī ʿani l-ḥāli l-ṭabīʿiyyati *Ḥummayāt 256.2-3 (cf. Ullmann Proportionalgefüge, 237)* ⟼ καὶ τοῖς οὔλοις δ᾽ ἀπονεμήσεις ὁμοίως πέμπει *Galen Nerv. diss. 837.5* = wa-yanbaʿiṯu (*sc.* al-qismu l-āḫaru) minhu ilā l-liṯati ayḍan ʿalā ḏālika l-miṯāli *102.10.*

1.2 ἐκπέμπω (*to send out, emit*): οὕτως δὲ καὶ τὸ ὁρᾶν πασχούσης τῆς ὄψεως γίνεσθαι, ἀλλ᾽ οὐχὶ ἐκπεμπούσης τι καὶ ποιούσης *Alex. An mant.* [*Vis.*] *141.32* = ka-ḏālika (*sc.* yaḥduṯu) l-ibṣāru bi-nfiʿāli l-ʿayni lā bi-annahā tafʿalu šayʾan aw yanbaʿiṯu minhā šayʾun *147.5.*

2. προΐεμαι *med.* (*to send forward from oneself, emit*) **(a)** *abs.* : Πυθαγόρας Ἐπίκουρος Δημόκριτος καὶ τὸ θῆλυ προΐεσθαι σπέρμα *Ps.-Plut. Placita 418a6* = Fūṯāġūras wa-Abīqūrus wa-Ḏīmūqrīṭūs yarawna anna li-l-ināṯi maniyy (*sic ed. pro* maniyyan) yanbaʿiṯu *64.19*⊗ **(b)** inbaʿaṯa *c.* min *or* ʿan : ἀκινητίζει τε φοβούμενα (*sc.* τὰ ἄναιμα) καὶ προΐεται περιττώματα *Galen An. virt. 53.7* (= *Arist. Part. anim. II 4, 650b32*) = iḏā faziʿat (*sc.* al-ḥayawānu l-ʿadīmu l-dami) fa-baʿḍuhā yabṭulu ḥarakatuhū wa-rubbamā nbaʿaṯat min baʿḍihā fuḍūlun *25.11* ⟼ Ἀριστοτέλης καὶ Ζήνων ὕλην μὲν ὑγρὰν προΐεσθαι (*sc.* τὸ θῆλυ) οἱονεὶ ... ἱδρῶτας *Ps.-Plut. Placita 418a11* = wa-ammā Arisṭūṭālīs wa-Zīnūn fa-yarayāni annahū yanbaʿiṯu mina l-ināṯi ʿunṣurun raṭbun ka-l-ʿaraqi *64.22;* οἱ Στωικοὶ ... προΐεσθαι δὲ καὶ τὴν γυναῖκα σπέρμα *423a5*

= wa-ammā l-Riwāqiyyūna fa-yarawna ... anna l-nisāʾa yanbaʿiṯu minhunna maniyyun *67.25; 418a3 = 64.18.*

3. διατείνω (*to stretch out, spread from*) : ἀκοὴ δὲ πνεῦμα διατεῖνον ἀπὸ τοῦ ἡγεμονικοῦ μέχρις ὤτων, ὄσφρησις δὲ πνεῦμα διατεῖνον ἀπὸ τοῦ ἡγεμονικοῦ μέχρι μυκτήρων *Ps.-Plut. Placita 411a5-7* = wa-l-samʿu huwa rūḥun tanbaʿiṯu min hāḏā l-ǧuzʾi l-raʾīsi ilā l-uḏunayni wa-l-šammu huwa rūḥun tanbaʿiṯu min hāḏā l-ǧuzʾi l-raʾīsi ilā l-manḫarayni *60.22f.; 411a15 = 60.26.*

4. διήκω (*to extend, spread from*) : τῶν νεωτέρων τινὲς διήκειν (*sc.* τὸ τῆς ψυχῆς ἡγεμονικὸν) ἀπὸ κεφαλῆς μέχρι τοῦ διαφράγματος *Ps.-Plut. Placita 391a21* = wa-qawmun mina l-ḥadaṯi yarawna annahū (*sc.* al-ǧuzʾa l-raʾīsa min aǧzāʾi l-nafsi) yanbaʿiṯu mina l-dimāġi ilā l-ḥiǧābi *52.10.*

5. ῥέω (*to flow*) : διὰ τί ἀποστλεγγισαμένοις μᾶλλον ῥεῖ ὁ ἱδρὼς ἢ ἐῶσιν ἐπιμεῖναι; *Ps.-Arist. Probl. phys. II 12, 867b4* = mā bālunā iḏā masaḥnā l-ʿaraqa wa-iḏā naššafnāhū ʿan abdāninā yanbaʿiṯu akṯara mimmā iḏā lam namsaḥhu wa-taraknāhu ʿalā l-badani *III 12, 140.1.*

6. προχέομαι *pass.* (*to be poured forth*) : προχέονται δ' ἐκ τῆς ὄψεως ἀκτῖνες μέλαιναι, οὐχὶ πύριναι (μέλαιναι ... πύριναι *Arab.* : πύριναι, οὐχὶ μέλαιναι *codd., ed.*) *Ps.-Plut. Placita 406a11** = wa-qad yanbaʿiṯu mina l-baṣari ayḍan šuʿāʿātun sūdun lā ḍiyāʾiyyatun *57.17.*

7. ἐκφύω *c. gen.* (*to grow out from*) : ἀπὸ δὲ τοῦ ἡγεμονικοῦ ἑπτὰ μέρη ἐστὶ τῆς ψυχῆς ἐκπεφυκότα *Ps.-Plut. Placita 410a31* = wa-li hāḏā l-ǧuzʾi l-raʾīsi sabʿatu aǧzāʾin tanbaʿiṯu mina l-nafsi *60.17.*

8. γεννῶμαι *pass.* (*to be produced, brought forth*) : τὸ δὲ ὡς μιᾶς ... αἴτιον ἀνάγκη πρὸ τῶν πάντων εἶναι, καὶ ἀπ' αὐτοῦ πάντα ... γεννᾶσθαι *Proclus El. theol. 21 : 24.20* = wa-huwa (*sc.* al-wāḥidu llaḏī huwa ʿillatun) qabla l-ašyāʾi ... iḍṭirāran wa-kulluhā minhu yanbaʿiṯu *21.16.*

9. ἐπαγωγός (*bringing on, producing*) : ἔστιν ἡ κράμβη γυναιξὶν ἐμμήνων ἐπαγωγός *Cass. Bass. Geopon. XII, 17.3* = wa-iḏā taʾaḫḫara ṭamṯu mraʾatin ... fa-ṭubiḫa l-karanbu wa-suqiyat minhu tilka l-marʾatu ... inbaʿaṯat ṭamṯuhā *WGAÜ Suppl. I, 373.10.*

10. *paraphr.* συνάπτω *intrans., c.* εἰς (*to some into connection with*): διὰ τὸ συνάπτειν τὰς ἀπὸ τοῦ στόματος (στόματος *Arab.* : σώματος *codd., ed.*) εἰς αὐτὴν φλέβας *Ps.-Plut. Placita 407a17** = bi-l-ʿurūqi llatī tanbaʿiṯu ilayhi mina l-fami *58.17.*

انبعاث VII. inbiʿāṯun *maṣdar*

1. *transl.* ὁρμή (*impulse*) *and its derivatives*

1.1 ὁρμή (*impulse*) : παρὰ τὴν ὁρμὴν *Arist. Metaph. Λ 7, 1072b12* = ġayru l-inbiʿāṯi *1608v3* ⟼ Μητρόδωρος ἐξ (ἐξ *B, Arab.* : *om. codd. cett., ed.*) ὑδατώδους (ὑδατώδους *om. Arab.*) ἀναθυμιάσεως διὰ τὴν ἡλιακὴν ἔκκαυσιν γίνεσθαι <ἀφ'> (*Arab. ut vid.*) ὁρμὴν πνευμάτων (*sc.* τοὺς ἀνέμους) *Ps.-Plut. Placita 375a7** = wa-ammā Miṭrūḏurus fa-yarā anna l-riyāḥa taḥduṯu min inbiʿāṯi l-hawāʾi llaḏī yakūnu ʿani l-buḫāri l-kāʾini ʿan iḥrāqi l-šamsi *43.26;* τὰ μὲν ὑγρότερα (ὑγρότερα *coni. Reiske ex Arab.* : οἰκειότερα *ed.*) εἰς τὸ ὕδωρ τὴν ὁρμὴν ἔχειν *431a8** = fa-mā kāna minhā akṯara ruṭūbatan kāna nbiʿāṯuhū ilā al-māʾi *72.26; 410a28 = 60.16.*

1.2 *sem.; etym.;* ὁρμητικός (*impulsive*) = lahu nbiʿāṯun : τὰ γὰρ ζῷα ὁρμητικὰ εἶναι καὶ αἰσθητικά *Ps.-Plut. Placita 438a13* = li-anna l-ḥayawānāti lahā nbiʿāṯun wa-lahā ḥissun *76.7;* τινὰ γὰρ ψυχῆς ὁρμητικῆς εἶναι καὶ ἐπιθυμητικῆς *438a16* = li-anna kulla nafsin lahā nbiʿāṯun wa-lahā šahwatun *76.10.*

2. ῥύσις (*flow*) : τοῦ μὲν γὰρ ἦρος, τὰ μελαγχολικά, καὶ τὰ μανικά, καὶ τὰ ἐπιληπτικά, <καὶ τὰ ἀποπληκτικά> (*add. Arab.* : *om. codd., ed.*), καὶ αἵματος ῥύσιες *Hippocr. Aphor. III.20** = qad yaʿriḍu fī l-rabīʿi l-waswāsu l-sawdāwiyyu wa-l-ǧunūnu wa-l-ṣarʿu wa-l-saktatu wa-nbiʿāṯu l-dami *25.2.*

3. *sem.; etym.; transl.* ῥήγνυμι *intrans.* (*to break forth, be let loose*)

3.1 αἱμορραγία (*haemorrhage, violent bleeding*) = inbiʿāṯu l-dami : καὶ γὰρ φλεγμοναὶ ἐπιγίγνονται τούτοισι καὶ αἱμορραγίαι *Hippocr. Progn. 226.5* = wa-ḏālika annahū qad tatbaʿu ḏālika awrāmun wa-nbiʿāṯu l-dami *229.4.*

3.2 αἱμορρήγνυμι (*to bleed violently*) = lā yazālu l-damu yanbaʿiṯu : αἱμορραγοῦντες γὰρ διὰ τοῦ στόματος καὶ τῶν μυκτήρων ... οὕτως ἀπόλλυνται *Galen Ther. Pis. 234.13* = lā yazālu l-damu yanbaʿiṯu min minḫarayhi wa-famihī ... ḥattā yahliku *111b9.*

4. ἀγωγή (*carrying away, moving on*) : καὶ τὰς τοῦ αἵματος ἀγωγὰς ἐπέχει *Galen Simpl. medic. XI, 819.4* = wa-yaḥbisu nbiʿāṯa l-dami *versio A WGAÜ, 72.14.*

5. ἀπόκρισις (*excretion*) : καὶ τὰς ἀμέτρους τῶν αἱμάτων ἀποκρίσεις εἴωθεν ἐπέχειν *Galen Ther. Pis. 274.4* = wa-yaḥbisu nbiʿāṯa l-dami l-mufriṭa *124b3.*

6. εἴσκρισις (*intromission*) : κατὰ εἴσκρισιν ἀκτίνων οὐκ εἰδώλων *Ps.-Plut. Placita 423a23* = ʿalā qadri nbiʿāṯi l-šuʿāʿāti lā nbiʿāṯi l-ṣuwari *68.11.*

منبعث **VII. munbaʿiṯun** *act. part.*

1. ἠγμένος *pass. part. of* ἄγομαι. (*to be carried away, sent forth from*) : Πλάτων τὴν φωνὴν ὁρίζεται πνεῦμα διὰ στόματος ἀπὸ διανοίας ἠγμένον *Ps.-Plut. Placita 408a1* = inna Aflāṭūn yaḥuddu l-ṣawta bi-annahū rīḥun yaḫruǧu mina l-fami munbaʿiṯun ʿani l-fikri *58.21.*

2. τεταμένος *pass. part. of* τείνομαι (*to be stretched out*) : αἰσθητήρια λέγεται πνεύματα νοερὰ ἀπὸ τοῦ ἡγεμονικοῦ ἐπὶ τὰ ὄργανα τεταμένα *Ps.-Plut. Placita 394a8* = qīla fī l-rūḥi l-ʿaqliyyi l-munbaʿiṯi mina l-ʿuḍwi l-raʾīsi ilā l-ālāti innahū ḥawāssun *53.6.*

بعد

بعد **I. baʿuda** *abs. or c.* min *or* ʿan

1. *transl. various compound verbs and expressions with the prep.* ἀπό *which lends them the meaning of "away from"*

1.1 ἀπέχω (*to be at a distance, far from*) **(a)** *abs.* : ταὐτὸ δ' ἐπιστάμεθα ... κατ' ἀναλογίαν, ὡς ἂν ἀπέχοντες πλεῖστον *Theophr. Princ. 9a7* = wa-qad naqifu ʿalā anna l-šayʾa wāḥidun bi-ʿaynihī ... bi-l-muqāyasati iḏ kunnā nabʿudu bihā buʿdan kaṯīran *202.9* **(b)** *c.* ʿan : ὁ (*sc.* λόγος) περὶ ... τοῦ πεινῶντος καὶ διψῶντος σφόδρα μέν, ὁμοίως δέ, καὶ τῶν ἐδωδίμων καὶ ποτῶν ἴσον ἀπέχοντος *Arist. Cael. II 13, 295b34* = mā qīla fī l-ʿaṭšāni wa-l-ǧāʾiʿi ǧiddan, wa-qad baʿuda ʿanhu l-ṭaʿāmu wa-l-šarābu bi-l-sawāʾi *versio B 292.1 Badawī* **(c)** *in hend.* naʾā wa-baʿuda minhu : τί γὰρ διαφέρει τὸ τοσονδὶ φάναι μῆκος ἀπέχειν ἢ τοσονδί; *Arist. Cael. I 8, 276b24* = wa-ḏālika anna l-ǧirma iḏā naʾā wa baʿuda min mawḍiʿihī, qalīlan kāna aw kaṯīran, lam yaḫtalif fī ṣūratihī l-batatta *versio C 181.3 Badawī.*

1.2 ἀφίσταμαι *med.* (*to stand away from*) **(a)** baʿuda *c.* min : πλησίον μὲν γὰρ ὄντος τοῦ ἡλίου ὁ τῆς ἀτμίδος ἄνω ῥεῖ ποταμός, ἀφισταμένου δὲ ὁ τοῦ ὕδατος κάτω *Arist. Meteor. I 9, 347a4* = fa-iḏā qarubati l-šamsu mina l-buḫāri ʿalā (*sc.* al-māʾu) ṣāʿidan wa-iḏā baʿudat minhu habaṭa nāzilan *278* ⟷ καὶ τὸ οἴεσθαι μὲν δεῖν πράττειν ... τὰ καλὰ ... ἀφίστασθαι δὲ αὐτῶν διὰ τὰς ἡδονάς *Ps.-Arist. Virt. 6, 1251a27* = wa-ḥīna yufakkiru fī stiʿmāli l-ašyāʾi l-ǧamīlati ... yabʿudu minhā ṭāʿatan li-šahwatin wa-taʿabbudin lahā *versio T 61.16* **(b)** *in hend.;* ḫālafa *c. acc.* wa-baʿuda *c.* ʿan : ὁμοιοῦται μὲν (*sc.* ὁ περισσάρτιος) τῷ ἀρτιοπερίσσῳ, ἀφίσταται δὲ τοῦ ἀρτιάκις ἀρτίου *Nicom. Arithm. 22.14* = fa-innahū (*sc.* zawǧu zawǧi l-fardi) yušbihu ... zawǧa l-fardi wa-yuwāfiquhū wa-yuḫālifu ... zawǧa l-zawǧi wa-yabʿudu ʿanhu *26.14.*

1.3 ἀποχωρίζω (*to separate from*) : τῶν συνδούντων (*sc.* τῶν ὀστῶν) αὐτὰ διασπασθέντων ἀποχωρισθῇ πλεῖστον ἀπ' ἀλλήλων *Galen In De off. med. 887.16* = fa-yatanaḥḥā bi-hāḏā l-sababi ʿaẓmun ʿan ʿaẓmin ḥattā yabʿudu ʿanhu ǧiddan *64.16.*

1.4 ἀποχωρέω (*to go, keep away from*) : μάλιστα δὲ τῶν ῥιζῶν ἀποχωρεῖν πειρῶ *Galen Anat. admin. II, 353.8* = wa-l-yakun akṯaru ḥirṣika wa-ʿināyatika an tabʿuda min uṣūli l-ʿaṣabi *146.5 Garofalo.*

1.5 ἀποτυγχάνω (*to miss* [*one's goal*]) : τοὺς ἀθλητὰς ... διὰ τὴν τοῦ σώματος ἀφυίαν ... ὁρῶμεν ἀποτυγχάνοντας τοῦ τέλους *Galen Med. phil. 3.11* = fa-qad narā l-ṣirrīʿīna yabʿudūna min ġaraḍihim ... li-anna ṭabīʿata abdānihim ġayru mutahayyiʾatin li-l-ṣirāʿi *43.*

1.6 ἀποικέω (*to dwell far from*) : ἦθος κακοῦργον μακρὸν ἀπῴκισται (μακρὸν ἀπῴκισται *mss. S, Vat. gr. 1276, cf. A. Meineke, Fragmenta Comicorum Graecorum, vol. IV* [*Berlin 1841*], *372, Pernigotti, 277* : μακρὰν οἰκίζει *edd. Jaekel, Pernigotti*) θεοῦ *Men. Mon. 319** = al-ḫuluqu l-sayyiʾu yabʿudu mina llāhi wa-mina l-kāffati *II, 20 : 66.1.*

1.7 ἀπολύομαι *med.* (*to be separated from, lose contact*) = *in hend.* fāraqahū wa-baʿuda ʿanhu : οὐδέποτ' ἀπολυθήσεται (*sc.* ἡ ΓΔ γραμμή) τῇ Ε *Arist. Cael. I 5, 272b26* = lam yumkin an yufāriqa l-ḫaṭṭu llaḏī ʿinda ḥarfi l-hāʾi l-battata wa-yabʿuda ʿanhu (*sc.* al-ḫaṭṭi llaḏī ʿinda ḥarfi l-ǧīmi wa-harfi l-dāli) *versio C 157.3 Badawī.*

1.8 ἀπὸ τρόπου (*off the proper way, i.e., unreasonably, in a far-fetched way*) : οὐκ ἄν τις ἀπὸ τρόπου φαίη *Galen Puls. introd. 470.18* = wa-lā yabʿudu (*sic leg. pro* yubʿidu *Ullmann*) man qāla *versio A WGAÜ Suppl. II, 493.22**.

2. *transl. adverbs meaning "far"*

2.1 *transl.* πόρρω (*far off*) *and its derivatives*

2.1.1 πόρρω (*far off, at a distance*) : νεοττεύει δὲ γένος τι αὐτῶν (*sc.* τῶν ἱεράκων) πόρρω *Arist. Hist. anim. VI 7, 564a6* = wa-ǧinsun min aǧnāsi l-buzāti yuʿaššišu fī amākina tabʿudu ʿan sabīli l-nāsi *258.10.*

2.1.2 πορρώτερον/πορρωτέρω *comp.* (*farther from*) : τὸ ἐγγύτερον (*sc.* τῆς ἁπλῆς καὶ πρώτης περιφορᾶς) ... τὸ δὲ πορρώτερον *Arist. Cael. II 10, 291b6* = mā qaruba minhu (*sc.* mina l-kawākibi) mina l-ḥarakati l-ūlā l-basīṭati ... mā baʿuda minhu *versio B 268.4 Badawī* ⟼ ὥσπερ ὁ καθεύδων γεωμέτρης τοῦ ἐγρηγορότος πορρωτέρω *Arist. Gener. anim. II 1, 735a11* = miṯla l-massāḥi l-nāʾimi fa-innahū yuqālu innahū yabʿudu mina l-massāḥi l-mustayqiẓi *59.14* (*where the translator misinterpreted the genitive of comparison as genitive of respect*)*;* πορρωτέρω τῶν οἰκείων ἐστὶν ἀρχῶν (*sc.* ἡ ἀπόδειξις) *II 8, 747b29* = baʿuda (*sc.* al-īḍāḥu) mina l-awāʾili l-ahliyyati *92.15* ⟼ ἡ τοῦ ἡλίου φορὰ διακρίνουσα καὶ συγκρίνουσα τῷ γίγνεσθαι πλησίον ἢ πορρώτερον *Arist. Meteor. I 9, 346b23* ≅ wa-qad taqrubu l-šamsu wa-tabʿudu minhā *265;* φερομένου δὴ τοῦ ἡλίου κύκλῳ, ... πορρωτέρω δὲ γιγνομένου ... συνισταμένης πάλιν τῆς ἀναχθείσης ἀτμίδος εἰς ὕδωρ *II 4, 359b35* = fa-iḏā dārati l-šamsu fī falakihā ... fa-iḏā baʿudat minhā ǧtamaʿa ḏālika l-buḫāru l-ʿālī wa-kaṯufa wa-staḥāla māʾan *608.*

2.1.3 πορρωτάτω *superl.* (*farthest from*) : τὸ μὲν γὰρ (*sc.* ἄστρον) ἐγγυτάτω (*sc.* τῆς ἁπλῆς καὶ πρώτης περιφορᾶς) μάλιστα κρατεῖται, τὸ δὲ πορρωτάτω πάντων ἥκιστα δὶα τὴν ἀπόστασιν *Arist. Cael. II 10, 291b7* = li-anna mā qaruba minhā mina l-ḥarakati l-ūlā l-mabsūṭati (al-basīṭati *versio C*) yalzamu minhā luzūman akṯara, wa-mā baʿuda minhā yalzamu minhā luzūman ḍaʿīfan li-ḥāli buʿdihā minhā *versio B/C 268.4 Badawī* ⟼ αἱ γὰρ ... πορρωτάτω τοῦ ἑνὸς (*sc.* δυνάμεις) ... πεπερασμέναι πάντως εἰσίν *Proclus El. theol. 86 : 80.1* = fa-ṣārati l-ašyāʾu llatī tabʿudu mina l-wāḥidi mutanāhiyatan *86.11.*

2.1.4 πόρρωθεν (*from afar*) : λέγεται γὰρ ὀξὺ ὁρᾶν ... τὸ πόρρωθεν δύνασθαι ὁρᾶν *Arist. Gener. anim. V 1, 780b16* = fa-innahū yuqālu inna l-baṣara ḥāddun iḏā qawiya ʿalā an yubṣira mā baʿuda ʿanhu *179.9;* τὰ μὲν γὰρ ἐξόφθαλμα οὐκ εὐωπὰ πόρρωθεν *780b36* = fa-inna al-ʿayna l-nātiʾata (al-nātiʾata *nos* : al-bāʾinata *ed.*) lā tubṣiru mā baʿuda ʿanhā baṣaran ǧayyidan *179.21*; 781a1 = 179.22; etc.*

2.2 μακράν (*far from*) : οἱ βουβῶνες οὐ μακρὰν τῶν αἰδοίων (*lac. post* αἰδοίων *indic. Pack* : <εἰσὶ> *suppl. Hercher* : *sine lac. fort. Arab.*) οὐδὲ διάφορόν τι σημαίνουσιν *Artem. Onirocr. 52.18** = al-urbiyyatāni lā yabʿudu dalīluhumā min dalīli l-iḥlīli wa-lā baynahū wa-baynahumā ḫtilāfun *99.9.*

3. *sem. concentr.* διάστασιν ἔχειν (*to be separate from*) : κατὰ γὰρ τὰς διαφορὰς δι' ἃς ταῦτα χωρίζουσι καὶ ἄλλα φανεῖται μόρια μείζω (μείζω *om. Arab.*) διάστασιν ἔχοντα τούτων *Arist. De an. III 9, 432a28* = li-annahū bi-qadri l-fuṣūli llatī faṣṣalū lahā fa-ʿarrafū baʿḍahā min baʿḍin bi-qadri ḏālika baʿudati l-aǧzāʾu l-bāqiyatu baʿḍuhā min baʿḍin *80.5.*

4. *paraphr.* πρόειμι *abs.* (*to go forward, proceed*) : πᾶσι δὲ τοῖς μὴ εὐθυεντέροις προϊοῦσιν εὐρύτερον γίνεται τὸ μόριον τοῦτο *Arist. Part. anim. III 14, 675b6* = fa-ammā l-ḥayawānu llaḏī laysa bi-mustaqīmi l-miʿāʾi fa-kullamā baʿuda miʿāʾuhū mina l-baṭni ṣāra awsaʿa *97.7.*

تبعيد II. tabʿīdun *maṣdar*

1. ἀποφορά (*taking away, removal*) : ἀποφάσει γὰρ καὶ ἀποφορᾷ δηλοῖ τὸ ἐναντίον *Arist. Metaph. Θ 2, 1046b14* = fa-innahū (*sic pro* innahū *leg.*) yudallu ʿalā l-ḍiddi bi-l-sālibati wa-bi-l-tabʿīdi (wa-bi-l-tabʿīdi *scripsit Bouyges* : *ms. parum clare; cf. app. crit. ad loc.*) *1115.7*.*

باعد III. bāʿada *c. acc. or* bi- *and* ʿan / min

1. ἀπάγω *transitive* (*to keep s.th. at a distance from s.th.*) **(a)** bāʿada *c. acc. et* ʿan : δύο μύες, ὁ μὲν ἀπάγων (*sc.* τὸν μέγαν δάκτυλον) ἐπὶ πλεῖστον ἁπάντων τῶν δακτύλων *Galen Anat. admin. II, 264.14* = ʿaḍalatāni ... iḥdāhumā tubāʿiduhā (*sc.* al-iṣbaʿa l-ʿuẓmā) ʿan ǧamīʿi l-aṣābiʿi mubāʿadatan kaṯīratan *56.18 Garofalo* **(b)** *in hend.* ḏahaba *c.* bi- ... wa-bāʿada *c. acc. et* ʿan : ὁ τοῦ μεγάλου δακτύλου (*sc.* μῦς) ..., ὁ τῶν ἄλλων αὐτὸν ἐπὶ πλεῖστον ἀπάγων *Galen Anat. admin. II, 269.3* = ʿaḍalati l-iṣbaʿi l-ʿuẓmā llatī taḏhabu bi-hāḏihi l-iṣbaʿi wa-tubāʿiduhā ʿani l-aṣābiʿi l-uḫari ilā buʿdin kaṯīrin *62.4 Garofalo.*

2. ἀπαρτάω (*to detach, separate*) : δεῖ δὲ ... μήτε μακρὰν ἀπαρτᾶν μήτε σύνδεσμον πρὸ συνδέσμου ἀποδιδόναι *Arist. Rhet. III 5, 1407a24* = fa-qad yanbaġī allā yubāʿida (*post* yubāʿida *lac. indic. Lyons* : baynahā *add. Badawī* : *an* ṭawīlan = μακράν *addendum?*) (*sc.* al-mutakallimu) wa-allā yaḍaʿa ribāṭan *186.4*.*

3. ἐξαιρέω (*to remove, take out of*) : ὀρθῶς ἔοικεν ἡ φύσις τὸ μέλλον ἔσεσθαι ἀγένητον καὶ ἄφθαρτον ἐξελέσθαι ἐκ τῶν ἐναντίων *Arist. Cael.*

I 3, 270a21 = fa-qad waffaqati l-ṭabīʿatu ḥīna ṣayyarat hāḏā l-badana l-karīma ġayra mukawwanin wa-bāʿada bihī mina l-aḍdādi *versio B*.

4. μακράν, *sc.* ποιέω (*[to make] long*) : Πλάτων δὲ καὶ οἱ Πυθαγόρειοι μακρὰν τὴν ἀπόστασιν (*sc.* ποιοῦσιν) *Theophr. Princ. 11a27* = fa-ammā Aflāṭun wa-šīʿat Fūṯāġūras fa-innahum bāʿadū l-amra buʿdan kaṯīran *220.3*.

5. ἐκποδών *adv.* (*removed from, out of the way*) : ὅκου δεῖ (*sc.* τὰ ὄργανα)· μὴ ἐμποδὼν τῷ ἔργῳ, μηδὲ ἐκποδὼν τῇ ἀναιρέσει *Hippocr. Off. med. 33.12* = wa-ammā ḥayṯu (*sc.* al-ālātu) lā yakūnu šayʾun yaʿūqu ʿani l-ʿamali wa-laysa (*sic leg. pro* fa-laysa) yakūnu šayʾun (*sic leg. pro* šayʾan) yubāʿidu l-tanāwula *5.5**.

مباعدة **III. mubāʿadatun** *maṣdar*

1. *used as cognate accusative following* bāʿada, *see above,* bāʿada 1a.

أبعد **IV. abʿada** *c. acc. and* ʿan / min

1. *transl. various compound verbs with the prep.* ἀπό *which lends them the meaning of "away from"*

1.1. ἀφίστημι *act.* (*to set apart at a distance*) : τὴν φύσιν ... ὅτι πλεῖστον ἀποστῆσαι (*sc.* τὰ ἄστρα) τῶν ἐχόντων ὄργανα πρὸς κίνησιν *Arist. Cael. II 8, 290a34* = an takūna (*sc.* l-ṭabīʿatu) ... abʿadathā (*sc.* al-nuǧūma) mina l-ašyāʾi llatī lahā ālatun li-ḥarakatihā *versio B 261.15 Badawī*.

1.2 ἀπέχω (*to stand away from s.th., i.e., protrude*) : κατὰ δὲ τὸ μέσον τῆς γονῆς τῷ πνεύματι δίοδος ... καὶ ταύτῃ (τοῦτο, *scil.* τὸ πνεῦμα, *ut intell. Arab.*) τοῦ ὑμένος ἀπέχει τι λεπτὸν (τὸ λεπτὸν *ut intell. Arab.*) καὶ τῆς γονῆς *Hippocr. Nat. puer. 55.1* = wa-yakūnu fī wasaṭi l-maniyyi li-l-rūḥi ṭarīqun ... wa-hāḏihi l-rīḥu hiya tubʿidu riqāqa l-ḥuǧubi ʿani l-maniyyi *48.13* (*where the translator misunderstood the precise meaning of* ἀπέχω *and misread both* ταύτῃ *and* τι).

2. παρατρέχω (*to run by, i.e., slight s.o.*) : ξένους πένητας μὴ παραδράμῃς ἰδών *Men. Mon. 542* = iḏā raʾayta ġurabāʾa fuqarāʾa fa-lā tubʿidhum *WGAÜ Suppl. II, 55.9*.

تباعد **VI. tabāʿada** *abs. and c.* min / ʿan

1. *transl. various compound verbs with the prep.* ἀπό *which lends them the meaning of "away from"*

1.1 ἀφίστημι *intrans. in 2. aor. and 2. perf. act., and in med.* (*to stand away from, be separated*) **(a)** tabāʿada *c.* min *or* ʿan : ἄμφω γὰρ αὗται (*sc.* ἀρετή τις καὶ ἡ ἐλευθεριότης) τοῦ μὲν μεγάλου ἀφεστᾶσι *Arist. Eth. Nic. IV 4, 1125b4* = fa-inna hātayni l-faḍīlatayni kiltayhimā qad tabāʿadatā mina l-amri l-ʿaẓīmi *269.15* ⟼ τῶν ψαυόντων μὲν ἀλλήλων ὀστῶν φύσει ..., ἀποστάντων δὲ διά τι πάθημα *Galen In De off. med. 887.9* = al-ʿiẓām allatī tumāssu aḥaduhā l-āḫara bi-l-ṭabʿi ... illā annahā qad tabāʿadat wāḥidan (*sic ed. pro* wāḥidun) ʿani l-āḫari bi-sababi āfatin aṣābathā *64.11*⊗ **(b)** *in hend.* tanaḥḥā wa-tabāʿada *c.* ʿan : ἀφίσταται γὰρ αὕτη (αὕτη, *sc.* ἡ τῶν μυῶν συζυγία, *A, Arab., Garofalo* : αὐτὴ *P, Kühn*) κατὰ βραχὺ τοῦ περιτοναίου *Galen Anat. admin. II, 520.3** = wa-hāḏā l-zawǧu yatanaḥḥā ʿani l-ṣifāqi qalīlan qalīlan wa-yatabāʿadu *320.14 Garofalo.*

1.2 ἀπέχω *c. gen.* (*to keep away from, abstain*) : καὶ τὸ μὲν (*sc.* τῆς ψυχῆς) διὰ μοχθηρίαν ἀλγεῖ ἀπεχόμενόν τινων *Arist. Eth. Nic. IX 4, 1166b20* = fa-baʿḍu anfusihim taʾallama li-l-radāʾati iḏā tabāʿada ʿan ašyāʾa *499.7* ⟼ ἰσχυέτω (*sc.* ὁ ἀνήρ) καὶ ὑγιαινέτω καὶ σιτίων ἀπεχέσθω τῶν μὴ ξυμφερόντων τῷ πρήγματι *Hippocr. Superf. 90.11* = wa-l-yakun (*sc.* al-raǧulu) ṣaḥīḥan ġayra saqīmin wa-yatabāʿad mina l-aġḏiyati l-ġalīẓati l-laziǧati l-ḥirrīfati *17.11.*

1.3. ἀπάγω *intrans.* (*to draw o.s. away from*) : πολὺ γὰρ ἀπάγοντες τοῦ ἁμαρτάνειν εἰς τὸ μέσον ἥξομεν *Arist. Eth. Nic. II 9, 1109b5* = fa-innā kulla-mā tabāʿadnā mina l-ḫaṭaʾi qarubnā mina l-tawassuṭi *183.4.*

1.4 ἀποχωρέω (*to depart, retreat from*) : διὸ δεῖ τὸν στοχαζόμενον τοῦ μέσου πρῶτον μὲν ἀποχωρεῖν τοῦ μᾶλλον ἐναντίου *Arist. Eth. Nic. II 9, 1109a31* = fa-li-ḏālika yanbaġī li-man qaṣada qaṣda l-mutawassiṭi an yatabāʿada min akṯari l-ṭarafayni muḍāddatan li-l-mutawassiṭi *181.12.*

1.5 ἀπαλλάσσομαι *med.* (*to depart; in context*: *leave home*) = tabāʿada ʿan ābāʾihī : ὅταν μετὰ πολλῶν ἀνατραφῇ φροντίδων, ἀπαλλάσσεται (*sc.* ἡ θυγάτηρ) *Artem. Onirocr. 222.3* = fa-iḏā šabbat (*sc.* al-ibnatu) wa-adrakat baʿda hammin kaṯīrin tabāʿadat ʿan ābāʾihā *407.2.*

2. *transl.* διΐσταμαι (*to stand apart*) *and its deribvatives*

2.1 διΐσταμαι *med.* (*to stand apart from one another*) : πλὴν ὅσον ἀποχωροῦσί τε (*sc.* οἱ ὑμένες) καὶ διΐστανται κατ' ἐκεῖνο τὸ μέρος, ἵνα περ ἡ καρδία κεῖται *Galen Anat. admin. II, 521.15* = ġayra annahā (*sc.

al-aġšiyata) tatafarraqu baʿḍun min baʿḍin wa-tatabāʿadu fī l-mawḍiʿi llaḏī fīhi l-qalbu mawḍūʿun *322.15 Garofalo.*

2.2 *sem. concentr.;* γίγνεται διάστασις (*to diverge, draw apart*) : ἤδη γὰρ ἄν ἐγεγόνει διάστασις τῶν ἄστρων ἐν τῷ ἀπείρῳ χρόνῳ *Arist. Cael. II 6, 288b10* = la-tabāʿadati l-kawākibu baʿḍuhā ʿan baʿḍin fī ṭūli l-dahri ... fa-tatabāʿadu l-kawākibu baʿḍuhā min baʿḍin *versio B 251.2, 6 Badawī; sim. versio A 71a8, 13.*

3. ἐξίσταμαι (*to stand aside from, leave*) : τὸ γὰρ μεταβάλλον, ἐξ οὗ μεταβάλλει, ἐξίσταται ἢ ἀπολείπει αὐτό *Arist. Phys. VI 5, 235b9* = wa-ḏālika anna l-mutaġayyira yatabāʿadu ʿammā minhu taġayyara aw yufāriquhū *666.7.*

4. *sem. concentr.;* πορρωτέρω διέρχομαι, γίγνομαι **(a)** *abs.* : πάντα γὰρ τοῦ βιασαμένου πορρωτέρω γιγνόμενα βραδύτερον φέρεται. *Arist. Cael. I 8, 277b7* = li-anna kulla šayʾin tabāʿada min dāfiʿihī wa-ḍāġiṭihī yakūnu sulūkuhū sulūkan baṭīʾan *versio B 185.13 Badawī* **(b)** ǧāwaza wa-tabāʿada (*where* tabaʿāda *transl.* πόρρω διέρχομαι *and* ǧāwaza *renders the comparative in* πορρωτέρω) : οὐκ ἐνδέχεται πορρωτέρω διελθεῖν τοῦ μέσου (*sc.* τὸ ὑφιστάμενον [σῶμα]) *Arist. Cael. I 6, 273a12* = lam yumkin an yuǧāwiza (yaǧūza *versio B*) l-wasaṭa (*sc.* al-šayʾu l-rāsibu) wa-lā yatabāʿada minhu *versio B/C 159.1 Badawī.*

5. *sem. metathesis; neg. / affirm. conceptual transformation* : μὴ σφόδρα ἐγγύς (*not very close*) = tabāʿada buʿdan laysa bi-l-kaṯīri (*not very far from each other*) : καὶ τὰς ῥίζας ἀλλήλαις συμπλέκειν, κἂν μὴ σφόδρα ἐγγὺς οὖσαι τυγχάνωσιν *Cass. Bass. Geopon. X, 29.5* = wa-ḫtalaṭat ʿurūquhumā wa-in tabāʿadā buʿdan laysa bi-l-kaṯīri *WGAÜ Suppl. I, 306.21.*

تباعد **VI. tabāʿudun** *maṣdar*

1. *transl. various compound verbs with the prep.* ἀπό *which lends them the meaning of "away from"*

1.1 ἀφίσταμαι *med.* (*to set off, i.e., a starting point; to stand away*) **(a)** *abs.* : εἴπερ καὶ τὸ μικρὸν παραβῆναι τῆς ἀληθείας ἀφισταμένοις γίνεται πόρρω μυριοπλάσιον *Arist. Cael. I 5, 271b9* = li-anna man ǧāwaza l-ḥaqqa qalīlan kāna tabāʿuduhū ribwātin kaṯīratan *versio B* **(b)** *in hend.* rafḍun wa-tabāʿudun min : Ἀνδρέου δὲ καὶ τῶν ὁμοίως ἀλαζόνων ἀφίστασθαι χρή *Galen Simpl. medic. XI, 796.8* = wa-ammā kutubu Andriyās wa-ašbāhihī min ahli l-ʿuǧbi bi-raʾyihim fa-yanbaġī lakum rafḍuhā wa-l-tabāʿudu minhā *versio A WGAÜ, 152.7.*

1.2 ἀπέχω (*to be at a distance from*) **(a)** *abs.* : οἷον τὰ κατὰ διάμετρον· ἀπέχει γὰρ πλεῖστον *Arist. Phys. VIII 8, 264b16* = <miṯālu> ḏālika mā kāna ʿalā l-quṭri fa-inna l-tabāʿuda baynahumā abʿadu mā yakūnu *911.12* **(b)** *sem. amplif.; used as cognate accus. to* mutabāʿidun *transl.* ἀπέχω *below,* mutabāʿidun 2.

1.3 ἀπολύομαι *med.* (*to be separated, apart*) = *in hend.* iftirāqun wa-tabāʿudun : εἰ μὲν οὖν ἄμφω (*sc.* ἡ τὸ Α φερομένη γραμμὴ παρὰ τὴν Β) κινοῖντο εἰς τοὐναντίον, θᾶττον ἂν ἀπολύοιντο *Arist. Cael. I 5, 272a26* = fa-in kānat ḥarakatu aḥadihimā (*sc.* al-ḫaṭṭayni) muqābilatan li-ḥarakati l-āḫari (*sic leg. cum mss.*) fa-ftirāquhumā wa-tabāʿuduhumā yakūnu asraʿa firāqan *versio C 153.7 Badawī.*

1.4 ἀπών *act. part. of* ἄπειμι (*to be absent*) : ἀλλ᾽ ὅταν καὶ ἀπόντα ποθῇ (πάθῃ *ut intell. Arab.* [*Arberry*]) καὶ τῆς παρουσίας ἐπιθυμῇ *Arist. Eth. Nic. IX 5, 1167a6** = bal iḏā uṣība bi-tabāʿudihī štahā qurbahū ayḍan *501.4.*

1.5 ἀποφορά (*taking away, removal*) : ἡ γὰρ στέρησις ἡ πρώτη τὸ ἐναντίον, αὕτη δὲ ἀποφορὰ θατέρου *Arist. Metaph. Θ 2, 1046b15* = fa-inna l-ʿadama l-awwala huwa l-ḍiddu wa-hāḏā huwa tabāʿudu aḥadihimā *1115.8.*

1.6 ἀποβάλλομαι *pass.* (*to be removed, rejected*) : ἐπειδὰν δὲ ἀποκριθῶσιν (*sc.* οἱ ἕλμινθες), ἀποβληθῆναι τοὺς τοιούτους ἀνθρώπους σημαίνουσι *Artem. Onirocr. 207.23* = fa-iḏā raʾā l-insānu ka-annahā (*sc.* ḥayyāti l-baṭni) taḫruğu minhu fa-innahā tadullu ʿalā tabāʿudi qawmin širārin munağissīna (munağissīna *corr. Endress, p. 344* : nağisīna *ed.*) *375.8**.

2. διΐστημι *intrans.* 2nd *perf.* (*to stand apart, be separate*) : διὰ τὸ πλεῖστον ἀλλήλων διεστάναι τό τε συμβεβηκὸς καὶ τὸ ᾧ συμβέβηκεν *Porph. Isag. 21.6* = wa-ḏālika li-kaṯrati l-tabāʿudi bayna l-ʿaraḍi wa-l-šayʾi llaḏī yaʿriḍu lahū *1102.9 / fol. 156a.*

3. *paraphr.;* ξενικός (*for a foreigner*; *in context, s.o. distant*) = *in expr.* ʿalā l-tabāʿudi : ἡ δὲ ξενικὴ φιλία ἡ ἀπὸ συστάσεως καὶ διὰ γραμμάτων γινομένη *Ps.-Arist. Div. 3a10* = wa-l-maḥabbatu llatī takūnu ʿalā l-tabāʿudi hiya llatī takūnu bi-l-mukātabāti wa-l-mulāṭafāti *versio T 56.22.*

متباعد **VI. mutabāʿidun** *act. part.*

1. διΐστημι *intrans.* 2nd *perf. and pluperf.* (*to stand apart, be separate*) : μανὸν δὲ τῷ διεστάναι (*sc.* τὰ μόρια) ἀπ᾽ ἀλλήλων *Arist. Cat. 8, 10a21* = wa-yuqālu mutaḫalḫilun bi-anna ağzāʾahū mutabāʿidatun baʿḍuhā min baʿḍin *58.21 / fol. 171a* ⊣ τὰς δὲ διαφορὰς ... θεωρητέον ... καὶ ἐξ ἄλλου πρὸς ἄλλο τῶν μὴ πολὺ λίαν διεστηκότων, οἷον τίνι αἴσθησις ἐπιστήμης· ἐπὶ μὲν γὰρ τῶν πολὺ διεστηκότων κατάδηλοι παντελῶς αἱ διαφοραί *Arist. Top. I 16, 108a4-5* = wa-yağibu an nanẓura (*sic leg. pro* yunẓara *ed.*) fī ḥāli l-fuṣūli ... ayḍan fī llatī min ğinsin bi-l-qiyāsi ilā llatī min ğinsin āḫara ġayrihī min ġayri an yakūna baʿḍuhā min baʿḍin mutabāʿidan buʿdan kaṯīran ka-qawlinā bi-māḏā yuḫālifu l-ḥissu l-ʿilma li-anna l-fuṣūla fī l-ašyāʾi l-mutabāʿidati buʿdan kaṯīran bayyinatun ğiddan *518.13*-14 / fol. 252b.*

2. ἀπέχω (*to be at a distance, far from*) : δῆλον γὰρ ὡς ἀνάλογον ἔχει, καθάπερ ὕδωρ πρὸς γῆν, καὶ τὰ πλεῖον ἀεὶ ἀπέχοντα τῶν στοιχείων (στοιχείων JS^1, *Arab.* : συστοίχων EHS^p, *ed.*) *Arist. Cael. II 4, 287b21** = wa-hāḏā bayyinun wāḍiḥun wa-ḏālika annahū ka-mā bayna buʿdi samki l-māʾi min samki l-arḍi, wa-ka-buʿdi samki l-usṭuqussāti l-mutabāʿidati tabāʿudan kaṯīran, fa-ka-ḏālika buʿdu samki ğirmi l-samāʾi min sāʾiri l-ağrāmi *versio B 245.15* ⊣ τὰ μὲν γὰρ γένει διαφέροντα ... ἀπέχει πλέον *Arist. Metaph. I 4, 1055a7* = fa-innahū ammā llatī tuḫālifu bi-l-ğinsi fa-... hiya mutabāʿidatun akṯara *1300.13.*

3. πόρρω *adv.* (*far off, at a distance*) : ἐν οἷς οὐκ ἔστ' (ἔστ' *Arab., Garofalo* : ἐτ' *P, ed.*) ἀγγεῖα μεγάλα καὶ πόρρω τὰ σπλάγχνα *Galen Anat. admin. II, 566.4** = ḥayṯu laysa ʿurūqun wa-širyānātun kabīratun (*sic leg. c. Garofalo in app. crit. pro* kaṯīratun *ed.*) wa-ḥayṯu l-aḥšāʾu mutabāʿidatun *378.2* Garofalo.*

4. *sem. amplif.;* ἀκρότης (*an extreme of s.th.*) = mutabāʿidun fī l-ṭarafi : ὡς οὖν ἀκροτήτων δύο, κύβου τε καὶ σκαληνοῦ *Nicom. Arithm. 108.1* = fa-yakūnu l-nawʿāni llaḏāni ḏakarnā nawʿayni mutabāʿidayni fī l-ṭarafi aʿnī nawʿa l-mukaʿʿabati wa-nawʿa l-šakli llaḏī yuqālu lahū siqālīnūs (*sic leg.*) *84.9**.

بَعْدَ **baʿda** *prep.*

A. 1-10. translates prepositions with the basic meaning "after"

B. 11-35. translates adverbs, adjectives (including participles), and conjunctions expressing or implying posteriority or succession

C. 36-38. used in expressions translating Greek phrases expressing posteriority and succession

min baʿdi *c. gen.*
baʿda an *conj.*

بَعْدَ ba‘da *prep.*

A. *transl. prepositions meaning explicitly or implicitly "after"*

1. *transl.* μετά (*after*) *alone and in compounds*

1.1 μετά *c. acc.* (*after, of time and place*) : ὁ γὰρ ἄνθρωπος μόνον ... μετὰ τὴν προσπεσοῦσαν αὐτῷ φαντασίαν περί τινος ὡς πρακτέου οἷός τε ζητεῖν *Alex. An. mant. [Lib. arb.] 172.26* = wa-ḏālika anna l-insāna waḥdahū ... yumkinuhū ba‘da l-taḫayyuli llaḏī yalqāhu an yabḥaṯa ‘an ğamī‘i mā yağibu an yuf‘ala (*or* yaf‘ala) *193.13* ⟼ ὥστε μετὰ τὸ γεγονέναι τὸ γίνεσθαι ὑπάρχειν ἐν τοῖς πράγμασιν *Arist. An. post. II 12, 95b2* = ḥattā yakūna ma‘nā annahū yakūnu mawğūdan fī l-umūri ba‘da ma‘nā qad kāna *457.5 / fol. 232a; II 13, 96b19 = 464.1 / fol. 234b* ⟼ μετὰ τὰς πρώτας οὐσίας ... τὰ εἴδη καὶ τὰ γένη δεύτεραι οὐσίαι λέγονται *Arist. Cat. 2, 2b29* = al-anwā‘u wa-l-ağnāsu ... tuqālu ba‘da l-ğawhari l-awwali ğawāhira ṯawāniya *38.11 / fol. 162a* ⟼ μετὰ τὰς τῶν καρπῶν συγκομιδάς *Arist. Eth. Nic. VIII 9, 1160a26* = ba‘da (ba‘da *ms., cf. Ullmann NE I, 66ult.* : ‘inda *ed.*) ğam‘i l-ṯimāri *459.3*; ἆρ' οὖν μετὰ τοῦτο ἐπισκεπτέον *X 9, 1180b28* = fa-hal ba‘da hāḏā yanbaġī an nafḥaṣa *577.14* ⟼ μικρᾶς ἀρχῆς μετακινουμένης πολλὰ συμμεταβάλλειν εἴωθε τῶν μετὰ τὴν ἀρχήν *Arist. Gener. anim. I 2, 716b4* = iḏā taġayyara šay'un yasīrun mina l-bādi'i l-awwali yataġayyaru bi-taġayyurihī ašyā'u kaṯīratun mina llaḏī ba‘da ḏālika l-awwali *5.9; I 4, 717b3 = 8.6; etc.* ⟼ μετὰ δὲ ταῦτα περὶ τῶν πεζῶν λεκτέον *Arist. Hist. anim. V 1, 539a13* = wa-ba‘dahū na'ḫuḏu fī ḏikri ... l-ḥayawāni l-maššā'i *202.5; V 14, 545a13 = 224.17; etc.* ⟼ μετὰ γὰρ (γὰρ *cet. codd., Arab.* : δὲ *Z²U², Louis*) τὴν κοιλίαν ἡ τῶν ἐντέρων ἔγκειται φύσις πᾶσι τοῖς ζῴοις *Arist. Part. anim. III 14, 675a31** = a‘nī li-anna ṭibā‘a l-mi‘ā'i mawḍū‘un ba‘da l-baṭni fī ğamī‘i l-ḥayawāni *96.16*; μετὰ δὲ τὸ στόμα τοῖς μαλακίοις ἐστὶ στόμαχος μακρός *IV 5, 678b25* = wa-li-l-ḥayawāni llaḏī yusammā bi-l-yūnāniyyati mālāqiyā ma‘idatun ṭawīlatun ba‘da l-fami *107.2; sim. 682a16 = 117.2; III 14, 675b9 = 97.9*; *etc.* ⟼ μετὰ τοῦτο θεωρητέον τίνι διαφέρει ὁ μαθηματικὸς τοῦ φυσικοῦ *Arist. Phys. I 2, 193b22* = fa-qad yanbaġī an nanẓura ba‘da ḏālika fī l-farqi bayna l-ta‘ālīmiyyi wa-bayna l-ṭabī‘iyyi mā huwa *90.5;* τί μετὰ τί γίγνεται *II 7, 198a34* = ayyu šay'in ba‘da ayyi šay'in yakūnu *139.15; V 3, 226b29 = 540.17 (v. supra* atā *c.* bi- *7, I 25.25)* ⟼ οὐ γάρ ποτε ἐρεῖ τις ὡς οὐ μετὰ τὴν ὄψιν αὐτὴν ἀποβαίνει τὰ τοιαῦτα *Artem. Onirocr. 6.9* = wa-ḏālika annahū lā yumkinu aḥadan (aḥadan *ms., cf. Rosenthal, 141* : aḥad *ed.*) an yaqūla inna hāḏihi l-ašyā'a ... laysa innamā takūnu ba‘da l-ru'yā *13.4*;*

87.12 = 161.10; etc. ⟼ μετὰ τὴν κάθαρσιν *Diosc. Mat. med. I, 250.5 =* baʿda ṭuhrihā *vetus transl. Ullmann Unters., 184* ⟼ μετὰ δὲ τοῦτο οἴνου μὲν γεύεσθαι *Galen An. virt. 68.6 =* wa-ammā baʿda ḏālika fa-l-yašrabū l-šarāba *35.18; 55.16 = 27.6* (*v. supra* āḫaru 1.3.1, *I 102.15*) ⟼ ποικίλη δὲ καὶ ἡ μετὰ τὰς φρένας νομὴ τῶν νεύρων τούτων *Galen Nerv. diss. 842.16 =* wa-qismatu hāḏihi l-aʿṣābi fī-mā baʿda l-ḥiǧābi qismatun mutafanninatun *107.1; 851.16 = 114.4; etc.* ⟼ μετὰ τὸ δῆγμα *Galen Ther. Pis. 215.12 =* baʿda l-nahšati *105b7; 239.16 = 113a9; etc.* ⟼ μετὰ ... τὴν ἑβδόμην *Hippocr. Diaet. acut. 44.9 =* baʿda l-yawmi l-sābiʿi *11.8* ⟼ μετὰ τὴν νοῦσον χρόνῳ τήκεται τὸ σῶμα *Hippocr. Nat. hom. 198.11 =* baʿda maraḍihī yaḏūbu (*sc.* al-badanu) ʿalā ṭūli l-zamāni *21.18* ⟼ μετὰ τὸ πρῶτον κύημα *Hippocr. Superf. 72.10 =* baʿda l-ḥabali l-awwali *1.11; 96.7 = 24.1* ⟼ καὶ τούτων αὐτῶν ἡγήσεται μὲν διπλάσιος, μετ' αὐτὸν δὲ τριπλάσιος *Nicom. Arithm. 66.4 =* wa-llaḏī yatawalladu minhā awwalan hāḏā l-ḍiʿfu wa-baʿda ḏālika l-ṯalāṯatu l-amṯāli *56.9; 97.9(bis) = 76.22(bis); etc.* ⟼ *Ps.-Arist. Mund. 2, 392a33 = F 89a4* (*v. supra* āfatun 1.5b, *I 604.19*) ⟼ τοῦ δ' ὁρατοῦ κόσμου προτέραν μὲν εἶναι τὴν ψυχήν, μετὰ δὲ ταύτην τὸ σωματοειδές *Ps.-Plut. Placita 334a13 =* wa-awwalu mā ʿumila mina l-ʿālami l-mubṣari huwa l-nafsu wa-baʿdahā l-šaklu l-ǧusmāniyyu *26.21; 336a9 = 27.12; 345a9 = 31.7* ⟼ τὸ δὲ μετὰ ταῦτ' ἤδη λόγου δεῖται πλείονος *Theophr. Princ. 5a13 =* wa-ammā mā baʿda ḏālika fa-yuḥtāǧu fīhi ilā qawlin ablaġa min hāḏā l-qawli *174.10;* τὰ μετὰ τὰς ἀρχάς *6b19, 7a3 =* mā baʿda l-mabādiʾi *188.7, 190.2.*

1.2 μετά *c. gen.* (*along with*) : ὅταν μετὰ πολλῶν ἀνατραφῇ φροντίδων (*sc.* ἡ θυγάτηρ) ἀπαλλάσσεται *Artem. Onirocr. 222.2 =* fa-iḏā šabbat (*sc.* al-ibnatu) wa-adrakat baʿda hammin kaṯīrin tabāʿadat ʿan ābāʾihā *407.1.*

1.3 *sem.; etym.; transl.* μετά *in* οἱ μεταγενέστεροι (*the later generations*) **(a)** allaḏīna baʿdahum : τούτοις μὲν οὖν τοῖς λόγοις ἐπείθοντο οἱ πρῶτοι· οἱ δὲ μεταγενέστεροι ... *Artem. Onirocr. 111.10 =* wa-hāḏā kāna qawlu l-qudamāʾi l-awwalīna fī ḏālika fa-ammā llaḏīna baʿdahum fa-... *204.12* **(b)** *sem. amplif.* allaḏīna baʿdahum wa-qablanā bi-zumaynin yasīrin : οἱ μὲν πάνυ παλαιοὶ ... οἱ δὲ μεταγενέστεροι ... *Artem. Onirocr. 68.17 =* ammā l-qudamāʾu l-awwalūna mina l-nāsi fa-... wa-ammā llaḏīna baʿdahum wa-qablanā bi-zumaynin yasīrin fa-... *126.12-13.*

1.4 *sem.; etym.; transl.* μετά *in* μεταγιγνώσκω (*to feel repentant after changing one's mind*) = ʿaraḍa lahū baʿda ḏālika nadāmatun : καὶ εἰ μὲν ἀνιῷτο ἐπὶ τῇ συνουσίᾳ ἢ μεταγινώσκοι, φεύξεται τὴν πατρίδα *Artem. Onirocr. 93.13* = fa-in kāna yarā ka-annahū yuǧāmiʿuhā bi-ġayri šahwatin aw yaʿriḍu lahū baʿda ḏālika nadāmatun fa-innahū sa-yuharrabu min bilādihī *171.8.*

2. *transl.* ἐπί (*upon, after*) *alone and in compounds*

2.1 ἐπί *c. dat.* (*upon, after*) : οἰκεῖαι δ' εἰσὶν αἱ ἐπὶ τῇ ἐνεργείᾳ καθ' αὑτὴν γινόμεναι *Arist. Eth. Nic. X 5, 1175b21* = fa-inna l-ḫāṣṣiyyata llatī takūnu baʿda l-fiʿli bi-ʿaynihī *549.9* ⟞ οὔτε μὴν ἄλλα πεντήκοντα ἔτη ἐπὶ τοῖς ἑβδομήκοντα οἷόν τε ζῆσαι *Artem. Onirocr. 201.6* = wa-lākinnahū lā yumkinu an yaʿīša ḫamsīna sanatan baʿda l-sabʿīna sanatan *362.17* ⟞ πυρετὸν ἐπὶ σπασμῷ βέλτιον γενέσθαι ἢ σπασμὸν ἐπὶ πυρετῷ *Hippocr. Aphor. II : 26* = an yakūna (*nos* : anna kawn *A :* lā yakūnu *ed.*) l-ḥummā baʿda l-tašannuǧi ḫayrun (*sic leg.*) min an yakūna l-tašannuǧu baʿda l-ḥummā *14.3-4** ⟞ μετ' αὐτὸν δὲ τριπλάσιος, ἐπὶ δὲ τούτῳ τετραπλάσιος *Nicom. Arithm. 66.5* = wa-baʿda ḏālika l-ṯalāṯatu l-amṯāli wa-baʿda ḏālika l-arbaʿatu l-amṯāli *56.9;* τὸ πρώτιστον εἶδος ἡμιόλιος, ἐπὶ τούτῳ δὲ τὸ μετ' αὐτὸ ἐπίτριτος *66.8* = al-nawʿu l-awwalu minhu wa-huwa l-miṯlu wa-l-niṣfu wa-baʿdahu llaḏī yatlūhu wa-huwa l-miṯlu wa-l-ṯulṯu *56.12; 119.15 = 93.10; etc.* ⟞ ἐπὶ δ' αἰγοκερῆι ὑδροχόος ... τοὺς δὲ μέτα κριός, ταῦρος δ' ἐπὶ τῷ, ἐπ' αὐτῷ (*sic Arab. ut vid.* : ἐπ' αὐτῷ *om. codd., sed vid. app. crit. ad 294a7*) δίδυμοί τε *Ps.-Plut. Placita 294a9-13** (= Aratus *Phaenomena 545-549*) = wa-baʿda l-ǧadyi muskibu l-māʾi ... wa-baʿdahumā kabšun wa-baʿdahū ṯawrun wa-baʿda l-ṯawri tawʾamāni *10.24-26;* Ἐμπεδοκλῆς τὸν μὲν αἰθέρα πρῶτον διακριθῆναι, δεύτερον δὲ τὸ πῦρ ἐφ' ᾧ τὴν γῆν *334a3* = wa-ammā Anbāḏūqlīs fa-yarā anna awwala mā yumayyazu mina l-usṭuqussāti huwa l-aṯīru wa-baʿdahu l-nāru wa-baʿdahu l-arḍu *26.15; 344a16 = 30.25.*

2.2 *sem.; etym.; transl.* ἐπί *in* ἐπιβιβρώσκω (*to eat after s.th. else*) = akala baʿdahū : προβρωθέντα καὶ ἐπιβρωθέντα (καὶ ἐπιβρωθέντα *Paris. gr. 2183, Marc. Venetus 271, Arab.* : *om. codd. cett., ed.*) *Diosc. Mat. med. I, 114.4** = iḏā ukila qablahā aw baʿdahā *vetus transl. Ullmann Unters., 184.*

2.3 *sem.; etym.; transl.* ἐπί *in* ἐπικυέω (*to become pregnant after a preceding* [*pregnancy*]) = ḥamala marratan baʿda marratin : ἤδη γὰρ συνέβη γενομένης διαφθορᾶς καὶ δώδεκα ἐκπεσεῖν τὰ ἐπικυηθέντα *Arist. Hist. anim. VII 4, 585a11* = wa-qad ʿaraḍa fī-mā salafa saqṭun li-baʿḍi l-nisāʾi fa-asqaṭat iṯnā ʿašara (*sic ed. pro* iṯnay ʿašara) mimmā ḥamalat marratan baʿda marratin *473.7-8*⊗.

2.4 *sem. etym.; transl.* ἐπί *in* ἐπίταξις, *milit.* (*station behind* [*another line of soldiers*]) = tartībun baʿda tartībin : λέγεται δέ τις ... ὀρθία φάλαγξ ἢ λοξὴ φάλαγξ καὶ παρεμβολὴ καὶ πρόσταξις καὶ ἔνταξις καὶ ὑπόταξις καὶ ἐπίταξις *Aelian. Tact. 378b9* = mina l-mutaqaddimīna man ǧaʿala lahu smāʾa ... ǧayšin mustaqīmin wa-ǧayšin muwarrabin (*sic leg. pro* muʾarrab *ed.*) wa-raṣṣin (*sic leg. pro* wa-raḍḍ *ed.*) wa-taqaddumin wa-ḥašwin wa-rādifatin wa-tartībin baʿda tartībin *22.16-17**.

2.5 *sem.; etym.; transl.* ἐπί *in* ἐφ' ὁσονοῦν (*as far as it goes on*) = *sem. amplif.* mā baʿda ḏālika ʿalā hāḏā l-miṯāli : οἷον α, ς, ια ... καὶ ἐφ' ὁσονοῦν *Nicom. Arithm. 94.22* = miṯla l-wāḥidi wa-l-sittati wa-YĀ ... wa-mā baʿda ḏālika ʿalā hāḏā l-miṯāli *75.9.*

3. ὑπό *c. acc.* (*after; of order, grade, or place*) : ὑπὸ δὲ τὸ ὑπόζωμα κεῖται ἡ κοιλία *Arist. Part. anim. III 14, 674a9* = wa-baʿda l-ḥiǧābi wuḍiʿa l-baṭnu *93.6* ⟼ τούτων δὲ τοῖς μὲν οὐρανίοις ἀποδεδόσθαι τὴν κυκλικὴν κίνησιν, τῶν δὲ ὑπ' (ὑπ' *codd. cett.* : ἐπ' *B*) ἐκεῖνα τεταγμένων τοῖς μὲν κούφοις τὴν ἄνω *Ps.-Plut. Placita 336a17* = wa-anna l-samāwiyyata min hāḏihī uʿṭiyati l-ḥarakatu l-dawriyyatu wa-anna l-murattabata baʿda l-samāwiyyati mā kāna minhā ḫafīfan ǧuʿila lahu l-ḥarakatu ilā l-ʿuluwwi *27.17;* ἀνωτάτω μὲν πάντων τὸν ἥλιον τετάχθαι, μετ' αὐτὸν δὲ τὴν σελήνην, ὑπὸ δὲ αὐτοὺς τὰ ἀπλανῆ τῶν ἄστρων *345a10* = anna waḍʿa l-šamsi aʿlā ǧamīʿi l-ašyāʾi wa-baʿdahā l-qamaru wa-baʿdahumā l-kawākibu l-mutaḥayyiratu *31.7.*

4. διά *c. gen.* (*after; of time*) : ἀφίησι δὲ καὶ περιττώματα τὰ μὲν εὐθὺς τὰ δὲ διὰ ταχέων *Arist. Hist. anim. VII 10, 587a29* = wa-rubbamā alqā l-mawlūdu faḍlatan min sāʿatihī wa-rubbamā faʿala ḏālika baʿda ḥīnin yasīrin *481.4* ⟼ διὰ πολλῆς ἐπιμελείας *Galen Ther. Pis. 286.14* = baʿda ǧahdin wa-kaddin *128a4* ⟼ οὔτε γὰρ ἐπιμήνιος κάθαρσις αὐτέῃσι γίγνεται ὡς χρεὼν ἐστιν, ἀλλ' ὀλίγον καὶ διὰ χρόνου *Hippocr. Aer. 72.4* = wa-ḏālika anna ṭahūrahunna lā yakūnu illā qalīlan baʿda zamānin ṭawīlin *147.9* ⟼ τὰ ἐπιμήνια μὴ φαίνεται πάμπαν ἢ ἐλάσσονα καὶ διὰ πλείονος χρόνου *Hippocr. Superf. 88.15* = hiya lā taṭmuṯu wa-in ṭamaṯat fa-šayʾan (fa-šayʾan *corr. Ullmann, p. 268* : šayʾan *ed.*) qalīlan baʿda dahrin ṭawīlin *16.5**.

5. ἀπό *c. gen.* (*after*) : ἀπὸ δείπνου *Diosc. Mat. med. I, 207.7* = baʿda l-ʿašāʾi *vetus transl. Ullmann Unters., 184* ⟼ ὅμοια δὲ τούτοις καὶ τὰ κατὰ τὴν ἐχομένην ῥῆσιν ἀπ' αὐτοῦ (ἀπ' αὐτοῦ *Arab. ut vid.* : ὑπ' αὐτοῦ *codd., secl. Mueller*) *Galen An. virt. 62.7** = wa-qad ḏakara ayḍan fī l-kalāmi llaḏī baʿda hāḏā šayʾan šabīhan bi-hāḏā *31.8* ⟼ ἐν δὲ τῷ α´ ἔτει ἀπὸ τῆς Ἀλεξάνδρου τελευτῆς *Ptol. Hypoth. 96.27* = fī awwali sanatin baʿda mawti l-Iskandar *45.17.*

6. παρά *c. acc.* (*next to, after; of order*) : ἔνταξις δέ ἐστιν, ἐάν τις προαιρῆται τοὺς ψιλοὺς εἰς τὰ διαστήματα τῆς φάλαγγος ἐντάσσειν, ἄνδρα παρ' ἄνδρα *Aelian. Tact. 412b12* = wa-ammā l-ḥašwu fa-yakūnu iḏā rattaba l-qāʾidu l-ʿuzla fī furaǧi l-ǧayši raǧulan baʿda raǧulin *24.4.*

7. κατά *c. acc.* (*during a period* [*of time*], *i.e., after its start*) : Ἱπποκράτης τὰς πρὸ κυνὸς καὶ κατὰ κύνα φαρμακίας ἐργώδεας εἶναι λέγει *Galen Ther. Pis. 285.14* = qāla Buqrāṭ qad yanbaġī an namnaʿa min šurbi l-dawāʾi qabla ṭulūʿi l-šiʿrā l-ʿabūri wa-baʿda ṭulūʿihā *127b11.*

8. ὑπέρ *c. acc.* (*beyond, over* [*a certain time*]) = baʿda tamāmi *c. gen.*: ὅταν ὑπὲρ τὰς εἴκοσιν ἡ ἐκκόλαψις γίνηται τῶν ᾠῶν *Arist. Hist. anim. VI 3, 561b29* = in kasara (*sc.* aḥadun) al-bayḍata baʿda tamāmi l-ʿišrīna yawman *251.8.*

9. *sem.; etym.; transl.* πρό (*forwards, forth*) *in* προιών (*proceeding, going forward; i.e., with what comes next, later*) = aḫaḏa fī-mā baʿda ḏālika : οὗτοι δὲ τῶν ἀπὸ μονάδος εὐτάκτων τετραπλάσιοί εἰσι προϊόντες ἐφ' ὅσον ἂν εὐτονῇ τις ἕπεσθαι *Nicom. Arithm. 48.10* = hiya arbaʿatu aḍʿāfi l-aʿdādi l-mubtadiʾati mina l-wāḥidi wa-hiya taʾḫuḏu fī-mā baʿda ḏālika ilā mawḍiʿin arāda l-murīdu *43.23;* ἐπίπεδοι ... οἱ ἀπὸ τριάδος ἀρχόμενοι ... καὶ διὰ τῶν ἑξῆς συνεχῶν ἀριθμῶν προιόντες *87.2* = al-aʿdādu l-musaṭṭaḥatu ... allatī yabtadiʾu asāsuhā ... min ʿadadi l-ṯalāṯati wa-taʾḫuḏu fī-mā baʿda ḏālika mutazayyidan ... ʿalā ḥasabi marātibi l-aʿdādi l-mutawāliyati *70.7.*

10. *paraphr.;* περί *c. acc.* (*about, around; of time*) = baʿda tamāmi *c. gen.* (*after completion* [*of a certain period of time*]) : παύεται δὲ ταῖς γυναιξὶ ταῖς μὲν πλείσταις τὰ καταμήνια περὶ τετταράκοντα ἔτη *Arist. Hist. anim. VII 5, 585b3* = wa-l-ṭamṯu yanqaṭiʿu ʿan kaṯīrin mina l-nisāʾi baʿda tamāmi l-arbaʿīna ʿāman *474.16.*

B. *transl. Greek adverbs, adjectives (including participles), and conjunctions expressing or implying posteriority or succession*

11. *transl.* ὕστερος (*coming after*) *alone and in compounds*

11.1 ὕστερος *adj.* (*coming after*) *and* ὕστερον *adv.* (*afterwards*) **(a)** baʿda *c. gen.* : οὐθὲν γὰρ παρὰ φύσιν ἀίδιον· ὕστερον δὲ τὸ παρὰ φύσιν τοῦ κατὰ φύσιν *Arist. Cael. II 3, 286a18* = li-annahū laysa šayʾun ḫāriǧun mina l-ṭabīʿati bi-dāʾimin fa-inna l-šayʾa l-ʿaraḍiyya huwa baʿda l-ṭabīʿiyyi *versio B 236.2 Badawī* ⟷ μικρὸν δ’ ὕστερον δακὼν τὸν καμηλίτην ἀπέκτεινεν (*sc.* ὁ πῶλος) *Arist. Hist. anim. IX 47, 630b35* = wa-baʿda ḥīnin qalīlin ʿaḍḍa (*sc.* al-bakru) ʿalā l-ǧammāli fa-qatalahū *451.9* ⟷ οἱ ὕστεροι *Arist. Phys. I 6, 189b15* = man atā baʿdahum *54.11* ⟷ περὶ μὲν οὖν τούτων ὀλίγον ὕστερον ἐπισκεψόμεθα *Galen An. virt. 46.8* = wa-sawfa afḥaṣu ʿan ḏālika baʿda qalīlin *20.7;* πρὸς τὸν ὀλίγον ὕστερον εἰρησόμενον λόγον *60.18* = fī-mā urīdu ḏikrahū baʿda qalīlin *30.13* ⟷ καίτοι τό γ’ ὑστέροις τῶν παλαιῶν ἡμῖν γεγονέναι ... οὐ σμικρὸν ἦν πλεονέκτημα *Galen Med. phil. 4.7* = ʿalā anna ... fī baqāʾinā baʿda l-qudamāʾi ... faḍlun laysa bi-l-yasīri *58* ⟷ καὶ τὰ ξύλα πῦρ μικρὸν ὕστερον γιγνόμενα *Galen Nat. fac. 6.9* = wa-l-ḥaṭabu llaḏī yaṣīru baʿda qalīlin nāran *WGAÜ Suppl. II, 566.14* ⟷ μικρὸν ὕστερον *Galen Nerv. diss. 836.10* = baʿda qalīlin *102.3* ⟷ ἐς τὸν αὐτὸν χρόνον καὶ μήτε πρότερον μήθ’ ὕστερον *Hippocr. Superf. 82.20* = fī waqtin wāḥidin ... wa-lā ... qabla ḏālika wa-lā baʿdahū *11.4* ⟷ οἱ ὕστερον *Paulus Aeg. III, 22.30* = al-ḥadaṯu baʿdahum *WGAÜ Suppl. II, 567.10* ⟷ ὅτι τὸ μὲν γένος πρὸ τῶν εἰδῶν, τὰ δὲ συμβεβηκότα τῶν εἰδῶν ὕστερα *Porph. Isag. 17.4* = anna l-ǧinsa aqdamu mina l-anwāʿi wa-l-aʿrāḍa baʿda l-anwāʿi (*in Ibn al-Ṭayyib*) *159.12 Gyekye* ⟷ μηδέ-τερον θατέρου πρότερον ἢ ὕστερον *Proclus El. theol. 5 : 4.30* = laysa l-wāḥidu qabla l-āḫari aw baʿdahū *5.10;* ἔσται τὸ πλῆθος πάντῃ τοῦ ἑνὸς ὕστερον *5 : 6.5* = kānati l-kaṯratu baʿda al-wāḥidi lā maḥālata *5.18* ⟷ ὃ δὴ πρότερον τῆς βροντῆς προσέβλεψεν (προσέβλεψεν *D*ᶜ *s”, Arab.* : προσέπεσεν *vel* συνέπεσεν *codd. cett., ed.*) ὕστερον γενόμενον *Ps.-Arist. Mund. 4, 395a17** = illā anna l-barqa yurā qabla an yusmaʿa l-raʿdu wa-huwa mutakawwinun baʿdahū *Y 298b23* ⟷ πηνίκα δὲ λέγειν ἐστὶ μήτε πρότερον μήτε ὕστερον (ὑστέρῳ *PV* : ὑστέρω *B*) *Ps.-Arist. Div. 22a7* = wa-fī l-ḥīni llaḏī yaǧibu fīhi an yuqāla fī awānihī lā qablahū wa-lā baʿdahu *versio T 51.22* **(b)** baʿda ḏālika : δεῖ γὰρ ἴσως ὑποτυπῶσαι πρῶτον, εἶθ’ ὕστερον ἀναγράψαι *Arist. Eth. Nic. I 7, 1098a21* = wa-ḫalīqun an yakūna yanbaġī an narsumahū (*sc.* al-ḫayra) awwalan ṯumma nuḥaṣṣilahā baʿda ḏālika *135.17* **(c)** *in hend.;* aḫīran baʿda : εἰ καὶ τὸ οὕτως ὂν ὄν τις λέγοι, ὕστερον ἔσται ἐκείνου ᾧ ὑπάρχει *Alex. Qu. I 11a* [*Univ.*] *22.5* = in sammāhu aḥadun šayʾan mawǧūdan fa-innahū innamā kāna mawǧūdan aḫīran baʿda ḏālika l-šayʾi <llaḏī huwa> (*nos*) l-mawǧūdu fīhi l-ʿāriḍu lahū *versio Esc. 29**.

11.2 *sem. etym.; transl.* ὕστερος *in* ὑστερογενής (*appearing after birth*) = baʿda l-wilādi : ἴσοι γὰρ οἱ τόποι εἰσὶν ἐν οἷς αἱ τρίχες ἐγγίνονται αἵ τε συγγενεῖς καὶ αἱ ὑστερογενεῖς *Arist. Hist. anim. III 11, 518a24** = fa-hāḏihī (*post* hāḏihī *add* <hiya> *Badawī*) l-amākinu llatī yakūnu fīhā šaʿrun maʿa l-wilādi wa-baʿda l-wilādi <musāwiyatun> (*nos*) *125.21-126.1**.

12. δεύτερος *adj.*, δεύτερον *adv.* (*second, secondary; i.e., after* [*the first*]) **(a)** baʿda *c. gen* : πᾶν πλῆθος δεύτερόν ἐστι τοῦ ἑνός *Proclus El. theol. 5 : 4.19* = inna kulla kaṯratin hiya baʿda l-wāḥidi *5.1* ⟝ Ἐμπεδοκλῆς τὸν μὲν αἰθέρα πρῶτον διακριθῆναι, δεύτερον δὲ τὸ πῦρ ἐφ᾽ ᾧ τὴν γῆν *Ps.-Plut. Placita 334a2* = wa-ammā Anbāḏūqlīs fa-yarā anna awwala mā yumayyazu mina l-usṭuqussāti huwa l-aṯīru wa-baʿdahu l-nāru wa-baʿdahu l-arḍu *26.15;* Φιλόλαος ... τὸ μὲν πῦρ μέσον, ... δευτέραν δὲ τὴν ἀντίχθονα *377a12* = wa-ammā Fīlūlāwus ... fa-yarā anna l-māʾa (*sic codd., ed.!*) fī l-wasaṭi ... wa-baʿdahu l-arḍu llatī yusammīhā anṭīḫtun *45.8** **(b)** *in hend.* ṯānin baʿdahū : τὸ δὲ ὁμώνυμον ὅμοιόν τε ἐκείνῳ δεύτερον, αἰσθητόν *Plato Tim. 52a5* = wa-ammā l-muwāfiqu lahū fī l-ismi fa-šabīhun bihī ṯānin baʿdahū maḥsūsun *Galen Comp. Tim. 14.7.*

13. τρίτος *adj.* (*third; i.e., next, after* [*the second*]) **(a)** baʿda ḏālika : ὑστερογενεῖς δ᾽ αἱ ἐπὶ τῆς ἥβης (*sc.* τρίχες) πρῶτον, ἔπειτα δ᾽ αἱ ἐπὶ τῆς μασχάλης, τρίται δ᾽ αἱ ἐπὶ τοῦ γενείου *Arist. Hist. anim. III 11, 518a22* = wa-ammā mā yanbutu minhu aḫīran fa-šaʿaru l-ʿānati yanbutu awwalan ṯumma yatbaʿuhū <šaʿaru> l-ibṭayni wa-baʿda ḏālika šaʿaru l-liḥyati *125.20* **(b)** *in hend.;* ṯumma ... baʿda ḏālika : τρίτον τὸ κατὰ τὴν ἰδέαν ὅπερ ἴδιον τῆς μορφῆς (ὅπερ ... μορφῆς *secl. Pack* : *habet Arab.) Artem. Onirocr. 55.7** = ṯumma yufḥaṣu baʿda ḏālika ʿan ḥāli l-nawʿi llaḏī huwa ṣūratu l-šayʾi *104.10.*

14. *transl.* ἑξῆς *adv.* (*next*) *and its compounds*

14.1 ἑξῆς (*next, what follows next*) **(a)** baʿda *c. gen. pron.* : πρῶτον μὲν μονάδες, εἶτα δυάδες ἐν ἄλλοις τρισίν, εἶτα τριάδες, καὶ ἑξῆς τετράδες *Nicom. Arithm. 65.24* = ammā awwalan fa-l-naǧʿalhā āḥādan ṯumma naǧʿal mā naḍaʿuhū fī ṯalāṯati ḥudūdin <iṯnatayi ṯnatayni ṯumma> (*nos*) ṯalāṯata ṯalāṯatin wa-baʿdahā arbaʿata rbaʿatin *56.5** ⟝ τούτων ὑποτυπωθέντων ἑξῆς ἐπελευσόμεθα καὶ τὰς τῶν πλανωμένων ὑποθέσεις *Ptol. Hypoth. 76.19* = fa-iḏ qad rasamnā hāḏihi l-ašyāʾa fa-innā naṣīru baʿdahā ilā l-qawli fī l-kawākibi l-mutaḥayyirati *21.12* **(b)** baʿda ḏālika : ὁ δὲ λδ τοῦ κη καὶ ϛ καὶ οἱ ἑξῆς ἀκολούθως *Nicom. Arithm. 98.26* = wa-ʿadadu l-arbaʿati wa-ṯalāṯīna mina l-ṯamāniyati wa-

ʿišrīna wa-l-sittatu wa-mā baʿda ḏālika ʿalā al-wilāʾi *78.4*; *96.8* = *76.5*; *105.20* = 83.1; *etc.* **(c)** *in hend.* baʿdahū wa-mā yatlūhu : τὸ δὲ τρίτον ζυγὸν καὶ τὰ ἑξῆς *Aelian. Tact. 314b15* = al-ṣaffu l-muqtarinu l-ṯāliṯu wa-man baʿdahū min sāʾiri l-ṣufūfi allatī tatlūhu *16.21* **(d)** *sem. amplif.* baʿda hāḏā l-qawli/mā qulnā : πρῶτον ἑξῆς δὲ περὶ δένδρων καὶ φυτῶν ποιήσομαι τὸν λόγον *Artem. Onirocr. 143.19* = wa-anā atakallamu baʿda hāḏā l-qawli fī l-šağari wa-l-nabāti *258.1;* περὶ δὲ τῶν οὐρανίων ἑξῆς ἐροῦμεν *160.24* = fa-ammā malāʾikatu l-samāʾi fa-innā nabtadiʾu bi-l-qawli fīhā baʿda mā qulnā *289.1.*

14.2 ἐφεξῆς (*afterwards, next in order*) **(a)** baʿda *c. gen.* : τῶν δ' ἐφεξῆς συζυγιῶν ἡ μὲν ἕκτη μετὰ τὸν πέμπτον ... ἀνίσχει σπόνδυλον *Galen Nerv. diss. 851.4* = wa-ammā l-azwāğu llatī baʿda hāḏā l-zawği fa-l-sādisu minhā yaḫruğu baʿda l-faqrati l-ḫāmisati *113.12* ⟼ οἷον δυάδι, τριάδι, τετράδι ἢ ἐφεξῆς *Nicom. Arithm. 108.22* = miṯla l-iṯnayni wa-l-ṯalāṯati wa-l-arbaʿati aw ġayri ḏālika mina l-aʿdādi baʿdahā *85.3* **(b)** mā baʿda ḏālika : εὐτάκτως ἐν ἑνὶ στίχῳ γ, ε, ζ, ... καὶ ἐφεξῆς *Nicom. Arithm. 23.18* = fī saṭrin wāḥidin ʿalā niẓāmihā kaḏā Ğ H Z ... wa-mā baʿda ḏālika *27.11; sim. 23.22* = *27.13* **(c)** *sem. amplif.* **(c1)** mā baʿda ḏālika ʿalā l-wilāʾi : καὶ συγκρινομένων ... πρώτου πρώτῳ, δευτέρου δευτέρῳ, τρίτου τρίτῳ, τετάρτου τετάρτῳ, καὶ ἐφεξῆς *Nicom. Arithm. 61.18* = wa-qīsati l-aʿdādu ... al-awwalu bi-l-awwali wa-l-ṯānī bi-l-ṯānī wa-l-ṯāliṯu bi-l-ṯāliṯi wa-l-rābiʿu bi-l-rābiʿi wa-mā baʿda ḏālika ʿalā l-wilāʾi *53.5; sim. 53.3* = *47.13-14* **(c2)** baʿda ḏālika ... mutawālin : τὸ δὲ πλείονα ἑνὸς ἄρχεται πάλιν ἀπὸ τοῦ β καὶ πρόεισιν ἐπὶ πάντας τοὺς ἐφεξῆς ἀριθμούς *Nicom. Arithm. 55.16* = akṯaru min ğuzʾin wāḥidin šayʾun yabtadiʾu mina l-iṯnayni wa-yamḍī ilā mā baʿda ḏālika ʿalā sabīli l-aʿdādi l-mutawāliyati *49.12.*

15. *transl.* εἶτα *adv.* (*then*) *and its compounds*

15.1 εἶτα (*then, after that*) **(a)** baʿda *c. gen. pron.* : πρῶτον περὶ τῆς κατὰ φύσιν ... συνουσίας, εἶτα περὶ τῆς ... παρὰ φύσιν *Artem. Onirocr. 86.19* = awwalan fī l-ğimāʿi llaḏī yakūnu bi-l-ṭabīʿati ... wa-baʿdahū fī llaḏī yakūnu ḫāriğan ʿani l-ṭabīʿati *160.7; 195.10* = *353.10* ⟼ εἶτα τούτων ἀμφοτέρων σύστημα ... ὁ διὰ πασῶν ἐφεξῆς αὐτοῖς κείμενος *Nicom. Arithm. 134.12* = wa-yatlū hāḏayni l-ittifāqayni baʿdahumā l-ittifāqu l-musāwī lahumā iḏā ğumiʿā wa-huwa l-ittifāqu llaḏī bi-l-kulli *103.21* ⟼ Πλάτων πῦρ πρῶτον εἶτ' αἰθέρα μεθ' ὃν ἀέρα *Ps.-Plut. Placita 336a8* = wa-ammā Aflāṭūn fa-innahū yarā anna l-awwala huwa l-nāru wa-baʿdahu l-aṯīru wa-baʿdahu l-hawāʾu *27.12* **(b)** baʿda ḏālika/hāḏā : πρότερόν τινα φόβον ... ἐπάγουσιν, εἶτα δὲ .... τελειοῦσι καὶ τὸ ἀγαθόν *174.24* = fa-innahum fī l-ibtidāʾi yadullūna ʿalā ḫawfin yaʿriḍu lahū wa-ʿalā annahū baʿda ḏālika ... yaṣīru amruhū ilā ḫayrin *Artem. Onirocr. 314.4* ⟼ ὡς πρῶτον μὲν ἐκείνου διαγλύφηται πολὺ ἐν αὐτῇ, εἶτα δὲ τὸ πᾶν *Galen Nerv. diss. 854.8* = ḥattā innahū awwalan yataqawwaru mina l-awwali taqwīran kaṯīran wa-baʿda ḏālika yataqawwaru kulluhū *115.12* ⟼ πρῶτον μὲν κατὰ τριγωνισμὸν ..., εἶτα ἀνάλογον ἀπὸ ἑξαγώνου καὶ ἑπταγώνου *Nicom. Arithm. 100.1* = ammā awwalan fa-ʿalā sabīli l-taṯlīṯi ... wa-ʿalā hāḏā l-sabīli yağrī l-amru fī l-maḫrūṭāti llatī baʿda hāḏihī aʿnī l-musaddasata l-qawāʿidi wa-l-musabbaʿata l-qawāʿidi *78.20*.

15.2 ἔπειτα (*thereafter*) **(a)** baʿda *c. gen. pron.* : φημὶ πρώτους εἶναι θεούς· ... ἔπειτα ἱερεῖς *Artem. Onirocr. 195.5* = aqūlu innahum awwalan al-malāʾikatu ... wa-baʿdahumu l-kahanatu *353.5* **(b)** baʿda ḏālika/hāḏā : ἔπειτα γόνιμα μὲν μικρὰ δὲ καὶ ἀτελῆ γεννῶσι *Arist. Hist. anim. VII 1, 582a17* = wa-baʿda ḏālika yakūnu minhu waladun wa-yakūnu ṣağīran laysa bi-tāmmin (*sic leg.*) *464.9** ⟼ καὶ ἑξῆς τετράδες, ἔπειτα πεντάδες *Nicom. Arithm. 65.24* = wa-baʿdahā arbaʿata arbaʿatin wa-baʿda hāḏihī ḫamsata ḫamsatin *56.5* ⟼ ἔπειτα φησὶ (*sc.* Εὐριπίδης) τὴν ἀνομίαν λυθῆναι νόμων εἰσαγωγῇ *Ps.-Plut. Placita 298a18* = wa-ḏakara (*sc.* Awrībīḏis) anna baʿda ḏālika baṭala l-fuğūru bi-waḍʿi l-nawāmīsi *13.1* ⟼ ἔπειτα ἕτερος κύκλος ὁμόκεντρος αὐτῷ περιφερέσθω *Ptol. Hypoth. 74.8* = wa-l-naḫuṭṭa baʿda ḏālika dāʾiratan yakūnu markazuhā markaza hāḏā l-falaki *19.6* **(c)** *in hend.* ṯumma ... baʿda ḏālika/hāḏā : καὶ τὸ μὲν πρῶτον λευκὸν καὶ μικρὸν φαίνεται, ἔπειτα ἐρυθρὸν καὶ αἱματῶδες *Arist. Hist. anim. VI 2, 559b9* = wa-yaẓharu ḏālika ... awwalan abyaḍa ṣağīran ṯumma yaẓharu aḥmara damiyyan baʿda ḏālika *245.10* ⟼ λεκτέον δὴ πρῶτον μὲν ..., ἔπειτα περὶ τοῦ ἀναγκαίου *Arist. Phys. II 8, 198b11* = fa-yanbağī l-āna an nağʿala kalāmanā awwalan fī ... ṯumma natakallamu baʿda ḏālika fī l-ḍarūriyyi *142.5-6* ⟼ ἔπειτα δὲ καὶ τὸ μέγεθος τῆς βλάβης ... *Galen Anat. admin. II, 671.3* = ṯumma yuḥtāğu an taʿlama baʿda hāḏā anna miqdāra l-ḍarari ... *506.4-5 Garofalo* ⟼ τὸ μὲν πρῶτον μικρόν, ἔπειτα <δὲ> μεῖζον γίγνεται *Hippocr. Aer. 44.26* = yakūnu fī awwali šaʾnihī yasīran ṯumma baʿda ḏālika yaʿẓumu *versio A 87.3* = *versio B 87.12* ⟼ ἔπειτα δὲ ῥεῖ (*sc.* τὸ αἷμα) φλεγματωδέστερόν τε καὶ χολωδέστερον *Hippocr. Nat. hom. 182.2* = ṯumma yağrī minhum baʿda ḏālika damun balġamiyyun fa-iḏā kāna bi-aḫaratin ğarā minhu l-damu llaḏī l-ġālibu ʿalayhi l-marāru *10.8-9*.

15.3 μετέπειτα (*then afterwards*) = ṯumma baʿda ḏālika : τὸ μὲν γὰρ πρῶτον ..., μετέπειτα δ' οὐ τοιαύτη ἡ ἐνέργεια *Arist. Eth. Nic. X 4, 1175a9* = fa-inna awwalan ... ṯumma baʿda ḏālika lā yakūnu fiʿlun miṯla hāḏā *545.10.*

16. *transl.* ἔτι *adv.* (*hereafter*) *and its compounds*

16.1 ἔτι (*hereafter*) = baʿda hāḏā : πότερον οὖν ὑπὲρ ὀνομάτων ἔτι διενεθήσῃ καὶ ληρήσεις ἐρίζων *Galen Med. phil. 7.25* = a-fa-turāka baʿda hāḏā tunāziʿunī fī l-asmāʾi wa-tastaʿmilu l-haḏayāna wa-l-mumārāta *126.*

16.2 οὐκέτι, οὐ ... ἔτι (*no longer*) = lā ... baʿda ḏālika : οὐ γὰρ ἔτι φίλοι εἰσίν *Arist. Eth. Nic. VIII 7, 1158b34* = min aǧli annahum lā yakūnūna baʿda ḏālika aṣdiqāʾa *449.15* ⟼ ὁ μὲν γὰρ οὐκέτι ὄψεται τὰ περὶ αὐτὸν κακά *Artem. Onirocr. 33.2* = wa-ḏālika annahū ... lā yarā baʿda ḏālika šayʾan mimmā huwa fīhi mina l-šarri *62.6.*

17. ἐπιών *pres. part.* (*following, succeeding*) *of* ἔπειμι = baʿda *c. gen.* : τούτων τὰς αἰτίας ὁ ἐπιὼν παρέξει λόγος *Artem. Onirocr. 43.6* = wa-ammā asbābu ḏālika fa-uʿlimuhā fī l-maqālati llatī baʿda hāḏihī *81.2;* τὴν δὲ αἰτίαν ὁ ἐπιὼν λόγος δηλώσει *66.2* = wa-sanubayyinu sababa ḏālika fī l-maqālati llatī baʿda hāḏihī *122.6* ⟼ ἡ νὺξ δύσφορος, ἡ πρὸ τοῦ παροξυσμοῦ, ἡ δὲ ἐπιοῦσα εὐφορωτέρη *Hippocr. Aphor. II : 13* = qad yaṣʿubu ... maraḍuhū fī l-laylati llatī qabla nawbati l-ḥummā ... ṯumma fī l-laylati llatī baʿdahā yakūnu aḫaffa *12.1.*

18. *transl.* λοιπός (*remaining, next*) *in various forms*

18.1 λοιπόν *adv.* (*hereafter*) = baʿda ḏālika : μὴ εὑρεθήσεσθαι αὐτὰς λοιπὸν ἐν ἐκείνῳ τῷ χωρίῳ *Cass. Bass. Geopon. XIII, 3.2* = lam yaṣir ilā tilka l-qaryati baʿda ḏālika šayʾun min hāḏihi l-dawābbi *WGAÜ Suppl. I, 640ult.*

18.2 οἱ λοιποί *substantivized adj.* (*the rest; i.e., those that come later*) = mā baʿda ḏālika : ἐπιτετράπεμπτος, εἶτα ἐπιπένθεκτος καὶ παραπλησίως ἐπὶ τῶν λοιπῶν *Nicom. Arithm. 58.7* = al-zāʾidu ṯalāṯata arbāʿin ṯumma l-zāʾidu ḫamsata asdāsin wa-mā baʿda ḏālika ʿalā hāḏā l-miṯāli *51.2;* ὁ τρίτος δευτέρῳ καὶ ὁ τέταρτος τρίτῳ καὶ ἀκολούθως οἱ λοιποί *116.8* = wa-l-ṯāliṯu min tilka bi-l-ṯānī min hāḏihī wa-<l-rābiʿu minhā bi-> (*nos*) l-ṯāliṯi wa-mā baʿda ḏālika ʿalā l-wilāʾi *90.13**.

19. εὐθύς *adv.* (*straightway, immediately next*) = baʿda qalīlin : ὡς εὐθὺς εἰσόμεθα *Nicom. Arithm. 46.11* = wa-sa-nubayyinu ḏālika baʿda qalīlin *42.19.*

20. ὀψέ *adv.* (*after some time*) **(a)** baʿda zamānin : καὶ ἐνυπνιαζόμενον δῆλον μὲν γίνεται, μνημονεύει δ' ὀψὲ τὰς φαντασίας *Arist. Hist. anim.VII 10, 587b11* = wa-huwa yarā fī nawmihi l-aḥlāma ... wa-rubbamā ṯabatat lahū fī ḏihnihī baʿda zamānin *481.15* **(b)** *in hend.* bi-ibṭāʾin wa-baʿda zamānin kaṯīrin : ὀψὲ γὰρ παύεται (*sc.* ὁ ἐγκέφαλος) τῆς ψυχρότητος καὶ τῆς ὑγρότητος *Arist. Gener. anim. II 6, 744a22* = min aǧli anna l-burūdata wa-l-ruṭūbata llatī (*sic ed. pro* allatāni) fīhi (*sc.* al-dimāġi) lā takuffu illā bi-ibṭāʾin wa-baʿda zamānin kaṯīrin *83.17*⊗.

21. χρονιώτερος (*later, after a long time*) = baʿda zamānin : τὸ δὲ ἡδὺ καὶ ὠφέλιμον ὕστερα καὶ χρονιώτερα *Arist. Rhet. I 12, 1372b15* = yakūnu ... al-laḏīḏu l-nāfiʿu mutaʾaḫḫiran wa-baʿda zamānin *63.14*.

22. τότε *adv.* (*then, next*) = baʿda ḏālika : ὥσπερ δὲ οἱ γραμματικοὶ τῶν στοιχείων ἐπειδὰν τὰς δυνάμεις διδάξωσι τοὺς παῖδας, τότε <ὁπότε> (ὁπότε *Arab., suppl. Browne, p. 220*) καὶ ὅπως (*post* ὅπως *add.* ὁμοῦ πᾶσι *ed.* : *om. Arab.*) χρῆσθαι δεῖ ὑποτίθενται *Artem Onirocr. 234.10** = fa-ka-mā anna muʿallimī l-aḥrufi yuʿallimūna l-mutaʿallimīna badʾan quwwata l-aḥrufi wa-yubayyinūna lahum baʿda ḏālika matā wa-kayfa yanbaġī lahum an yastaʿmilūhā *433.2*.

23. ἐπάν *conj.* (*after, when*) : οἱ μὲν οὖν ἐν ταῖς πόλεσιν ἄρχοντες ὑπὸ τῶν πολιτῶν ἐπὰν αἱρεθῶσι, κατὰ νόμον ἄρχουσιν *Ps.-Arist. Div. 18a6* = fa-l-musallaṭu baʿda ḫtiyāri l-ʿāmmati iyyāhu huwa l-raʾīsu bi-l-mašīʾati *versio Q 35.8*.

24. πλησίος *adj.* (*nearby, next*) : ἀλλ' ὥρισται πρὸς τὸ πλησίον (*sc.* σῶμα) ἁφῇ *Arist. Cael. I 1, 268b7* = ġayra anna lahū ḥaddan yumāssu mā baʿdahū mina l-aǧrāmi *versio B*.

25. κατωτέρω *adv.* (*afterwards, below*) = fī-mā baʿda hāḏā l-kalāmi : καὶ κατωτέρω τοῦ συγγράμματος ἀποφαινόμενος τὴν αὐτὴν δόξαν ἔγραψεν *Galen An. virt. 52.6* = wa-qad bayyana hāḏā l-raʾya ayḍan fī-mā baʿda hāḏā l-kalāmi min hāḏihi l-maqālati *24.19*.

26. ἔξω *adv.* (*ouside of, beyond*) : τὸ γὰρ τέλος τὸ περιέχον τὸν τῆς ἑκάστου ζωῆς χρόνον, οὗ μηθὲν ἔξω κατὰ φύσιν, αἰὼν ἑκάστου κέκληται *Arist. Cael. I 9, 279a24* = wa-ḏālika annahum qālū inna l-zamāna l-muḥīṭa bi-ḥayāti kulli wāḥidin mina l-mawǧūdāti llatī lahā ḥayātun, wa-laysa baʿdahū zamānun āḫaru ṭabīʿiyyun, fa-huwa l-dahru l-abadiyyu *versio A 111b1*.

27. *transl. derivatives of* νέος (*recent*)

27.1 νεώτερος *comp.* (*what is more recent, later*) = al-šayʾu baʿda l-šayʾi : νεώτερον λέγεται καὶ ὑστερογενέστερον *Nicom. Arithm. 10.2* =

yuqālu inna l-šayʾa baʿda l-šayʾi aw innahū mutaʾaḫḫirun (mutaʾaḫḫirun *cod.* : taʾaḫḫara *Kutsch*) ʿanhu bi-l-ṭabīʿati *17.4**.

27.2 οἱ νεωτερικοί (*the later ones, the moderns*) = man kāna baʿda l-qudamāʾi : τετάρτη δὲ ἐν τῇ τῶν νεωτερικῶν ἐκθέσει *Nicom. Arithm. 144.2* = al-rābiʿu mina l-tawassuṭāti llatī waḍaʿahā man kāna baʿda l-qudamāʾi *110. 20.*

28. *sem. metathesis; affirm. / neg. transformation* : βραδέως (*slowly*) = lā ... illā baʿda ḥīnin ṭawīlin (*not ... except after a long time*) : βραδέως πεπαινόμενον *Diosc. Mat. med. I, 109.17* = lā yanḍağu illā baʿda ḥīnin ṭawīlin *vetus transl. Ullmann Unters., 184.*

29. *sem. metathesis; neg. / affirm. transformation* : οὐ βιώσιμος (*not likely to live* [*of a newborn*]) = māta baʿda l-ḫurūji (*dies after birth*) : κίνδυνος τὸ παιδίον τεθνηκὸς ἀπολυθῆναι, ἢ οὐ βιώσιμον γενέσθαι *Hippocr. Superf. 78.12* = yutaḫawwafu ʿalā l-ğanīni an yaḫruğa mayyitan aw yamūta baʿda ḫurūğihī *6.13;* αὗται ἢ τεθνηκότα τίκτουσιν, ἢ ζῶντα πονηρὰ καὶ οὐ βιώσιμα *80.3* = immā an talida ğanīnahā mayyitan wa-immā marīḍan mudnifan ṯumma yamūtu baʿda ḏālika *8.4.*

30. *sem.; expr.;* μόλις (*scarcely*) = lā ... illā baʿda šiddatin/ʿusrin : βραδύτερα γὰρ καὶ δυσκολώτερα καὶ μόλις ἐσόμενα τὰ ἀγαθὰ σημαίνει τὸ διὰ γῆς δοκεῖν πλεῖν *Artem. Onirocr. 140.13* = wa-ḏālika anna l-sayra (<fī safīnatin> *add. frustra Fahd*) fī l-barri yadullu ʿalā anna l-ḫayra yakūnu baṭīʾan maʿa ʿusratin (*sic leg.*) wa-lā yatimmu illā baʿda šiddatin *252.15** ⟼ καὶ ἐν γαστρὶ ἴσχουσι μόλις καὶ τίκτουσι χαλεπῶς *Hippocr. Aer. 36.15* = fa-lā yaḥbalna illā baʿda ʿusrin wa-lā yalidna illā bi-mašaqqatin *versio A 55.1* = *versio B 55.9.*

31. *morph.; transl. the past tense of aorist and perfect participles*

31.1 ἀποκοπέντων *aorist part.* (*having been cut off*) = baʿda qaṭʿihī (*after its having been cut off*) : εἰ δὲ βλέποις ἐν αὐτοῖς ἀποκοπέντων τῶν μερῶν ὑπολειπομένην κίνησίν τινα *Galen Ther. Pis. 266.2-3* = wa-iḏā raʾaytahā baʿda qaṭʿi l-ṭarafayni kaṯīrata l-taḥarruki *122b2.*

31.2 πεποιημένον *perf. part.* (*having been made*) = baʿda farāğihī minhu (*after it was completed*) : ἡ μὲν οἰκοδομικὴ καὶ ναυπηγικὴ (*sc.* ἐπιστῆμαι) ποιητικαί εἰσιν· ἔστι γὰρ αὐτῶν ἰδεῖν ἔργον πεποιημένον *Ps.-Arist. Div. 8a4* = fa-ammā l-ʿilmu l-ṣāniʿu fa-ka-l-tāğiri wa-l-ṣāniʿi l-mawğūdi fiʿluhū ʿalaynā (*sic leg. pro* ʿynʾ *ed.*) qāʾiman baʿda farāğihī minhu *versio Q 37.20*;* αὐλητικὴ καὶ κιθαριστικὴ ... πρακτικαί (*sc.* ἐπιστῆμαί εἰσιν)· οὐ γὰρ ἔστιν ἰδεῖν ἔργον αὐτῶν πεποιημένον *8a8* =

wa-ammā l-ʿilmu l-fāʿilu fa-ka-l-muġannī wa-l-zāmiri llaḏayni lā yabqā fiʿluhumā baʿda farāġihimā minhū (minhu *nos* : šayʾan *ed.*) *versio Q 36.2**.

32. *paraphr.;* συνεχής (*successive*) = baʿda ḏālika : παρεκτεθῇ αὐτῷ ... ὁ ἀπὸ τῆς ἑνάδος ἀρχόμενος κατὰ ἑνάδος προκοπὴν συνεχῶν ἀριθμῶν (συνεχῶν ἀριθμῶν *C Arab.* : συνεχὴς ἀριθμός *codd. cett., ed.*) *Nicom. Arithm. 61.24** = wuḍiʿat ilā ǧānibihī ... al-aʿdādu l-mubtadiʾatu mina l-tisʿati llati tuzuyyida fīhā baʿda ḏālika bi-tisʿatin tisʿatin (*sic leg. pro* bi-tisʿatin bi-tisʿatin) *53.9**.

33. *paraphr.;* τὸ διαλεῖπον *pres. part.* (*being at an interval from*) *of* διαλείπω = baʿda *c. gen.*: τὸν δ' ἀπ' ἐκείνου δύο διαλείποντα (*sc.* ἀριθμόν) *Nicom. Arithm. 32.5* = al-ʿadadu ... llaḏī baʿda l-ʿadadi llaḏī ḏakarnā bi-ʿadadayni *33.1; sim. 32.7 = 33.3.*

34. *paraphr.; transl.* νῦν *adv.* (*now*), *in context, coming after s.th. that happened* πρότερον (*previously*) =*in hend.* ṯumma ... baʿda ḏālika : λέγεται δ' ἀγένητον ἕνα μὲν τρόπον ἐὰν ᾖ τι νῦν πρότερον μὴ ὂν ἄνευ γενέσεως καὶ μεταβολῆς *Arist. Cael. I 10, 280b6* = al-šayʾu qad yuqālu ġayra mukawwanin ʿalā ǧihātin šattā, aḥaduhā (*sic ed. pro* iḥdāhā) iḏā kāna l-šayʾu awwalan laysa, ṯumma kāna baʿda ḏālika aysa bi-ġayri kawnin wa-lā stiḥālatin *versio B 203.1 Badawī* ⊗.

35. *paraphr.; transl.* πάλιν *adv.* (*again*) *and its compounds*

35.1 πάλιν (*again*) : καὶ εἰ μέν τις ἀναβαίνειν πάλιν ἐξ Ἅιδου ὑπολάβοι *Artem. Onirocr. 184.15* = fa-in raʾā l-insānu ka-annahū yaṣʿadu mina l-āḫirati baʿda nuzūlihī fīhā *334.15*

35.2 *sem.; etym.; transl.* πάλιν *in* παλινίδρυσις (*settling down* [*after having arisen*]) : σκεπτέα ταῦτα· ... σχήματα, κίνησις, μετεωρισμὸς, παλινίδρυσις *Hippocr. Humor. 2.4* = yanbaġī an tanẓura wa-taftaqida hāḏihi l-ašyāʾa ... al-aškālu wa-l-ḥarakatu wa-l-istiqlālu wa-l-istiqrāru baʿdahū *3.10.*

C. *used in expressions translating Greek phrases denoting posteriority and succession*

36. *sem. amplif.;* οὐκ εἰς μακράν (*not long after*) **(a)** baʿda muddatin laysat bi-l-kaṯīrati : καὶ οὐκ εἰς μακρὰν αὐτῷ ἐπεστάλη περὶ τούτου (*sc.* τοῦ θανάτου *ut intell. Arab.*) *Artem. Onirocr. 34.4* = fa-lammā kāna baʿda muddatin laysat bi-l-kaṯīrati māta *64.5* **(b)** *sem. metathesis;*

neg. / affirm. transformation; baʿda zamānin yasīrin : ἐδόκει ἐλέφαντι ὀχεῖσθαι, καὶ οὐκ εἰς μακρὰν ἀπέθανεν *Artem. Onirocr. 123.18* = fa-raʾat ka-annahā rākibatun fīlan fa-mātat baʿda zamānin yasīrin *225.3.*

37. *sem.; expr.; used in expressions transl. Greek adverbial phrases meaning, "indefinitely, endlessly"*

37.1 ἐπ' ἄπειρον (*indefinitely, ad infinitum*) **(a)** mā baʿda ḏālika ilā mā lā nihāyata : ἑξάγωνοι καὶ ἑπτάγωνοι καὶ ἐπ' ἄπειρον *Nicom. Arithm. 87.5-6* = al-musaddasu wa-l-musabbaʿu wa-mā baʿda ḏālika ilā mā lā nihāyata *70.10*; *60.16* = *52.8-9*; *93.16* = *74.13-14*; *127.2* = *98.8*; *etc.* **(b)** fī-mā baʿda ḏālika dāʾiman : καὶ ἐπ' ἄπειρον τῷ αὐτῷ τρόπῳ *Nicom. Arithm. 32.10* = wa-ʿalā hāḏā l-miṯāli yaǧrī l-amru fī-mā baʿda ḏālika dāʾiman *33.7* **(c)** mā baʿda ḏālika ʿalā hāḏā l-miṯāli yaǧrī dāʾiman : ὁ δὲ γ τριπλάσιος, ὁ δὲ δ τετραπλάσιος καὶ ὁ ε πενταπλάσιος (καὶ ὁ ε πενταπλάσιος *PC Arab.* : *om. Hoche*), καὶ ἐπ' ἄπειρον *Nicom. Arithm. 47.1** = wa-l-ṯalāṯatu ṯalāṯata amṯālihī wa-l-arbaʿatu arbaʿata amṯālihī wa-l-ḫamsatu ḫamsata amṯālihī wa-mā baʿda ḏālika ʿalā hāḏā l-miṯāli yaǧrī dāʾiman *42.23* **(d)** *periphr.;* fī-mā baʿda ḏālika : καὶ ὀκταπλασίοις ἕνα παρὰ τρεῖς, καὶ ἐπ' ἄπειρον οὕτως ἀνάλογον ἡ προκοπή *Nicom. Arithm. 48.17* = wa-l-ṯamāniyatu l-amṯāli mā ǧarā ʿalā tarki ṯalāṯatin wāḥidin wāḥidin wa-ʿalā hāḏihi l-sabīli yaǧrī l-amru fī-mā baʿda ḏālika *44.6.*

37.2 μέχρις ἀπείρου (*indefinitely, ad infinitum*) = mā baʿda ḏālika ilā mā lā nihāyata : προχωροῦντες μέχρις ἀπείρου καθ' ἑκάστην *Nicom. Arithm. 103.16* = naʾḫuḏu fī-mā baʿda ḏālika ilā mā lā nihāyata *81.9.*

37.3 μέχρι παντός (*and so on throughout*) = wa-mā baʿda ḏālika ḥayṯu mā balaġa l-insānu *or sim.*: οἷον ... ὁ ιβ τοῦ η, ὁ ιε τοῦ ι, καὶ μέχρι παντός *Nicom. Arithm. 53.19* = miṯla ... l-iṯnay ʿašara mina l-ṯamāniyati wa-l-ḫamsata ʿašara mina l-ʿašarati wa-mā baʿda ḏālika ʿalā hāḏā l-miṯāli ḥayṯu mā balaġa l-insānu *48.3*; καὶ ἐν πενταπλασίῳ τετράκις καὶ τοῦτο μέχρι παντός *128.11* = wa-in kānati l-nisbatu ḫamsata amṯālin fa-inna ḏālika yakūnu arbaʿa marrātin miṯla mā qulnā wa-mā baʿda ḏālika ilā ḥayṯu mā arāda l-murīdu *99.11-12.*

37.4 καὶ ἀεὶ οὕτως (*and so on always*) = wa-mā baʿda ḏālika ʿalā hāḏā l-miṯāli dāʾiman *or sim.*: τεσσάρων (*sc.* ἄλφα) ... τετράδος καὶ πέντε πεντάδος καὶ ἀεὶ οὕτως *Nicom. Arithm. 83.25* = wa-l-arbaʿu alifātin ʿalā arbaʿatin wa-l-ḫamsatu alifātin ʿalā ḫamsatin wa-mā baʿda ḏālika ʿalā hāḏā l-mithāli dāʾiman *68. 10-11*; μονὰς μὲν γὰρ τοῦ δυνάμει πρωτίστου πενταγώνου ὑπάρχει τοῦ ἑνός, τοῦ δὲ τῶν ἐκκειμένων δευτέρου τοῦ ιβ πλευρὰ τριὰς ... καὶ ἀεὶ οὕτως *92.12* = wa-ammā l-wāḥidu fa-huwa ḍilʿu l-muḫammasi llaḏī huwa bi-l-quwwati muḫammasun wa-ammā ḍilʿu l-muḫammasi l-ṯānī ... wa-huwa l-iṯnā ʿašara fa-huwa l-ṯalāṯatu ... wa-mā baʿda ḏālika ʿalā hāḏā l-mithāli *73.23; sim. 104.21 = 82.5.*

38. *sem.; expr.; used in expressions transl. Greek phrases meaning, "one thing after another"*

38.1 ἄλλοτε ἄλλος (*now this now that*) = šayʾun baʿda šayʾin : τίνος γὰρ ἕνεκα ... πρὸς ἄλλοτ᾽ ἄλλο μεταβολαὶ καὶ φθοραὶ καὶ γενέσεις *Theophr. Princ. 10b3* = al-sabab allaḏī lahū ṣāra ... al-taġāyīr allatī taʿriḍu ... ilā šayʾin baʿda šayʾin wa-aṣnāf al-kawn wa-l-fasād *214.2.*

38.2 ἄλλος καὶ ἄλλος (*one thing after another*) **(a)** šayʾun baʿda šayʾin : πολλαχῶς τὸ εἶναι, ὥσπερ ἡ ἡμέρα ἔστι καὶ ὁ ἀγὼν τῷ ἀεὶ ἄλλο καὶ ἄλλο γίγνεσθαι *Arist. Phys. III 6, 206a22* = kāna l-mawǧūdu yuqālu ʿalā anḥāʾin šattā fa-ka-mā yuqālu inna l-nahāra mawǧūdun wa-l-ǧihādu mawǧūdun min ṭarīqi annahū dāʾimu l-takawwuni šayʾan baʿda šayʾin *251.7;* ὅλως μὲν γὰρ οὕτως ἔστιν τὸ ἄπειρον, τῷ ἀεὶ ἄλλο καὶ ἄλλο λαμβάνεσθαι *206a28* = fa-inna bi-l-ǧumlati hāḏihī ṣifatu mā lā nihāyata lahū anna laka an taʾḫuḏa minhu dāʾiman šayʾan baʿda šayʾin *251.13; VI 7, 238b7 = 700.15* **(b)** wāḥidun baʿda āḫara : ὥσπερ ἡ κίνησις αἰεὶ ἄλλη καὶ ἄλλη *Arist. Phys. IV 11, 219b9* = ka-mā anna l-ḥarakata takūnu abadan wāḥidatun baʿda uḫrā *420.11-12;* ἄλλος οὖν (*sc.* ὁ χρόνος) ἢ ὁ αὐτὸς πολλάκις; *IV 13, 222a30* = wa-hal huwa (*sc.* al-zamānu) wāḥidun baʿda āḫara aw wāḥidun bi-ʿaynihī marrātin kaṯīratan *464.8 (where the translator interpreted* ἄλλος *correctly in the sense of* ἄλλος καὶ ἄλλος*); sim. IV 10, 218a10 = 406.1; etc.* **(c)** āḫaru baʿda āḫara : ᾗ μὲν γὰρ ἐν ἄλλῳ καὶ ἄλλῳ (*sc.* τὸ νῦν), ἕτερον *Arist. Phys. IV 11, 219b13-14* = wa-ḏālika anna min ǧihati annahū (*sc.* al-āna) fī āḫara baʿda āḫara fa-innahū muḫtalifun *421.5.*

38.3 ἕτερος καὶ ἕτερος *or sim.* (*one thing after another*) **(a)** wāḥidun baʿda āḫara : εἰ μὲν γὰρ αἰεὶ ἕτερον καὶ ἕτερον (*sc.* τὸ νῦν) *Arist. Phys. IV 10, 218a11* = fa-innahū in kāna (*sc.* al-ānu) abadan wāḥidan baʿda āḫara ġayrahū *406.2;* οὕτως καὶ ὁ χρόνος ἀεὶ ἐν ἀρχῇ καὶ τελευτῇ καὶ διὰ τοῦτο δοκεῖ ἀεὶ ἕτερος *IV 13, 222b4* = ka-ḏālika l-zamānu ayḍan abadan huwa fī btidāʾin wa-taqaḍḍin wa-li-ḏālika qad yuẓannu annahū abadan wāḥidun baʿda āḫara *465.4-5 (where the translator interpreted* ἕτερος *correctly in the sense of* ἕτερος καὶ ἕτερος*)* **(b)** *incorporating the context:* baṭnun baʿda baṭnin : ἡ τῶν κοιλιῶν ἑτέρα πρὸς ἑτέρας δεχομένη τὴν τροφήν *Arist. Part. anim. III 14, 674b11* = qabilahū (*sc.* al-ṭaʿāma) baṭnun baʿda baṭnin *94.13.*

38.4 πάλιν καὶ πάλιν (*again and again*) = marratan baʿda marratin : ὡς ἐνδέχεται κίνησιν εἶναι τὴν αὐτὴν καὶ μίαν πάλιν καὶ πάλιν, οὕτω καὶ χρόνον *Arist. Phys. IV 12, 220b13* = ka-mā yumkinu an takūna l-ḥarakatu l-wāḥidatu bi-ʿaynihā tatakarraru marratan baʿda marratin ka-ḏālika qad yumkinu hāḏā fī l-zamāni ayḍan *442.9-10.*

من بعدِ **min baʿdi** *c. gen.*; *prep.*

1. *transl.* μετά *prep.* (*after*) *alone and in compounds*

1.1 μετά *c. acc.* (*after, next*) : εἶτα μετὰ τοῦτο ὅσα ἕπεται τῷ πράγματι *Arist. An. pr. I 27, 43b3* = ṯumma min baʿdi ḏālika kullu mā yalḥaqu l-šayʾa *215.3 / fol. 94b* ⟼ μετὰ δὲ τὰς εἰρημένας φιλοσοφίας ἡ Πλάτωνος ἐπεγένετο πραγματεία *Arist. Metaph. α 6, 987a29* = wa-min baʿdi mā ḏukira min anwāʿi l-falsafati wuǧidat falsafatu Aflāṭūn *62.16;* μετὰ ταῦτα ὅτι οὐ γίγνεται οὔτε ἡ ὕλη οὔτε τὸ εἶδος *Λ 3, 1069b35* = wa-min baʿdi hāḏihī annahū lā l-māddatu takūnu wa-lā l-ṣūratu *1452.6, sim. versio Usṭāṯ 1452v2; 1070a4 = 1456.2* ⟼ οὗ μετὰ τὴν ἀρχὴν ὄντος *Arist. Phys. V 3, 226b34* = al-šayʾ allaḏī huwa min baʿdi l-mabdaʾi *542.15;* μετὰ γὰρ τὸ γενέσθαι πρῶτον ἀλλοίωσις καὶ αὔξησις *VIII 7, 260b32* = wa-ḏālika annahā innamā takūnu min baʿdi an yakūna (*sic leg. pro* takūna *ed.*) awwalan istiḥālatun wa-numuwwun *881.7** ⟼ μετὰ τὸ ἀποξηρανθῆναι *Diosc. Mat. med. I, 255.8* = min baʿdi mā yuyabbasu *vetus transl. Ullmann Unters., 184* ⟼ μία μὲν αὕτη ῥῆσις ... εἶτα πάλιν μετ᾽ οὐ πολύ ... καὶ μετὰ τοῦτο πάλιν ... καὶ πάλιν οὐ μετὰ πολύ ... *Galen An. virt. 55.16-56.17* = fa-hāḏā wāḥidun min aqāwīlihī ... wa-min baʿdi hāḏā l-kalāmi bi-qalīlin qāla ... wa-min baʿdi ḏālika ayḍan qāla ... wa-min baʿdi hāḏā bi-qalīlin *27.6-28.2;* καὶ μέντοι καὶ μετ᾽ ὀλίγα πάλιν οὕτως εἶπεν *59.9* = wa-min baʿdi hāḏā bi-qalīlin yaqūlu ayḍan *29.18-19;* καὶ μετὰ ταῦτα πάλιν ἐν ἑτέρᾳ ῥήσει γράφει ταυτί ... *59.18* = wa-min baʿdi hāḏā ayḍan fī mawḍiʿin āḫara mina l-kalāmi yaqūlu ... *29.23; etc.* ⟼ ᾗτινι ἂν ἡ μήτρη ἔμπυος γένηται ... μετὰ τόκον *Hippocr. Superf. 84.15* = in ʿaraḍat fī fami l-raḥimi middatun min baʿdi mā talidu (talidu *corr. Ullmann, p. 266* : tulqī *ed.*) *12.7** ⟼ ἡ γὰρ κίνησις φύσει μετὰ τὴν μονήν *Nicom. Arithm. 11.14* = wa-ḏālika anna l-ḥarakata hiya bi-l-ṭabīʿati min baʿdi l-sukūni *18.10;* μετὰ ... τὸ διχασθῆναι ἕκαστον τούτων *19.16* = kulla wāḥidin min hāḏihi l-aʿdādi min baʿdi an yanqasima *24.9; 76.16 = 62.13; 89.11 = 72.5; etc.*

1.2 *sem.; etym.; transl.* μετά *in* μεταγενέστερος (*later in origin*) = kāna min baʿdi *c. gen.*: ἐκδηλότερόν γε μὴν ἡ σφαιρικὴ (*sc.* ἐπιστήμη) ... ὅτι γεωμετρίας μεταγενεστέρα ἐστιν *Nicom. Arithm. 11.13* = wa-ammā l-amru fī ʿilmi l-kurati ... fa-huwa amrun bayyinun ... min qibali anna hāḏā l-ʿilma innamā yakūnu min baʿdi ʿilmi l-handasati *18.10.*

2. ἀπό *prep. c. gen.* (*since* [*of time*], *i.e., after*) : ἐν δὲ τῷ αὐτῷ πρώτῳ ἔτει ἀπὸ τῆς Ἀλεξάνδρου τελευτῆς *Ptol. Hypoth. 84.15* = fī hāḏihi l-sanati l-ūlā llatī min baʿdi mawti l-Iskandar *31.14; sim. 88.23 = 37.5.*

3. ἐπί *prep. c. dat.* (*thereupon, after*) : τὸ πρώτιστον εἶδος ἡμιόλιος, ἐπὶ τούτῳ δὲ τὸ μετ' αὐτὸ ἐπίτριτος, ἐπὶ δὲ τούτοις ὁ τάξει ἑξῆς *Nicom. Arithm. 66.9* = al-nawʿu l-awwalu minhu wa-huwa l-miṯlu wa-l-niṣfu wa-baʿdahu llaḏī yatlūhu wa-huwa l-miṯlu wa-l-ṯulṯu wa-min baʿdi hāḏayni l-nawʿu llaḏī yatlūhumā fī l-martabati *56.12;* ἕπεται δ' εὐθὺς ἐπὶ τούτῳ τὸ ἐπιτριμερές *66.13* = wa-yatlūhu min baʿdihi l-zāʾidu ṯalāṯata ağzāʾ*in 56.15; 93.10 = 74.12; 119.19 = 93.13* (*v. supra* āna 1, *I 732.8*).

4. *transl.* ἑξῆς *adv.* (*next*) *and its compounds*

4.1 ἑξῆς (*next*) **(a)** min baʿdi ḏālika : ἀλλ' ἐπισωρεύω τὸν ἑξῆς (*sc.* ἀριθμόν) τὸν ις *Nicom. Arithm. 43.12* = lākinnā naḍaʿu ilayhi min baʿdi ḏālika ʿadada l-sittati ʿašara *40.23;* ἐκκείσθω ἐν μὲν τῷ πρώτῳ στίχῳ ὁ ἀπὸ μονάδος φυσικὸς ἀριθμός, εἶτα ἑξῆς οἱ κελευσθέντες τῶν τοῦ πολλαπλασίου εἰδῶν *52.1* = naḍaʿu (*sic leg. pro* naṣnaʿu) fī awwali saṭrin ... al-aʿdāda l-mubtadiʾata mina l-wāḥidi ʿalā wuğūhihā wa-ṭabīʿatihā ṯumma naḍaʿu fīhā min baʿdi ḏālika sāʾira mā qad umira bi-waḍʿihī min anwāʿi ḏawāti l-aḍʿāfi *45.22*; 97.10 =76.22; etc.* **(b)** min baʿdi mā qulnā : ἑξῆς ὑποθησόμεθα πῶς δεῖ κρίνειν τοὺς ὀνείρους *Artem. Onirocr. 19.5* = wa-min baʿdi mā qulnā raʾaynā an naʾḫuḏa fī nafsi taʿbīri l-ruʾyā *36.14;* ἑξῆς δὲ περὶ κυνηγίου καλῶς ἔχον εἶναί μοι δοκεῖ διασαφῆσαι *117.4* = mā yalīqu binā an natakallama fīhi min baʿdi mā qulnā huwa amru l-ṣaydi *213.14; 145.19 = 261.10; etc.*

4.2 ἐφεξῆς (*afterwards, next in order*) = min baʿdi ḏālika : καὶ δὴ καὶ τούτων ἐφεξῆς τάδε γράφει *Galen An. virt. 56.10* = wa-min baʿdi ḏālika yaḍaʿu hāḏā l-qawla *27.18;* ἐν μέν γε τῷ Τιμαίῳ κατὰ τὰ πρῶτα τῶν λόγων ἔγραψε ..., ἀλλὰ καὶ συνάπτων ἐφεξῆς ... *65.10* = minhā qawluhu llaḏī waḍaʿahū fī awwali kitābi Ṭīmāwus fa-innahū qāla ... wa-min baʿdi ḏālika atbaʿa mā qaddama fa-qāla *33.15; 66.1 = 34.1; etc.*

5. *transl.* εἶτα *adv.* (*then*) *and its compounds*

5.1 εἶτα (*then, after that*) = *in hend.* ṯumma min baʿdi ḏālika : μετὰ δὲ ἀμφοτέρους πενταγώνων, εἶτα ἑξαγώνων, εἶτα ἑπταγώνων *Nicom.*

Arithm. 97.10 = wa-llaḏī baʿda hāḏayni li-l-muḫammasāti ṯumma min baʿdi ḏālika li-l-musaddasāti (*sic leg. pro* al-musaddasātu *ed.*) ṯumma li-l-musabbaʿāti *76.22**.

5.2 ἔπειτα (*thereafter*) **(a)** min baʿdi ḏālika : ἔπειτα προελθὼν ἐπὶ πλέον περὶ τῶν αὐτῶν ὡδί πως διεξέρχεται *Galen An. virt. 57.21* = min baʿdi ḏālika lammā nbasaṭa fī l-kalāmi aṭnaba fī l-šarḥi *28.19* **(b)** *in hend.* ṯumma ... min baʿdi ḏālika : *Artem. Onirocr. 65.17* = *121.10-11 (v. supra* ayḍan 14.2, *I 730.2*) ⟼ ἔπειτα σιτία παντοδαπὰ ἐσθιέτω *Hippocr. Nat. hom. 214.1* = ṯumma yaʾkulu min baʿdi ḏālika aṭʿimatan muḫtalifatan min kulli ḍarbin *31.16.*

5.3 κἄπειτα (*and thereafter*) = *in hend.* ṯumma min baʿdi ḏālika : κἄπειτα ἐκ μὲν τῶν ὑποκαθιζόντων ἐγεννήθη ἡ γῆ *Ps.-Plut. Placita 290a24* = ṯumma min baʿdi ḏālika takawwanat al-arḍu mina l-aǧzāʾi llatī rasabat *9.5.*

6. ὕστερον *adv.* (*later, afterwards*) = min baʿdi ḏālika : οἱ ἐγχώριοι ... ἐκάλουν τὴν ἐσθῆτα τημένειον ἐπώνυμον Τημένου τοῦ εὑρόντος· ὕστερον δὲ τῷ χρόνῳ παραφθαρέντος τοῦ ὀνόματος τήβεννος ἐκλήθη *Artem. Onirocr. 104.14* = sammaw (*sc.* ahlu l-bilādi) hāḏā l-libāsa ṭīmāniyūn bi-smin muštaqqin mini smi l-raǧuli llaḏī abdaʿahū fa-ammā min baʿdi ḏālika bi-zamānin fa-innahum lammā nasū hāḏā l-isma sammawhu tībānun *192.16.*

7. νυνί *adv.* (*now; i.e., next*) = min baʿdi hāḏā : καὶ ταῦτα μὲν περὶ ἀνατροφῆς· νυνὶ δὲ περὶ σώματος καὶ τῶν ἐν τῷ σώματι μερῶν ... ποιήσομαι τὸν λόγον *Artem. Onirocr. 25.15* = fa-hāḏā mā naktafī bihī mina l-qawli fī hāḏihi l-ruʾyāti wa-ammā min baʿdi hāḏā fa-innī aṣīru ilā l-qawli fī aʿḍāʾi l-badani *49.1.*

8. ἔτι *adv.* (*hereafter*), *c. neg.* (*no longer*) = lā ... min baʿdi ḏālika : οὐ γὰρ ἔτι φίλοι ἔσονται αὐτοῖς *Arist. Eth. Nic. VIII 7, 1159a7* = fa-innahū ... lā yakūnūna min baʿdi ḏālika aṣdiqāʾa *451.5.*

9. *paraphr.;* οἱ νεώτεροι (*the more recent ones*) *Nicom. Arithm. 122.17* = man atā min baʿdi l-qudamāʾi *95.4.*

10. *paraphr.;* ἀπόβασις (*outcome, an event succeeding s.th. else*) = al-ʿāriḍu llaḏī ʿaraḍa min baʿdi šayʾin : ἐπιστεύθησαν τῷ τὰς ἀποβάσεις ἐοικέναι τοῖς ὀνείροις *Artem. Onirocr. 101.9* = fa-wuǧidat ḥaqqan wa-ḏālika anna al-ʿāriḍa llaḏī ʿaraḍa min baʿdihā (*sc.* al-ruʾyaʾāti) kāna mušākilan lahā *21.10-11.*

بعد أن baʿda an *conj.*

1. ἐπί *prep. c. dat.* (*after, subsequent to*) : καὶ γὰρ τὸν Προμηθέα λέγουσιν ἐπὶ τῷ πλάσαι τοὺς ἀνθρώπους ... ἀπολέσθαι *Artem. Onirocr. 211.18* = wa-ḏālika annahū yuqālu fī l-luġzi inna Barāmītiyūs baʿda an ʿamila unāsan ... māta *383.6.*

2. πρότερον *adv.* (*previously*) : φίλον δὲ ὁ περαίνων εἰς ἔχθραν αὐτῷ καταστήσεται βλαβεὶς (βλαβεὶς *LV Arab.* : βλαβέντι *Hercher, Pack; v. Festugière p. 88, n. 12*) πρότερον ὑπ' αὐτοῦ *Artem. Onirocr. 91.3** = fa-in raʾā ka-annahū yuǧāmiʿu ṣadīqan lahū fa-inna ḏālika yadullu ʿalā muʿādāti ṣadīqihī baʿda an yanālahū minhu maḍarratun *167.9.*

3. ἔτι *adv.* (*hereafter*) : νυνὶ δ' οἷς ἐξ ἀρχῆς προὐθέμην, προσθήσω τὰ λείποντα τοσοῦτον ἔτι πάλιν ἐπειπών, ὡς ... *Galen An. virt. 46.10* = wa-ammā l-sāʿata fa-innī zāʾidun ʿalā mā badaʾtu bihī mā yuḥtāǧu ilayhi baʿda an aqūla innahū ... *20.8.*

4. παρὰ *prep. c. acc.* (*beside, contrary to s.th.; after*) : φαμὲν γὰρ καὶ ἐν τῇ συνηθείᾳ τὸν παρὰ προσδοκίαν σωθέντα ἐξ Ἅιδου ἀναβεβηκέναι *Artem. Onirocr. 185.1* = wa-ḏālika annā naqūlu ʿalā mā ǧarat bihi l-ʿādatu iḏā raʾaynā man qad naǧā baʿda an lam yakun yurǧā innahū qad raǧaʿa mina l-āḫirati *335.10.*

5. *sem. metathesis; transformation of a conditional clause into a temporal one;* ἐάν (*if s.th. happens*) = baʿda an (*after s.th. has happened*) : αἱ πλεῖσται (*sc.* τῶν γυναικῶν, *sic interpunxit Arab.*) διαλύονταί τε γάρ, ἐὰν πίωσι, καὶ ἀδυνατοῦσιν *Arist. Hist. anim. VII 5, 585a33* = li-anna kaṯīran minhunna baʿda an yašrabna šarāban yataḥallalna wa-yaḍʿufna *474.11.*

6. *sem. metathesis; transformation of a conceptual/logical condition into a temporal one;* μόνον, μόνον ἵνα (*provided only that*) = baʿda an (... faqaṭ) (*only after that*) **(a)** *abs.* : καὶ ἐπ' ἄπειρον, μόνον ἵνα μονάδι μείζων ἡ ἑτέρα πλευρὰ τῆς λοιπῆς ᾖ *Nicom. Arithm. 108.19* = wa-mā baʿda ḏālika ilā mā lā nihāyata baʿda an yakūna aḥadu l-ḍilʿayni yazīdu ʿalā l-āḫari wāḥidan *85.1;* οἷον τρὶς γ ἑπτάκις ἢ ὀκτάκις ἢ ἐνάκις ἢ ὁσακισοῦν μόνον ὑπερβαλλόντως *111.1* = miṯla l-ṯalāṯati fī l-ṯalāṯati wa-mā ǧtamaʿa fī sabʿatin aw fī <ṯamā>niyatin (*nos*) aw fī tisʿatin aw (aw *nos* : wa *ed.*) fī ayyi ʿadadin kāna baʿda an (baʿda an *nos* : buʿdan *ed.*) yakūna zāʾidan ʿalā kulli wāḥidin mina l-ʿadadayni l-awwalayni *86.16** **(b)** baʿda an ... faqaṭ : δοθέντων σοι τριῶν ὅρων ἐν ᾑτινιοῦν σχέσει καὶ ἀναλογίᾳ, ... μόνον ἵνα ἐν τῷ αὐτῷ λόγῳ ὁ μέσος πρὸς τὸν ἐλάττονα θεωρῆται ἐν ᾧ ὁ μείζων πρὸς τὸν μέσον *Nicom. Arithm. 74.19* = iḏā kānat ṯalāṯatu ḥudūdin maʿlūmatin wa-kānat ʿalā nisbatin wāḥidatin ... baʿda an takūna nisbatu l-awsaṭi ilā l-aṣġari ka-nisbati l-aʿẓami ilā l-awsaṭi faqaṭ *61.2*.

7. *synt.; transl. the temporal relation or circumstantiality implied by a participium coniunctum or a genitive absolute* : οἳ μὲν (*sc.* γονεῖς) γὰρ εὐθὺς γενόμενα στέργουσιν (*sc.* τὰ τέκνα), τὰ δὲ προελθόντος χρόνου τοὺς γονεῖς *Arist. Eth. Nic. VIII 12, 1161b25* = min aǧli anna l-ābāʾa yuḥibbūna l-awlāda ḥīna tūladu (*sic leg.*) min sāʿatihā wa-ammā l-awlādu fa-innahā tuḥibbu baʿda an yamḍiya zamānun *467.1-2** ⊣ πρῶτον μὲν οὖν ὕδρωψ ἐξέρχεται ..., ἔπειτα τὸ ἔμβρυον ... τοῦ ὑστέρου τὰ ἔσω ἐκτὸς ἴσχοντος *Arist. Hist. anim. VII 9, 587a8* = wa-awwalu mā yaḫruǧu mina l-marʾati māʾun ... ṯumma yaḫruǧu l-ǧanīnu ... baʿda an tanqaliba l-mašīmatu wa-yakūna mā dāḫilun minhā ḫāriǧan *480.6* ⊣ τοῦτο γὰρ μᾶλλόν ἐστιν ἀξιοπίστων ἀκοῦσαι λεγόντων ἢ τὸ περὶ τὴν κεφαλήν, ὡς ἀποκοπεῖσα φθέγγεται τῶν ἀνθρώπων *Arist. Part. anim. III 10, 673a14* = wa-yanbaġī lanā an nuḥaqqiqa hāḏā l-qawla akṯara min qawli llaḏīna yazʿumūna anna raʾsa l-insāni yatakallamu baʿda an yuqṭaʿa *90.17; sim. 673a29 = 91.6* ⊣ εἰς κρατῆρα μέλιτι κατακεχρισμένον *Diosc. Mat med. I, 42.14* = baʿda an tuṭlā l-iǧǧānatu bi-ʿasalin *vetus transl. Ullmann Unters., 184* ⊣ μάλιστα δὲ τῶν ῥιζῶν ἀποχωρεῖν πειρῶ γινώσκων ὅτι ... *Galen Anat. admin. II, 353.8* = wa-l-yakun akṯaru ḥirṣika wa-ʿināyatika an tabʿuda min uṣūli l-ʿaṣabi baʿda an taʿlama annahū ... *146.5 Garofalo;* ἀφῃρημένου τοῦ δέρματος *514.3* = baʿda an takšiṭa l-ǧilda *314.1 Garofalo* ⊣ οἴνῳ Φαλερίνῳ ἀναλάμβανε, ὀποβαλσάμου παραπτόμενος ἐν τῷ ἀναλαμβάνειν *Galen Ther. Pis. 263.4* = wa-yuʿǧanu bi-ḫamrin fālārīnus wa-yuʿǧanu bi-l-aṣābiʿi baʿda an tumassiḥahā bi-labani l-balasāni *121b7* ⊣ οἱ μέν τι καὶ τὴν γνώμην βλαβέντες (*sc.* θνῄσκουσιν) *Hippocr. Diaet. acut. 43.3* = wa-baʿḍuhum yamūtu baʿda an tadḫula ʿalayhi l-āfatu fī ḏihnihī *9.11* ⊣ ὁ δὲ Δημόκριτος πάντα μετέχειν φησὶ ψυχῆς ποιᾶς, ... διότι ἀεὶ διαφανῶς (διαφανοῦς *Arab. ut vid., prop. Daiber*) τινος θερμοῦ καὶ αἰσθητικοῦ μετέχει τοῦ πλείονος διαπνεομένου *Ps.-Plut. Placita 390a23** = wa-ammā Ḏīmūqrīṭūs fa-innahū yarā anna l-nafsa mawǧūdatun fī ǧamīʿi l-ašyāʾi ... wa-li-ḏālika fīhā šayʾun muḍīʾun ḥārrun ḥassāsun baʿda an qad nuffisa minhā akṯaru ḏālika *51.21* ⊣ ὅπερ Ἀρχύτας ποτ' ἔφη ποιεῖν Εὔρυτον διατιθέντα τινὰς ψήφους *Theophr. Princ. 6a20* =

wa-huwa mā qālahū marratan Arḫūṭas an yaǧʿala mā yaǧʿaluhū salisa l-ǧaryi baʿda an yaṣīra lahū ḥiṣaṣun mā *186.1-2* (*cf. also Gutas, notes 78-79 ad loc.*).

بَعْدُ baʿdu *adv.*

A. 1-5. Basic meaning: yet, still

B. 6-12. Basic meaning: afterwards

fī-mā baʿdu *adv.*

min baʿdu *adv.*

A. *Basic meaning: yet, still*

1. ἔτι (*still*) **(a)** *abs., in affirm. sentences* : εἰ τὰ πρῶτά τις μοχθηρῶς ἐθισθείη παῖς ὢν ἔτι *Alex. An. mant.* [*Lib. arb.*] *175.12* = ini ʿtāda l-insānu fī awwali amrihī wa-huwa baʿdu ṣabiyyun ʿādātin radīʾatan *207.126* ⟼ ἐξέρχεται μὲν ἔτι μαλακόν (*sc.* τὸ ᾠόν), πόνον γὰρ ἂν παρεῖχε τικτόμενον *Arist. Gener. anim. III 2, 752a34* = taḫruǧu l-bayḍatu wa-hiya baʿdu layyinatun, wa-law kānat ǧāsiyatan ǧiddan la-kānat mūǧiʿatan muʾḏiyatan li-llaḏī taḫruǧu *(sic leg.)* minhu *104.20**; καὶ διὰ τοῦτο τῶν χελιδόνων ἐάν τις ἔτι νέων ὄντων ἐκκεντήσῃ τὰ ὄμματα πάλιν ὑγιάζονται *IV 6, 774b31* = wa-li-hāḏā l-sababi in aḫraǧa aḥadun ʿaynay firāḫi l-ḫuṭṭāfi bi-ḥadīdatin aw ġayri ḏālika wa-huwa ḥadaṯun baʿdu yaʿūdu ʿaynayhā (*sic ed. pro* taʿūdu ʿaynāhā) ilā ḥāli l-ṣiḥḥati l-ulā *163.20*⊗ ⟼ ἀνάγκαζε τρέχειν τὸ ζῶον ..., ὥστε ἀσθμαῖνον ἔτι (ἀσθμαῖνον ἔτι *P Arab.* : ἀσθμαίνοντι *Chart., Kühn, Garofalo*) τὴν πλευρὰν ἐκκόπτεσθαι *Galen Anat. admin. II, 702.11** = fa-taḍṭarru l-ḥayawāna ilā l-ʿadwi kay-mā yuqṭaʿa l-ḍilʿu wa-l-ḥayawānu baʿdu yalhaṯu *544.8 Garofalo* (=*WGAÜ Suppl. I, 408; cf. Ullmann, Coclusio a minori ad maius, # 73*) **(b)** *sem. metathesis; affirm. / neg. transformation* (*still ignorant = not yet knowing*): ἠγνόουν γὰρ ἔτι τοὺς ἐν ἄκροις τοῖς κώλοις μῦς τοὺς μικρούς *Galen Anat. admin. II, 234.17* = li-annī lam akun baʿdu ʿaraftu ḏāka l-ʿaḍala l-ṣiġāra llaḏī fī l-kaffi *24.6 Garofalo.*

2. *sem.; etym.; transl.* πω (*yet*) *with preceding neg. or in compounds*

2.1 μήπω or μηδέπω (*not yet*) **(a)** lam ... baʿdu : τὸ μήπω ἐφθαρμένον, ἐνδεχόμενον δ' ὕστερον μὴ εἶναι *Arist. Cael. I 11, 280b33* = iḏā kāna l-šayʾu lam yafsud baʿdu wa-yumkinu aḫīran an yakūna laysa *versio B 204.16 Badawī* = al-šayʾu llaḏī lam yafsud baʿdu wa-yumkinu fīhi aḫīran an yakūna ġayra mawǧūdin *versio A 101b18* ⟼ ὅταν γένηται κύημα τέλειον ζῷον δὲ μήπω τέλειον *Arist. Gener. anim. II 4, 737b9* = iḏā kāna minhu ḥamlun tāmmun wa-lam yakun baʿdu ḥayawānan tāmman *65.22* ⟼ ἰχὼρ δ᾽ ἐστὶν ἄπεπτον αἷμα ἢ τῷ μήπω πεπέφθαι ἢ τῷ διωρρῶσθαι *Arist. Hist. anim. III 19, 521b2* = wa-innamā yakūnu l-damu māʾiyyan immā li-annahū lam yanḍaǧ baʿdu nuḍǧan balīġan <wa-immā> li-annahū muftariqun bi-ḏātihī *139.8* ⟼ μηδέπω δὲ τοῦ ὀφθαλμοῦ βεβλαστηκότος *Diosc. Mat. med. I, 119.4* = wa-lam yatimma baʿdu qūḥuhū *vetus transl. Ullmann Unters., 184* ⟼ καὶ γὰρ ξηρότητος ἀδήκτου μετέχει καὶ ψύξεως μηδέπω ναρκούσης *Galen Simpl. medic. XI, 838.13* = wa-ḏālika anna lahū yubūsatan ġayra laḏḏāʿatin wa-burūdatan lam tabluġ baʿdu ilā ḥaddi l-burūdati llatī tuḫdiru *versio B WGAÜ, 418.22;* διὰ τὸ τινὰς μὲν τῶν λίθων μηδέπω τεθεᾶσθαι *XII, 227.10* = wa-ḏālika li-annī lam akun raʾaytu baʿdu afrādan mina l-ḥiǧārāti *WGAÜ, 418.23* ⟼ τὰ δὲ ἐπικυήματα ..., ἢν μήπω διάκρισιν ἔχῃ, ἀλλὰ σὰρξ ᾖ *Hippocr. Superf. 72.12* = fa-ammā l-ḥabalu ʿalā ḥabalin ... in kāna lam yataṣawwar baʿdu wa-innamā huwa laḥmun *1.12* **(b)** *sem. metathesis; neg. / affirm. transformation* (*not yet ripe = green*) : οὖα τὰ μηλίζοντα καὶ μήπω πέπειρα *Diosc. Mat. med. I, 111.10* = al-ġubayrā mā ǧuniya min šaǧarihī wa-huwa baʿdu ġaḍḍun aṣfaru *versio A WGAÜ Suppl. I, 687.ult.*

2.2 οὔπω, οὐδέπω, οὔ ... πω, *etc.* (*not yet*) **(a)** laysa ... baʿdu : τὸ γὰρ γεννώμενον οὐδέπω τὴν ἕξιν ἔχει τὴν αἰσθητικήν *Alex. Qu. III 3* [*Sens.*] *84.38* = fa-inna l-ḥayawāna llaḏī fī l-kawni laysa bi-mutaḥayyiʾin li-ḥissi l-ašyāʾi baʿdu *180.7* ⟼ ταῦτα ... ἀδικήματά ἐστιν, οὐ μέντοι πω ἄδικοι διὰ ταῦτα οὐδὲ πονηροί *Arist. Eth. Nic. V 8, 1135b23* = hiya lā ʿtidālātun illā annahum laysa hum baʿdu ḏawī lā ʿtidālin bi-hāḏihī wa-lā ašrāran *327.13* ⟼ ἔνια (ἔνια *codd.* : ἔνιοι *ut intell. Arab.*) δ᾽ οὐκ ἔχουσί πω ὅταν γεννῶσιν, οἷον τρίχωσιν πολιῶν ἢ γενείου *Arist. Gener. anim. I 18, 722a6* = wa-mina llaḏīna yalidūna man laysa lahū baʿdu šaʿarun <abyaḍu> (*suppl. nos*) wa-lā liḥyatun *22.5** ⟼ καὶ γὰρ ὁ τοῦ ἀνθρώπου λόγος, ἐὰν μὴ τὸ ἔστιν ἢ ἦν ἢ ἔσται (ἦν ἢ ἔσται *Βα*[d], *Arab.* : ἔσται Δ: ἔσται ἢ ἦν ς, *ed.*) ἤ τι τοιοῦτο προστεθῇ, οὔπω λόγος ἀποφαντικός *Arist. Int. 5, 17a12** = wa-ḏālika anna qawla l-insāni mā lam yustaṯna maʿahū annahu l-āna aw kāna aw yakūnu aw šayʾun min naẓāʾiri hāḏihī fa-laysa huwa baʿdu ǧāziman *103.19-20 / fol. 180b17* ⟼ ὥσπερ ἡ γῆ οὔπω ἀνδριὰς δυνάμει *Arist. Metaph. Θ 7, 1049a17* = miṯla l-arḍi llatī laysat baʿdu ṣanaman bi-l-quwwati *1166.7* ⟼ οἷον τῷ ΖΗ, ἐν τούτῳ τὸ Β οὔπω ἔσται πρὸς τῷ Δ *Arist. Phys. V 2, 232a30* = miṯālu ḏālika zamānu ZḤ laysa yalḥaqu fīhi baʿdu B ilā l-wuṣūli ilā D *617.10*

(b) lam ... baʿdu : ἐπιστήμη μὲν αὐτοῦ οὐκ ἔστιν οὐδέπω, αὐτὸ δὲ τὸ ἐπιστητὸν ἔστιν *Arist. Cat. 7, 7b33* = fa-ʿilmuhū lam yūǧad baʿdu, fa-ammā hāḏā l-maʿlūmu nafsuhū fa-anniyyatuhū qāʾimatun *52.9-10 / fol. 168a16* ⟼ ὥστε τὴν μὲν (*sc.* ἀρετὴν) ἤδη, τὴν δ' οὔπω εἰληφὼς ἔσται *Arist. Eth. Nic. VII 13, 1144b35* = ḥattā annahū qad yakūnu <baʿḍahā (*sc.* al-faḍāʾila) qad adrakahā> (*suppl. nos; lac. in cod.*) wa-baʿḍahā lam yudrikhā baʿdu *333.4** ⟼ περὶ γὰρ φρενῶν οὐδέν πω διώρισται *Arist. Part. anim. III 7, 670b30* = li-annā lam naḏkur baʿdu ḥāla ṭibāʿi l-ḥiǧābi *84.13* ⟼ οὔπω δ' ἐπικεχείρηται τὰ περὶ τὴν ὑπόκρισιν *Arist. Rhet. III 1, 1403b21* = ġayra anna l-ḥīlata fī l-aḫḏi bi-l-wuǧūhi lam tabtadiʾ an tuẓhara baʿdu *172.2;* οὔπω δὲ σύγκειται τέχνη περὶ αὐτῶν, ἐπεὶ καὶ τὸ περὶ τὴν λέξιν ὀψὲ προῆλθεν *III 1, 1403b35* = ġayra anna l-ṣināʿata awi l-ḥīlata fī ḏālika lam turakkab baʿdu li-anna l-ḥīlata fī l-maqālati ayḍan innamā balaġat aḫīran *172.19* ⟼ οὔπω δὲ νοσεῖν οἱ οὕτως ἔχοντες λέγονται *Galen Ars medica I, 362.3* = illā anna man ʿaraḍa lahū ḏālika lam yamraḍ baʿdu *WGAÜ, 482.20* ⟼ ἡμεῖς δὲ οὐδέπω πεῖραν αὐτῆς (*sc.* τῆς πόας) ἔχομεν *Galen Simpl. medic. XI, 840.12* = wa-ammā naḥnu fa-lam nuǧarribhā (*sc.* al-ʿušbata) wa-lam naḫtabirhā baʿdu *versio B WGAÜ, 481.21* ⟼ περὶ δὲ τοῦ θεωρητικοῦ νοῦ οὐδέν πω φανερόν *Them. In De an. 102.12* = fa-ammā l-ʿaqlu l-naẓariyyu fa-lam yatabayyan baʿdu šayʾun min amrihī *185.12; cf. also WGAÜ, 482.*

3. ἤδη *with preceding neg.* (*not yet*) = lam ... baʿdu : ἀναγκαῖον εἶναί τι καὶ τὸ μεταξὺ ἐν ᾧ μεταβάλλει (*sc.* ἡ τροφὴ ἐν τῇ κοιλίᾳ) καὶ οὔτ' ἔτι πρόσφατος οὔτ' ἤδη κόπρος *Arist. Part. anim. III 14, 675b32* = bi-iḍṭirārin ṣāra šayʾun āḫaru fī-mā bayna l-baṭnayni li-kay yataġayyara l-ṭaʿāmu hunālika wa-lā yaḫruǧa ḥadīṯan ṭariyyan li-annahū lam yaṣir baʿdu ziblan *98.7.*

4. *sem. amplif.; transl. the prospective outcome implied in* ἄπεπτος (*undigested*) = lam yanḍaǧ baʿdu (*not yet digested*) : ἔστι δ' ὁ πρόλοβος δέρμα κοῖλον καὶ μέγα, ἐν ᾧ ἡ τροφὴ πρώτη εἰσιοῦσα ἄπεπτός ἐστιν *Arist. Hist. anim. II 17, 508b29* = wa-innamā ḫilqatu l-ḥawṣalati min ǧildin ʿaẓīmin ʿamīqin yakūnu fīhi l-ṭaʿāmu llaḏī lam yanḍaǧ baʿdu *92.19* ⟼ τοῦτο γὰρ (ἡ νῆστις) μεταξὺ τῆς τ' ἄνω (*sc.* κοιλίας), ἐν ᾗ τὸ ἄπεπτον, καὶ τῆς κάτω, ἐν ᾗ τὸ ἄχρηστον *Arist. Part. anim. III 14, 675b35* = fa-hāḏā l-ʿuḍwu fī-mā bayna l-baṭni l-aʿlā wa-l-baṭni l-asfali wa-fīhi l-ṭaʿāmu llaḏī lam yanḍaǧ baʿdu wa-baʿdahu l-baṭnu l-asfalu llaḏī fīhi l-ṭaʿāmu l-fāsidu *98.10* ⟼ ἔστ' ἂν δὲ πυρρόν τε ᾖ τὸ οὖρον καὶ λεπτόν, ἄπεπτον σημαίνει τὸ νόσημα *Hippocr. Progn. 208.14* = wa-mā dāma l-bawlu aṣfara raqīqa l-qawāmi fa-innahū yadullu ʿalā anna l-maraḍa lam yanḍağ baʿdu *216.15*.

5. *sem. metathesis; affirm. / neg. transformation* : παίδιον νέον πάμπαν (*very young girl*) = ğāriyatun lam tabluġ baʿdu (*girl who has not yet reached puberty*) : τὰ δὲ λευκὰ (*sc.* καταμήνια) καὶ παιδίοις οὖσι γίνεται νέοις πάμπαν *Arist. Hist. anim. VII 1, 581b2* = fa-ammā l-ṭamṯu l-abyaḍu fa-huwa yaʿriḍu li-l-ğawārī llawātī lam yabluġna baʿdu *462.13*.

B. *Basic meaning: afterwards*

6. *transl.* ὕστερος (*later, afterwards, posterior*) *in various functions*

6.1 ὕστερος *adj., subst.* (*subsequent, posterior*) **(a)** *abs* : τὸ ἴσον ἔχειν καὶ πρότερον καὶ ὕστερον *Arist. Eth. Nic. V 7, 1132b20* = wa-li-l-musāwī qablu wa-baʿdu *311.3* ⟝ πρότερα καὶ ὕστερα λέγεται ἔνια *Arist. Metaph. Δ 11, 1018b9* = yuqālu qablu wa-baʿdu baʿḍu l-ašyāʾi *567.5;* τὸ δὲ πορρώτερον ὕστερον *1018b14* = wa-llaḏī huwa abʿadu min hāḏihī huwa baʿdu *567.10;* τὸ ὕστερον *1018b24* = allaḏī huwa baʿdu *568.8; sim. B 1, 995b22 = 172.15; etc.* **(b)** *with the article,* al-baʿdu : πῶς μὲν οὖν ἔχει περὶ ὅλου καὶ μέρους καὶ περὶ τοῦ προτέρου καὶ ὑστέρου, εἴρηται *Arist. Metaph. Z 10, 1036a13* = fa-qad qīla kayfa huwa fī l-kulli wa-l-ğuzʾi wa-fī l-qabli wa-l-baʿdi *914.2 (cf. ibid., 567.3)*.

6.2 ὕστερον *adv.* (*later, afterwards*) : δειχθήσεται δὲ περὶ αὐτῆς ἐν τοῖς ὕστερον *Arist. Eth. Nic. IV 9, 1128b35* = wa-sa-natakallamu fīhi fī-mā baʿdu; κἂν μηδὲν ὦσι χρήσιμοι μηδ᾽ εἰς ὕστερον γένοιντ᾽ ἂν *IX 7, 1167b33* = wa-in lam yakun yuntafaʿu bihim fī šayʾin wa-lā takūnu minhum manfaʿatun fī-mā baʿdu *507.3* (*see below,* fī-mā baʿdu 1.2 *and* 1.3); οὐ γάρ ἐστιν ἐνδεὴς (*sc.* ἡ ὅρασις) οὐδενὸς ὃ εἰς ὕστερον γινόμενον τελειώσει αὐτῆς τὸ εἶδος *Arist. Eth. Nic. X 4, 1174a15* = min ağli annahū (*sc.* al-baṣara) lā yaḥtāğu ilā šayʾini l-battata yakūnu min baʿdu li-yutimma ṣūratahū (*sic leg. pro* li-tatimma ṣūratuhū *ed.*) *539.11-12** (*see below,* min baʿdu 1.2).

7. *transl.* ἑξῆς (*thereafter*) *by itself and in compounds*

7.1 ἑξῆς *adv.* (*thereafter*) : διὰ τίνα δ᾽ αἰτίαν ... ἐν τοῖς ἑξῆς ῥηθήσεται *Arist. Eth. Nic. II 7, 1108a2* = wa-naḥnu naṣifu fī-mā baʿdu l-sababa *179.1* ⟝ ὅτι δὲ ... καὶ ἐν τοῖς ἑξῆς μὲν ποικιλώτερον εἰσόμεθα *Nicom. Arithm. 51.2* = wa-ammā ... fa-innahū amrun yatabayyanu fī-mā baʿdu bayānan šāfiyan *45.13* (*see below,* fī-mā baʿdu 4.2).

7.2 *sem.; etym.; transl.* ἑξῆς *in* ἐφεξῆς (*thereupon, subsequently*) : διὰ τοῦτ᾽ οὖν ἐφεξῆς φησι *Galen An. virt. 58.20* = wa-min ağli ḏālika qāla fī-mā ba‘du *29.12* (*see below,* fī-mā ba‘du 4.1) ⟼ πρὸς τὴν ἐξ ἀρχῆς μάθησιν καὶ πρὸς τὴν ἐφεξῆς ἄσκησιν *Galen Med. phil. 7.17* = fī ta‘allumihim ... awwalan ṯumma fī tadarrubihim min ba‘du *120* (*see below,* min ba‘du 1.3).

8. *transl.* αὖθις (*hereafter*) *by itself and in compounds*

8.1 αὖθις (*hereafter*) : τά τ' ἀποβλαστήματα τῆς κοίλης ... πάντα, περὶ ὧν αὖθις εἰρήσεται *Galen Anat. admin. II, 617.12* = ǧamī‘ šu‘abi l-‘irqi l-aǧwafi llatī anā ḏākiruhā ba‘du *440.13 Garofalo.*

8.2 *sem.; etym.; transl.* αὖθις *in* εἰσαῦθις (*in the hereafter*) : ἀλλὰ τοῦτο μὲν εἰσαῦθις ἐπισκεπτέον *Arist. Eth. Nic. I 5, 1097b14* = wa-lākinnā sa-nabḥaṯu ‘an hāḏā fī-mā ba‘du *133.5;* καὶ ἡδονῆς δ' ἕνεκα τῆς εἰσαῦθις μεγάλης (μεγάλης *om.* K^b*, Arab.*) μικρὰ λυπήσει *IV 12, 1127 a6** = wa-qad yaġummu ġamman yasīran bi-sababi l-laḏḏati llatī takūnu fī-mā ba‘du *279.11.*

9. εἶτα (*next, presently*) = *in hend.* ṯumma ... ba‘du : εἶτα ἀναπλεῖν *Diosc. Mat. med. I, 25.7* = ṯumma rtafa‘a ba‘du fawqahū *vetus transl. Ullmann Unters., 184.*

10. *sem. concentr.;* μετὰ τοῦτο (*after this*) : οἱ δὲ λαβόντες ἀρχὴν ψυχῆς ἀθάνατον, τὸ μετὰ τοῦτο θνητὸν σῶμα αὐτῇ περιετόρνευσαν *Them. In De an. 106.17* (= *Plato Tim. 69C6*) = hā'ulā'i taqabbalūhu fa-aḫaḏū mimmā huwa ladayhi mabda'an mina l-nafsi ġayra mā'itin fa-handamū ‘alayhi ba‘du badanan mā'itan wa-manaḥūhu l-badana kullahū murakkaban lahū *193.9.*

11. *sem. etym.; transl.* ἐπί *prep.* (*after, in addition*) *in compounds* : ἐπιφαίνομαι (*to show oneself in addition, later; supervene*) = ẓahara ba‘du : καὶ οὖρα καὶ ὑποχωρήματα καὶ ἱδρῶτες ... ἐπιφαινόμενα *Hippocr. Aphor. I : 12* = wa-l-bawlu wa-l-birāzu wa-l-‘araqu iḏā ẓaharat ba‘du *5.12.*

12. *sem.; def.;* ἕπομαι (*to come later*) = atā ba‘du : ὑπὲρ οὗ τὴν ἐπίσκεψιν ἐν τοῖς ἑπομένοις ποιησόμεθα *Arist. Eth. Nic. I 3, 1096a5* = wa-sa-nabḥaṯu ‘anhā fī-mā ya'tī ba‘du mina l-kalāmi *123.12.*

فيما بعدُ fī-mā ba‘du *adv.*

1. *transl.* ὕστερον *adv.* (*later, afterwards*) *by itself and in expr.*

1.1 ὕστερον *adv.* (*later, afterwards*) : ὕστερον δὲ ἀκριβέστερον περὶ αὐτῶν διορισθήσεται *Arist. Eth. Nic. II 7, 1107b15* = wa-sa-nastaqṣī tamyīzahā wa-taḥdīdahā fī-mā baʿdu *177.6*; ὕστερον ῥηθήσεται *II 7, 1107b21* = wa-sa-naṣifu ... fī-mā baʿdu *177.8* ⟼ Ἀριστοτέλης ... ἠκολούθησε δ' ὕστερον αὐτῷ καὶ ὁ ἀπὸ τῆς στοᾶς χορός *Galen Nat. fac. 8.7* = Arisṭūṭālīs wa-tabiʿahū fī-mā baʿdu aṣḥābu l-miẓallati *WGAÜ Suppl. II, 565.24* ⟼ πολλὰ δὲ καὶ ἄλλα ἐπίκαιρα παρεῖται ..., ἃ εἰρήσεται ὕστερον *Hippocr. Diaet. acut. 41.8* = wa-qad taraktu ḏikra ašyāʾa uḫara kaṯīratin ǧalīlati l-qadri ... anā wāṣifuhā fī-mā baʿdu *7.4* ⟼ ἐρέω δὲ ... ὀλίγον ἐπὶ τούτῳ ὕστερον *Hippocr. Nat. puer. 56.8* = sa-aqūlu ... fī-mā baʿdu *51.11* ⟼ φεῦγ' ἡδονὴν φέρουσαν ὕστερον βλάβην *Men. Mon. 806* = uhrub min laḏḏatin taʾūlu fī-mā baʿdu <ilā> maḍarratin *II, 85 : p. 72* (= *WGAÜ, 718.2*).

1.2 *in expr.; used in the transl. of* εἰς ὕστερον *adv.* (*later, afterwards*) = fī-mā baʿdu, *where* fī-mā *transl.* εἰς *and* baʿdu *transl.* ὕστερον : κἂν μηδὲν ὦσι χρήσιμοι μηδ' εἰς ὕστερον γένοιντ' ἄν *Arist. Eth. Nic. IX 7, 1167b33* = wa-in lam yakun yuntafaʿu bihim fī šayʾin wa-lā takūnu minhum manfaʿatun fī-mā baʿdu *507.3*.

1.3 *in expr.; used in the transl. of* ἐν τοῖς ὕστερον *adv.* (*later, afterwards*) = fī-mā baʿdu, *where* fī-mā *literally transl.* ἐν τοῖς *and* baʿdu *transl.* ὕστερον : δειχθήσεται δὲ περὶ αὐτῆς ἐν τοῖς ὕστερον *Arist. Eth. Nic. IV 9, 1128b35* = wa-sa-natakallamu fīhi fī-mā baʿdu *287.3*.

2. *transl.* αὖθις (*hereafter*) *by itself and in expr.*

2.1 αὖθις *adv.* (*hereafter*) : τὴν δὲ περίοδον αὖτις φράσω (φράσομεν *V, Arab. A*) τὴν τῶν ἡμερέων *Hippocr. Nat. hom. 186.16** = wa-innā nubayyinu (wa-anā mubayyinun *F*) l-adwāra mina l-ayyāmi llatī yanqaḍī fīhā l-amrāḍu fī-mā baʿdu *13.16*.

2.2 *in expr.; used in the transl. of* εἰσαῦθις (*in the hereafter*) = fī-mā baʿdu, *where* fī-mā *transl.* εἰς *and* baʿdu *transl.* αὖθις : ἀλλὰ τοῦτο μὲν εἰσαῦθις ἐπισκεπτέον *Arist. Eth. Nic. I 5, 1097b14* = wa-lākinnā sa-nabḥaṯu ʿan hāḏā fī-mā baʿdu *133.5;* καὶ ἡδονῆς δ' ἕνεκα τῆς εἰσαῦθις μεγάλης (μεγάλης *om.* K^b, *Arab.*) μικρὰ λυπήσει *IV 12, 1127a6** = wa-qad yaġummu ġamman yasīran bi-sababi l-laḏḏati llatī takūnu fī-mā baʿdu *279.11*.

3. ἔτι (*yet further* [*in the future*]) : καὶ οὐδὲν ἔτι τῷ τεθνεῶτι δοκεῖ οὔτ' ἀγαθὸν οὔτε κακὸν εἶναι *Arist. Eth. Nic. III 9, 1115a27* = wa-laysa yuẓannu anna l-mayyita yanāluhū fī-mā baʿdu šayʾun mina l-ḫayri aw mina l-šarri *215.4*.

4. *in expr.; used in the transl. of* ἐφεξῆς (*thereupon, subsequently*)

4.1 ἐφεξῆς (*thereupon, subsequently*) = fī-mā baʿdu, *where* fī-mā *transl.* ἐπί *and* baʿdu *transl.* ἑξῆς: διὰ τοῦτ' οὖν ἐφεξῆς φησι *Galen An. virt. 58.20* = wa-min aǧli ḏālika qāla fī-mā baʿdu *29.12*.

4.2 ἐν τοῖς ἑξῆς *adv.* (*in the hereafter, what comes next*) = fī-mā baʿdu, *where* fī-mā *literally transl.* ἐν τοῖς *and* baʿdu *transl.* ἑξῆς : διὰ τίνα δ' αἰτίαν ... ἐν τοῖς ἑξῆς ῥηθήσεται *Arist. Eth. Nic. II 7, 1108a2* = wa-naḥnu naṣifu fī-mā baʿdu l-sababa *179.1* ⟼ ὅτι δὲ ... καὶ ἐν τοῖς ἑξῆς μὲν ποικιλώτερον εἰσόμεθα *Nicom. Arithm. 51.2* = wa-ammā ... fa-innahū amrun yatabayyanu fī-mā baʿdu bayānan šāfiyan *45.13*.

5. *morph.; rendering the future tense of the Greek verb* **(a)** *abs.* : φιλοτιμοῦνται γὰρ πρὸς τοὺς εἰρημένους, πρὸς δὲ τοὺς μυριοστὸν ἔτος ὄντας ἢ πρὸς τοὺς ἐσομένους ... οὐδείς *Arist. Rhet. II 10, 1388a11* = wa-l-mukramūna (*fort.* fa-l-mukramūna *leg.*) ʿindahum humu llaḏīna waṣafnā fa-ammā llaḏīna qad ḫalat lahum sinūna kaṯīratun awi llaḏīna hum ātūna fī-mā baʿdu ... fa-laysa āḥadun minhum ka-ḏālika *117.12* ⟼ τὸ δ' ἁρμόζον ἐφ' ἑκάστοισι τῶν τρόπων εἰρήσεται *Hippocr. Diaet. acut. 40.24–5* = wa-anā muḫbirun bi-l-anfaʿi fī kulli wāḥidin mina l-aḥwāli fī-mā baʿdu *6.14*; οἷα γεγράψεται *57.15* = mā anā wāṣifuhū fī-mā baʿdu *29.11* ⟼ ὁ λόγος βεβαιώσει τὸ λεγόμενον *Nicom. Arithm. 87.21* = wa-ḏālika amrun yatabayyanu ǧamīʿuhū fī-mā baʿdu *70.20* **(b)** *in hend. with Arabic future marker* sa- : δείξομεν δέ, ὅτι ἡ πρώτη καὶ τετάρτη δύναμις ἴση ἐστὶ τῇ δευτέρᾳ καὶ τρίτῃ *Aelian. Tact. 298b16* = wa-sa-yaʾtī fī-mā baʿdu anna l-quwwata l-ūlā wa-l-rābiʿata musāwiyatun li-l-ṯāniyati wa-l-ṯāliṯati *14.12*.

مِن بَعد **min baʿdu** *adv.*

1. *transl.* ὕστερον *adv.* (*later, afterwards*) *by itself and in expr.*

1. ὕστερον *adv.* (*later, afterwards*) : ὕστερον δὲ οὐχ ὁμοίως *Arist. Eth. Nic. X 4, 1175a6* = wa-ammā min baʿdu fa-laysat ka-ḏālika *545.9* ⟼ ὥστ' εἰ μὲν ὕστερον διεληλύθει (*sc.* τὴν Α τὸ Ω) ἢ διῄει, διαιρετὴ ἂν εἴη (*sc.* ἡ κίνησις) *Arist. Phys. V 1, 232a2* = fa-wāǧibun, in kāna l-mutaḥarriku innamā yakūnu qad qaṭaʿa l-masāfata min baʿdu, iyyāhā (*sc.* al-ḥarakati) an takūna munqasimatan *611.9*.

1.2 *in expr.; used in the transl. of* εἰς ὕστερον (*later, afterwards*) = min baʿdu, *where* min *transl.* εἰς *and* baʿdu *transl.* ὕστερον: οὐ γάρ ἐστιν ἐνδεὴς (*sc.* ἡ ὅρασις) οὐδενὸς ὃ εἰς ὕστερον γινόμενον τελειώσει αὐτῆς τὸ εἶδος *Arist. Eth. Nic. X 4, 1174a15* = min aǧli annahū (*sc.* al-baṣara) lā yaḥtāǧu ilā šayʾini l-battata yakūnu min baʿdu li-yutimma ṣūratahū (*sic leg. pro* li-tatimma ṣūratuhū *ed.*) *539.11-12**.

1.3 *in expr.; used in the transl. of* ἐφεξῆς (*thereupon, subsequently*) = min baʿdu, *where* min *transl.* ἐπί *and* baʿdu *transl.* ἑξῆς; *in hend.;* ṯumma ... min baʿdu : πρὸς τὴν ἐξ ἀρχῆς μάθησιν καὶ πρὸς τὴν ἐφεξῆς ἄσκησιν *Galen Med. phil. 7.17* = fī taʿallumihim ... awwalan ṯumma fī tadarrubihim min baʿdu *120.*

2. εἶτα *adv.* (*then, after that*) : οὐδὲν γὰρ ὡς ἔτυχε κινεῖται, ἀλλὰ δεῖ τι ἀεὶ ὑπάρχειν ... εἶτα ποία πρώτη; *Arist. Metaph. Λ 6, 1017b36* = wa-ḏālika annahū wa-lā šayʾun mina l-ašyāʾi yataḥarraku lākin yanbaġī an yūǧada dāʾiman šayʾun ... wa-min baʿdu fa-ayyumā hiya l-ūlā *1565.3.*

3. πάλιν *adv.* (*again, i.e., after* [*the first occurrence*]) : τότε (τότε *Arab.* : πότε *ed.*) πάλιν ἥξει (*sc.* τὸ τῆς λέξεως μέτρον) *Arist. Rhet. III 8, 1408b24** = ṯumma yaʾtī bihī (*sc.* wazni l-maqālati) min baʿdu *192.10.*

4. *sem.; etym.; transl.* ἐπί *prep.* (*after, in addition*) *in compounds*

4.1 ἐπιγίγνομαι (*to come after*) = ṣāra min baʿdu : τελειοῖ δὲ τὴν ἐνέργειαν ἡ ἡδονὴ οὐχ ὡς ἕξις (ὡς ἕξις L^b M^b *Arab. ut vid.* : ὡς ἡ ἕξις *codd. cett., ed.*) ἐνυπάρχουσα, ἀλλ' ὡς ἐπιγινόμενόν τι τέλος *Arist. Eth. Nic. X 4, 1174b33** = tammamati l-laḏḏatu l-fiʿla lā ka-hayʾatin hiya fīhi bal ka-tamāmin mā yaṣīru fīhi min baʿdu *545.3.*

4.2 ἐπιφαίνομαι (*to appear in addition, later*) = ẓahara min baʿdu : ἀτὰρ καὶ τοῖσιν ἐπιφαινομένοισιν, οἷον ἐν πλευριτικοῖσι *Hippocr. Aphor. I : 12* = wa-l-ašyāʾu llatī taẓharu min baʿdu miṯālu ḏālika mā yaẓharu fī aṣḥabi ḏāti l-ǧanbi *5.8.*

5. *morph.; rendering the future tense of the Greek verb, in hend., with Arabic future marker* sa- : ὡς ἀπ' αὐτῶν τῶν ἐπιδειχθησομένων ἔσται δῆλον *Ptol. Hypoth. 74.4* = wa-ḏālika yatabayyanu bi-mā sa-nubarhinuhū min baʿdu *19.3.*

بُعد **buʿdun,** *pl.* **abʿādun**

1. *transl.* διΐστημι (*to set apart*) *and its derivatives*

1.1 διΐστημι *intransitive perf. act.* (*to be at a distance*) : τὰ μεγέθη τῶν σωμάτων μὴ πολὺ διέστηκεν *Arist. Gener. anim. II 4, 738b30* = aʿẓāmi l-ağsāmi llatī laysa baynahā buʿdun kaṯīrun *69.5.*

1.2 διεστηκώς *intransitive perf. act. part.* (*one that is at a distance, extended*) = budʿun *c. gen. or* lahū buʿdun : τὰ γὰρ πλεῖστον ἀλλήλων διεστηκότα τῶν ἐν τῷ αὐτῷ γένει ἐναντία ὁρίζονται *Arist. Cat. 6, 6a17*

= li-annahum innamā yaḥuddūna l-mutaḍāddāti bi-annahā llatī buʿduhā baʿḍihā min baʿḍin ġāyatu l-buʿdi *47.12 / fol. 166a* ⤚ ἄπειρον ... τὸ ἀπεράντως διεστηκός, ὥστε τὸ ἄπειρον σῶμα πανταχῇ ἔσται διεστηκὸς εἰς ἄπειρον *Arist. Phys. III 5, 204b21-22* = wa-ġayru l-mutanāhī huwa llaḏī lahū buʿdun lā nihāyata lahū fa-yaǧibu an yakūna l-ǧismu ġayru l-mutanāhī lahū buʿdun ilā l-ǧihāti kullihā bi-lā nihāyata *228.11-12.*

1.3 διάστημα (*interval, distance*) : νῦν δὲ καὶ περὶ τῶν διαστημάτων ... δηλώσομεν *Aelian. Tact. 304b10* = wa-qad yanbaġī an nuḫbira (*sic leg. pro* yuḫbara *ed.*) l-āna bi-l-buʿdi *15.17**; πρῶτον μὲν γὰρ τάσσονται (*sc.* οἱ ὁπλῖται) ἐν ἀραιοτέροις διαστήμασιν *304b17* = wa-ḏālika anna taʿbiyatahum (*sc.* aṣḥābi l-silāḥi) awwalan takūnu ʿalā buʿdin abʿada *15.18;* τὰ ἶσα ἀπ' ἀλλήλων διαστήματα *386b6* = yakūna buʿdu mā baynahum mutasāwiyan *23.7; etc.* ⤚ καὶ οὕτως τοῦ ἀέρος ἐπιλαμβάνει (*sc.* τὰ χρώματα), ὅσον δύναται ἀπὸ τοῦ τοσούτου διαστήματος ἐπιλαβεῖν *Alex. An mant.* [*Vis.*] *143.22* = wa-tanfuḏu (*sc.* al-alwānu) fī l-hawāʾi bi-miqdāri l-buʿdi llaḏī bayna l-baṣari wa-l-mubṣarāti (*sic leg.*) *151.56**; κινήσεως δὲ αἰσθάνεται τῷ διαστήματός τε καὶ ἀποστήματος αἰσθάνεσθαι *147.6* = wa-l-ʿaynu tuḥissu l-ḥarakata bi-iḥsāsihā l-buʿda wa-l-masāfata *161.153; 147.15 = 163.161* ⤚ λέγω δὲ μῆκος μὲν αὐτοῦ (*sc.* τοῦ παντός) τὸ κατὰ τοὺς πόλους διάστημα *Arist. Cael. II 2, 285b9* = inna ṭūla l-falaki huwa l-buʿdu allaḏī fīhi l-aflāku *versio B 232.13* ⤚ δῆλον δ' ἂν πολὺ διάστημα γένηται ἀρετῆς ἢ κακίας *Arist. Eth. Nic. VIII 9, 1158b33* = fa-bayyinun annahū yakūnu buʿdun kaṯīrun fī-mā bayna l-faḍīlati wa-l-radāʾati *449.14* ⤚ τὸ πνεῦμα τούτοις μὲν διάστημ' ἔχειν μέγα καὶ πολὺν ἀναγκάζεσθαι ἀέρα κινεῖν *Arist. Gener. anim. V 7, 787b4* = wa-iḏā kāna l-buʿdu kabīran bi-ḍṭirārin takūnu ḥarakatu l-hawāʾi kaṯīratan *195.8* ⤚ τὸ δὲ τῶν ἐσχάτων διάστημα μέγιστον *Arist. Metaph. I 4, 1055a9* = wa-buʿdu l-ašyāʾi l-uḫari (al-uḫari *cod., ed.* : *fort.* al-āḫirati *leg.*) akbaru l-abʿādi *1301.2**; οὔτε τοῦ ἑνὸς διαστήματος πλείω δυοῖν ἔσχατα *1055a21* = wa-lā yakūnu li-l-buʿdi l-wāḥidi akṯaru min nihāyatayni *1305.3* ⤚ τὸ αὐτὸ διάστημα *Arist. Phys. III 3, 202a18* = al-buʿd al-wāḥid bi-ʿaynihī *191.10;* ὁ τόπος ... ἢ ... μορφὴ ἢ ὕλη ἢ διάστημά τι τὸ μεταξὺ τῶν ἐσχάτων, ἢ τὰ ἔσχατα εἰ μὴ ἔστι μηδὲν διάστημα παρὰ τὸ τοῦ ἐγγιγνομένου σώματος μέγεθος *IV 4, 211b7-9* = al-makān ... immā ḫilqatun wa-immā hayūlā wa-immā buʿdun mā fī-mā bayna l-ġāyāti <wa-immā ġāyātun> iḏā lam yakun hāhunā buʿdun aṣlan siwā ḥaǧmi l-ǧismi llaḏī yakūnu fī l-šayʾi *309.8-9;* τὸ γὰρ κενὸν οὐ σῶμα ἀλλ' ἀσώματον (ἀλλ' ἀσώματον *Arab.* : ἀλλὰ σώματος *codd., ed.*) διάστημα βούλονται (βούλονται

E²GIJVS, Arab. : βούλεται *codd. cett., ed.*) εἶναι *IV 7, 214a20** = wa-ḏālika anna l-ḫalāʾa laysa ʿindahum ǧisman bal buʿdun ġayru ǧismiyyin *349.8; IV 14, 223a1 = 471.9; etc.* ⟼ νάφθα ... δύναμιν δὲ ἔχει ἁρπακτικὴν πυρὸς ὥστε καὶ ἐκ διαστήματος ἁρπάζειν τοῦτο *Diosc. Mat. med. I, 73.5* = lahū (*sc.* li-l-nifṭi) quwwatun yuḫtaṭafu bihā l-nāru ʿan buʿdin *versio B WGAÜ Suppl. I, 278.7* ⟼ καὶ παντὶ κέντρῳ καὶ διαστήματι κύκλον γράφεσθαι *Eucl. El. I. Post. 3 : i, 5.1* = wa-ʿalā an naḫuṭṭa dāʾiratan ʿalā kulli markazin wa-bi-kulli buʿdin *I.1, 20.9;* κέντρῳ μὲν τῷ Α διαστήματι δὲ τῷ ΑΒ κύκλος γεγράφθω ὁ ΒΓΔ, καὶ πάλιν κέντρῳ μὲν τῷ Β διαστήματι δὲ τῷ ΒΑ κύκλος γεγράφθω ὁ ΑΓΔ (ΑΓΔ *Arab.* : ΑΓΕ *PV* : ΓΑΕ *BFbpV*^corr.^) *I.1 : i, 7.7-8** = fa-l-naǧʿal nuqṭata Ā markazan wa-naḫuṭṭu bi-buʿdi ĀB dāʾirata BĞD ṯumma naǧʿalu B markazan wa-naḫuṭṭu bi-buʿdi BĀ dāʾirata ĀĞD *I.1, 42.6-7; I.2 : i, 8.19 = I.1, 48.8; etc.* ⟼ ἔσται οὖν ἡ μὲν μονὰς ... ἀρχὴ μὲν διαστημάτων καὶ ἀριθμῶν, οὔπω δὲ διάστημα οὐδὲ ἀριθμός, ὡς τὸ σημεῖον ἀρχὴ μὲν γραμμῆς καὶ διαστήματος, οὔπω δὲ γραμμὴ οὐδὲ διάστημα *Nicom. Arithm. 84.10-12* = wa-ḏālika anna l-wāḥida btidāʾu l-abʿādi wa-l-aʿdādi wa-laysa (*sic leg. pro* fa-laysa) huwa hāḏā wa-lā ʿadadan ka-mā anna l-nuqṭata btidāʾu l-ḫaṭṭi wa-l-buʿdi wa-laysat ḫaṭṭan wa-lā buʿdan *68.15-16**; διάστημα γάρ ἐστι δυεῖν ὅρων τὸ μεταξὺ θεωρούμενον. πρῶτον δὲ διάστημα γραμμὴ λέγεται *85.2-3* = wa-l-buʿdu huwa llaḏī yurā fī-mā bayna ḥaddayni wa-awwalu l-abʿādi l-ḫaṭṭu *69.1-2; 84.14 = 68.18; 84.25 = 68.24* (*v. supra* awwala mā 2.1, *I 653.7*); *etc.* ⟼ Πλάτων αἰῶνος εἰκόνα κινητὴν ἢ διάστημα τῆς τοῦ κόσμου κινήσεως *Ps.-Plut. Placita 318a5* = wa-ammā Aflāṭūn fa-innahū yarā anna l-zamāna huwa miṯālun li-l-dahri aw buʿdun li-ḥarakati l-ʿālami *20.12* ⟼ ἀλλά τις ἑτέρα φύσις ὁ νοῦς ἔξω παντελῶς σωματικοῦ διαστήματος *Them. In De an. 22.2* = bali l-ʿaqlu ... ṭabīʿatun mā uḫrā ḫāriǧatun aṣlan ʿan kulli buʿdin min abʿādi l-ǧismi *5.2;* μηδὲν ἐμποδίζοι τῶν ἔξωθεν, οἷον ἢ θέσις ἢ διάστημα ἀσύμμετρον *57.19* = lam yakun yaʿūquhā šayʾun min ḫāriǧin ka-l-waḍʿi awi l-buʿdi l-ḫāriǧi min ṭāqatihā *85.5;* οὐδὲ γὰρ ἔχει (*sc.* ἡ στιγμὴ καὶ τὸ νῦν) μορφὴν οἰκείαν· ἀλλὰ ἀφαιρούμενος τὸ διάστημα καὶ τὸ μέγεθος οὗ πέρατα ἦν *111.17* = laysa lahumā (*sc.* li-l-nuqṭati wa-l-āni) ḫilqatun taḫuṣṣuhumā bal innamā yaʿqiluhumā (*sc.* al-ʿaqlu, *sic leg. pro* yaʿqiluhā *ed.*) bi-rafʿi l-buʿdi wa-l-ʿiẓami llaḏayni humā ṭarafāhumā (ṭarafāhumā *vel* ṭarafuhumā *leg. pro* ṭarafāhu *ed.*) *203.7**; *etc.*

1.4 διάστασις (*dimension, extension, distance*) **(a)** *abs.* : τῶν μὲν οὖν ἐν μορίου εἴδει σωμάτων ... ἕκαστον ... πάσας ... ἔχει τὰς διαστάσεις *Arist. Cael. I 1, 268b6* = fa-ammā sāʾiru l-aǧrāmi llatī hiya ka-lağzāʾ fī anwāʿihā li-hādā l-kulli ... li-kulli wāḥidin minhā abʿādun talātatun *versio C 128.14 Badawī*; *cf.* τὸ μὲν ἐφ᾽ ἓν γραμμή, τὸ δ᾽ ἐπὶ δύο ἐπίπεδον, τὸ δ᾽ ἐπὶ τρία σῶμα *I 1, 268a7–8* = wa-ammā l-ʿiẓamu fa-mā kāna minhu dā buʿdin wāḥidin fa-huwa l-ḫaṭṭu, wa-mā kāna minhu dā buʿdayni fa-huwa l-saṭḥu, wa-mā kāna minhu dā talātati abʿādin fā-huwa l-ğirmu *versio C 126.1–3 Badawī*; κατὰ τὰς διαστάσεις τῶν μορίων ... τοσαῦτα εἰρήσθω *II 2, 285b33* = fa-qad laḫḫaṣnā wa-bayyannā abʿāda ağzāʾi l-samāʾi *versio B 234.11 Badawī* ⟼ διὰ τὸ πλείστην τῷ μέσῳ διάστασιν πρὸς τὰ πέρατα τοῦ κόσμου εἶναι *Arist. Cat. 6, 6a14* = li-anna l-buʿda bayna l-wasaṭi wa-bayna aṭrāfi l-ʿālami abʿadu l-buʿdi *47.10 / fol. 166a11* ⟼ ἐν μεγάλῃ δὲ διαστάσει μάλιστα δῆλον γίνεται *Arist. Eth. Nic. IX 3, 1165b25* = wa-innamā yatabayyanu dālika katīran fī l-buʿdi l-ʿaẓīmi *493.10* ⟼ σῶμα μὲν γάρ ἐστιν τὸ πάντῃ ἔχον διάστασιν *Arist. Phys. III 5, 204b20* = wa-dālika anna l-ğisma huwa lladī lahu buʿdu l-ğihāti kullihā *228.10;* τό τε ἄνω καὶ τὸ κάτω καὶ αἱ λοιπαὶ τῶν ἕξ διαστάσεων *IV 1, 208b14* = fawqu wa-asfalu wa-sāʾiru l-abʿādi l-sitti (*sic ed. pro* al-sittati) *272.14*⊗ ⟼ οἷον ὁ τοῦ σώματος ὁρισμὸς τὸ ἔχον τρεῖς διαστάςεις *Arist. Top. VI 5, 142b25* = mitālu dālika taḥdīdu l-ğismi annahu lladī lahū talātatu abʿādin *660.9 / fol. 300a* ⟼ εἴ τι γὰρ στερεόν ἐστιν, ἐκεῖνο τὰς τρεῖς διαστάσεις πάντως ἔχει *Nicom. Arithm. 85.18* = in kāna l-šayʾu muğassaman fa-inna lahū l-talātata l-abʿādi *69.10; sim. 85.20 = 69.11;* οὐκ ἄρα τὸ δύο μόνον ἔχον διαστάσεις ἔσται στερεόν *85.21* = wa-l-šayʾu lladī lahū buʿdāni faqaṭ laysa huwa bi-muğassamin *69.12; etc.* **(b)** *in hend.;* buʿdun wa-saʿatun : καὶ διὰ τοῦτο τοῖς μὲν θήλεσι τὸ μόριον τὸ δεκτικὸν οὐ πόρος ἐστίν, ἀλλ' ἔχουσι διάστασιν αἱ ὑστέραι *Arist. Gener. anim. II 4, 738b37* = wa-min ağli hādihi l-ʿillati l-ʿuḍwu lladī yakūnu fī l-ināti li-qabūli l-zarʿi (*sic leg. pro* al-qabūl li-l-zarʿi *ed.*) laysa huwa sabīlan bal fī l-arḥāmi buʿdun wa-saʿatun *69.11**.

1.5 *sem.; etym.;* διαστατός (*having dimension*) **(a)** dū l-buʿdi : γραμμὴ γάρ ἐστι τὸ ἐφ' ἓν διαστατόν· ... ἐπιφάνεια γάρ ἐστι τὸ διχῇ διαστατόν· ... στερεὸν γάρ ἐστι τὸ τριχῇ διαστατόν *Nicom. Arithm. 85.4-7* = wa-dālika anna l-ḫaṭṭa huwa dū l-buʿdi l-wāḥidi ... wa-dālika anna l-basīṭa huwa dū l-buʿdayni ... wa-dālika anna l-muğassama huwa <dū> (*supplevimus*) l-talātati l-abʿādi *69.2-4*; sim. 86.3 = 69.15; 101.6 = 79.18; etc.* **(b)** lahū buʿdun : ἐπιφάνειά τε γὰρ ὀρθῶς τὸ διχῇ διαστατὸν καὶ πάλιν τὸ διχῇ διαστατὸν πάντως ἐπιφάνεια ἔσται *Nicom. Arithm. 85.25-86.1* = anna l-basīṭa huwa lladī lahū buʿdāni wa-mā kāna innamā lahū buʿdāni fa-huwa abadan basīṭun *69.14.*

1.6 *sem.; etym.;* ἀδιάστατος (*having no dimension, without extension*) **(a)** laysa bi-ḏī abʿādin : ἀδιάστατον γὰρ ἀδιαστάτῳ συντεθὲν διάστημα οὐχ ἕξει *Nicom. Arithm. 84.14* = li-anna mā laysa bi-ḏī abʿādin iḏā rukkiba maʿa mā laysa bi-ḏī abʿādin lam yuḥdiṯ fīhi ḏālika buʿdan *68.17*; διὰ τοῦτο προελέχθη εἶναι ἀδιάστατον (*sc.* τὸ σημεῖον) *86.7* = wa-li-ḏālika qad qīla awwalan inna l-nuqṭata laysat bi-ḏāti abʿādin *69.18* **(b)** ġayru ḏī buʿdin : ἀδιάστατος ἄρα ἡ μονάς *Nicom. Arithm. 84.24* = fa-l-wāḥidu iḏan ġayru ḏī buʿdin *68.24.*

2. *transl.* ἀφίστημι (*to move or put away*) *and its derivatives*

2.1 ἀφίστημι *intransitive perf. act.* (*to stand away, keep far from*) = *in hend.* buʿdun wa-rtifāʿun *c. gen.* : τοσούτῳ τιμιωτέραν ἔχον τὴν φύσιν ὅσωπερ ἀφέστηκε τῶν ἐνταῦθα πλεῖον *Arist. Cael. I 2, 269b16* = wa-ṭabīʿatuhū akramu min ṭabāʾiʿihā ka-buʿdihī minhā wa-rtifāʿihī ʿanhā *versio B* = wa-ṭabīʿatuhū ašrafu min ṭabāʾiʿihā wa-aʿlā bi-ḥasabi buʿdihī minhā wa-rtifāʿihī ʿalayhā *versio C 136.7 Badawī.*

2.2 ἀφεστώς, *intransitive perf. act. part.* (*one that is standing away, at a distance*) = fī l-buʿdi *or* buʿdun *c. gen.* : διότι ἀφεστῶτες αἰσθανόμεθα τοῦ ὁρωμένου *Alex. An. mant.* [*Vis.*] *145.22* = anna idrāka l-mubṣari innamā yakūnu huwa fī l-buʿdi minnā fī l-mawāḍiʿi llatī nuḥissuhū <fīhā> *157.119* ⟼ Παρμενίδης Δημόκριτος διὰ τὸ πανταχόθεν ἴσον ἀφεστῶσαν ... μόνον μὲν κραδαίνεσθαι (*sc.* τὴν γῆν) μὴ κινεῖσθαι δέ *Ps.-Plut. Placita 380a14* = wa-ammā Barmānīḏus wa-Ḏīmūqrīṭūs fa-innahumā yarayāni anna l-arḍa lammā kāna buʿduhā mina l-ğihāti kullihā mutasāwiyan ... ṣārat tatamawwağu faqaṭ wa-lā tataḥarraku *47.5 (cf. also Ullmann Proportionalgefüge, # 133).*

2.3 ἀπόστασις (*distance, interval*) : λοξὴ δὲ ἡ τὸ μὲν ἕτερον κέρας, ὁπότερον ἂν προῄρηται, πλησίον τῶν πολεμίων ἔχουσα ... τὸ δὲ ἕτερον ἐν ἀποστάσει δι' ὑποστολῆς ἔχουσα *Aelian. Tact. 410b18* = wa-l-ğayšu l-muwarrabu huwa llaḏī maymanatuhū aw maysaratuhū, ayyahumā kāna, qarībatun mina l-ʿaduwwi ... wa-l-ğānibu l-āḫaru bi-l-buʿdi multaffun muğtamaʿun *23.23* ⟼ δοκεῖ ... οὐ δι' αὑτὸν ἀλλὰ διὰ τὴν ἀπόστασιν τῆς ἡμετέρας ὄψεως *Arist. Cael. II 8, 290a16* = wa-innamā ṣārat tuẓannu (*sic leg. cum mss.*) ʿalā hāḏihi l-ḥāli lā min ağlihā lākin li-buʿdihā min abṣārinā *versio B 260.10* Badawī*; ὑποθέμενοι ... τὰς ταχυτῆτας ἐκ τῶν ἀποστάσεων ἔχειν τοὺς τῶν συμφωνιῶν λόγους *II 9, 290b22* = fa-in ... kānat suraʿuhā ʿalā naḥwi buʿdihā baʿḍihā min baʿḍin, kāna lā maḥālata l-ṣawtu l-ʿāriḍu min sulūkihā l-mustadīri (ḏā hibatin *add. mss. versionis C*) muṭriban mulhiyan *versio B 263.9**; *II 10, 291b8, 9*

= *268.5*; μικρὰς ἔχοντας ἀφορμὰς καὶ τοσαύτην ἀπόστασιν ἔχοντας *II 12, 292a16* = li-qillati asbābi maʿrifatihā wa-buʿdihā *271.*13 ⟼ ὕστερον λέγομεν κατὰ τὴν πρὸς τὸ νῦν ἀπόστασιν *Arist. Phys. IV 14, 223a5* = naqūlu muta'aḫḫirun bi-ḥasabi buʿdihī ʿani l-āni *472.2;* ἐν ᾧ γὰρ τὸ νῦν, καὶ ἡ τοῦ νῦν ἀπόστασις *223a8* = wa-ḏālika anna l-šay'a llaḏī fīhi l-ānu fa-fīhi l-buʿdu ʿani l-āni *472.6* ⟼ ἢ παρὰ τὸ ἀσύμμετρον τῶν μορίων ὡς πρὸς τὴν ἀπόστασιν τῆς μήτρας *Ps.-Plut. Placita 421a18* = wa-immā min qibali ḫtilāfin fī mizāǧi l-aʿḍā'i wa-buʿdi baʿḍihā ʿan baʿḍin *66.24* ⟼ τὰ κατὰ τὰς φορὰς καὶ τὰ μεγέθη καὶ τὰ σχήματα καὶ τὰς ἀποστάσεις *Theophr. Princ. 9b26* = amra ḥarakātihā wa-maqādīrihā wa-aškālihā wa-abʿādihā *208.7; 11b1* = *220.3.*

2.4 ἀπόστημα (*distance*) : συμβαίνει δὲ κατὰ λόγον γίγνεσθαι τὰς ἑκάστου κινήσεις τοῖς ἀποστήμασι *Arist. Cael. II 10, 291a33* = qad yaʿriḍū bi-ḥaqqi kulli wāḥidin mina l-kawākibi an takūna ḥarakatuhū ʿalā naḥwi buʿdihī *versio B 267.9 Badawī*; *sim. 291a31* = *267.5*; οὐ προσλογιζόμενοι τὸ ... ἀπόστημα τοῦ ἡλίου *II 13, 294a4* = qālū hāḏā l-qawla bi-tarkihimi l-fikra fī buʿdi l-šamsi *versio B 281.4* ⟼ περὶ ἀποστημάτων τῆς σελήνης *Ps.-Plut. Placita 362a1* = fī abʿādi l-qamari *37.14.*

3. ἀπέχω *c. gen. or* ἀπό (*to be away or at a distance from*) **(a)** buʿdun *c. gen. and* min *or* ʿan : ἀεὶ γὰρ ἕκαστον ἀπέχειν τὴν εὐθεῖαν τίθεμεν *Arist. Cael. I 4, 271a13* = wa-ḏālika annā naḍaʿu dā'iman anna kulla wāḥidin minhumā (*sc.* al-ḥarakatayni) buʿduhū mina l-mustaqīmi buʿdun wāḥidun *versio C 144.4*; ἴσου γὰρ πάντῃ προστιθεμένου ἴσον ἀνάγκη ἀπέχειν τοῦ μέσου τὸ ἔσχατον *II 14, 297a24* = iḏā atat (*sc.* aǧzā'u l-arḍı ḏawātu l-ṯiqli) min ǧamīʿi l-nawāḥī bi-l-sawā'i, kāna buʿdu ǧamīʿi l-nawāḥī mina l-wasaṭi bi-l-sawā'i ḍṭirāran *versio B 298.18 Badawī* ⟼ τοσοῦτον ἀπέχουσι τοῦ περιπατεῖν *Galen Anat. admin. II, 222.13* = wa-bi-ḥasabi ḏālika buʿduhā ʿan an tamšiya *10.11 Garofalo* ⟼ ἴσον γὰρ ἀπέχει (*sc.* τὸ λα τεταρτημόριον καὶ τὸ αδ τεταρτημόριον) τοῦ ἰσημερινοῦ *Hyps. Anaph. 80* = li-anna buʿdahā (*sc.* rubʿi l-dā'irati llaḏī huwa LĀ wa-rubʿi l-dā'irati llaḏī huwa ĀD) ʿan ḫaṭṭi muʿaddali l-nahāri buʿdun mutasāwin *65;* καὶ αἱ ἴσον ἀπέχουσαι (*sc.* τοῦ ἰσημερινοῦ) ἐν ἴσῳ χρόνῳ ἀναφέρονται *108* = wa-l-qusīyu llatī buʿduhā ʿan ḫaṭṭi muʿaddali l-nahāri buʿdun mutasāwin taṭluʿu fī azmānin mutasāwiyatin *86* ⟼ Ἐμπεδοκλῆς διπλάσιον ἀπέχειν τὴν σελήνην ἀπὸ τοῦ ἡλίου ἤπερ ἀπὸ τῆς γῆς *Ps.-Plut. Placita 362a4* = ammā Anbāḏūqlīs fa-yarā anna buʿda l-qamari mina l-šamsi ḍiʿfu buʿdihī mina l-arḍi *37.15;* Ἐρατοσθένης τὸν ἥλιον ἀπέχειν ἀπὸ τῆς γῆς σταδίων μυριάδας τετρακοσίας καὶ ὀκτακισμυρίας, τὴν δὲ σελήνην ἀπέχειν τοῦ ἡλίου (τοῦ ἡλίου *Arab.* : τῆς γῆς *ed.*) μυριάδας ἑβδομήκοντα ὀκτὼ σταδίων *362a9–363a3** = ammā Arāṭūstānis fa-yarā anna buʿda l-šamsi mina l-arḍi arbaʿumiʾati alfin wa-ṯamāniyatu ālāfi asṭādiyatin wa-anna buʿda l-qamari mina l-šamsi ṯamāniyatun wa-sabʿūna alfa asṭādiyatin *37.19–20 (cf. Daiber, p. 28)* **(b)** kāna minhu ʿalā buʿdin : τούτου δή τι τοῦ ὑμένος κατʼ ἀρχὰς ὀμφαλῶδές ἐστι κατὰ τὸ ὀξὺ (*sc.* τῶν ᾠῶν) καὶ ἀπέχει ... οἷον αὐλός *Arist. Gener. anim. III 2, 752b3* = fa-baʿḍu hāḏā l-ṣifāqi yakūnu fī l-ibtidāʾi miṯla surratin fī-mā yalī l-nāḥiyata l-ḥāddata mina l-bayḍati wa-yakūnu minhā ʿalā buʿdin ... wa-yakūnu (*sic leg. pro* wa-takūnu) bi-manzilati unbūbatin *105.1** **(c)** *sem. amplif.;* iḫtalafa bi-ḥāli buʿdihī min : τὸ δʼ ἀξιοῦν ἄλλην εἶναι φύσιν τῶν ἁπλῶν σωμάτων ἂν ἀποσχῶσιν ἔλαττον ἢ πλεῖον τῶν οἰκείων τόπων, ἄλογον *Arist. Cael. I 8, 276b22* = fa-in qāla qāʾilun inna ṭabīʿata l-ağrāmi l-mabsūṭati (al-basīṭati *versio C*) llatī fī l-ʿawālimi l-kaṯīrati ḫtalafat bi-ḥāli buʿdihā min mawāḍiʿihā bi-l-aqalli wa-l-akṯari qulnā inna hāḏā l-qawla ḫāriğun mina l-qiyāsi *versio B/C 181.1* Badawī* (*sic leg. cum mss.*).

4. *transl.* πρό *prep. and adv.* (*before, forwards*) *and its derivatives*

4.1 πρὸ *prep.* (*before, of time*) : παντελῶς δὲ μικρᾷ (*sc.* γυναικὶ) καὶ πρὸ πολλοῦ τῆς ὥρας τῶν γάμων οὔσῃ θάνατον προμαντεύεται *Artem. Onirocr. 25.2* = fa-in kānat (*sc.* al-marʾatu) ṣağīratan ğiddan kaṯīrata l-buʿdi min waqti l-zawāği fa-inna hāḏihi l-ruʾyā tadullu ʿalā mawtihā *48.1.*

4.2 *sem.; etym.; transl.* πρό *in* πρότερος *comp. adj.* (*prior*) = ašaddu buʿdan : ἕτερα τὰ κυριώτατʼ ἂν εἴη καὶ πρότερα *Theophr. Princ. 10a7* = fa-l-umūru llatī hiya ağallu qadran wa-ašaddu buʿdan hiya ġayru hāḏihī *210.2.*

4.3 πόρρω *adv.* (*far off, far away*) **(a)** buʿdun *c. gen.* : γίνονται δʼ οἳ μὲν οἰκειότεροι οἳ δʼ ἀλλοτριώτεροι τῷ σύνεγγυς ἢ πόρρω τὸν ἀρχηγὸν εἶναι *Arist. Eth. Nic. VIII 14, 1162a3* = wa-yakūnu baʿḍuhum aḫaṣṣa wa-baʿḍuhum abʿada ʿalā qadri qurbi l-awwali llaḏī hum minhu wa-buʿdihī *467.11* **(b)** *in hend.* min buʿdin wa-taqādumin : διότι πόρρω ταῦτα (ταῦτα *ΘΠ Γ, Arab.* : ταὐτὰ *A, ed.*) μᾶλλον ἢ ἐγγὺς γιγνόμενα ἐντιμότερα καὶ εὐαλαζόνευτα *Arist. Rhet. II 15, 1390b20** = wa-min ağli anna hāḏā amrun yakūnu min buʿdin wa-taqādumin wa-laysa min qurbin, fa-qad yakūnu ağalla wa-akrama mimmā qaruba *126.9*

(c) *sem. amplif.* al-mustaqbalu ʿan buʿdin : καὶ ταῦτα ἐὰν μὴ πόρρω ἀλλὰ σύνεγγυς φαίνηται ὥστε μέλλειν *Arist. Rhet. II 5, 1382a25* = t̠umma mā kāna min hād̠ā laysa ka-l-mustaqbali ʿan buʿdin wa-lākin ka-llad̠ī yutawaqqaʿu min qurbin *97.6.*

4.4 *sem.; etym.; transl.* πόρρω (*far off*) *in* πόρρωθεν *adv.* (*from afar*) = min buʿdin: καὶ ταὐτὸν χρῶμα ἐγγύθεν τε καὶ πόρρωθεν φαινόμενον διάφορον φαίνεται· οὐ γὰρ ὁμοίως λευκὸν τὸ πόρρωθεν ὁρώμενον *Alex. An. mant.* [*Vis.*] *145.34-35* = wa-l-lawnu l-wāḥidu bi-ʿaynihī yurā min qurbin wa-min buʿdin muḫtalifan wa-d̠ālika anna l-abyaḍa llad̠ī huwa min qurbin laysa yurā ʿalā mit̠āli mā yurā l-abyaḍu min buʿdin *159.128-129* ↤ ἀλλὰ λίαν τὸ λέγειν οὕτω πόρρωθέν ἐστιν ἅπτεσθαι τῆς αἰτίας *Arist. Gener. anim. IV 1, 765b4* = wa-lākinna hād̠ā l-qawla šabīhun bi-qawli llad̠īna yadnūna min daraki l-ʿillati min buʿdin kat̠īrin *138.18* ↤ οἱ οὐ δύνανται διὰ πολλῶν συνορᾶν οὐδὲ λογίζεσθαι πόρρωθεν *Arist. Rhet. I 2, 1357a4* = allad̠īna lā yastaṭīʿūna an yubṣirū l-umūra ʿan marātiba kat̠īratin wa-lā yafʿalū l-salǧasata min buʿdin *11.16;* ἔτι δὲ οὐ πόρρωθεν δεῖ ἀλλ' ἐκ τῶν συγγενῶν καὶ τῶν ὁμοειδῶν μεταφέρειν *III 2, 1405a35* = t̠umma laysa yanbaġī an yakūna l-taġyīru min buʿdin lākin mina l-mušākilāti l-mutaqāribāti fī l-ṣuwari *179.1*; *III 3, 1406b8* = *183.8.*

4.5 προσωτέρω *comp.* (*at a greater distance*) = bi-l-buʿdi : δεῖ ... ταῦτα δὲ μὴ ἐγγὺς οὕτω κρίσιος, ἀλλὰ προσωτέρω *Hippocr. Humor. 6.34* = fa-lā yanbaġī an yakūna hād̠ā bi-l-qurbi mina l-buḥrāni lākin bi-l-buʿdi (bi-l-buʿdi *nos* : al-buʿd *cod., ed.*) minhu *15.14**.

5. *transl.* μακρός (*far*) *and derivatives*

5.1 ἐπὶ μακρόν *adv.* (*far, a long way*) = ilā buʿdin kat̠īrin : οὐκ ἐπὶ μακρὸν ἐκτείνοντες τὰς ἶνας (*sc.* οἱ ῥαχῖται μύες) *Galen Anat. admin. II, 451.18* = min ġayri an tamtadda awtāruhā (*sc.* ʿaḍalāti l-ṣulbi) ilā buʿdin kat̠īrin *246.6 Garofalo.*

5.2 *sem.; etym; transl.* μακρός *in* μακρόθεν (*from afar*) = min buʿdin : διὸ καὶ τὴν κώπην ἐν τῇ θαλάσσῃ μακρόθεν καμπτομένην ὁρῶμεν *Ps.-Plut. Placita 372a25* = wa-li-d̠ālika narā l-mirdā fī l-baḥri munḥaniyan id̠ā (*sic leg. pro* wa-id̠ā) raʾaynāhu min buʿdin *42.8**.

6. μῆκος (*length* [*i.e., of distance or duration*]) : πρὸς δὲ τοὺς μένοντας (*sc.* ἀστέρας) κραδαίνεται (*sc.* ἡ ὄψις) διὰ τὸ μῆκος, ἀποτεινομένη πόρρω λίαν *Arist. Cael. II 8, 290a22* = wa-lā yaqwā l-baṣaru (<ʿalā> *fort. addendum*) an yabluġa l-nuǧūma l-markūzata wa-yanālahā illā an yahtazza wa-yatamāyala li-mawqiʿi buʿdihā minhu *versio B 260.17**